W9-BOB-517

DEMOCRACY
in the
STATES

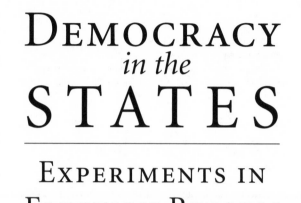

DEMOCRACY
in the
STATES

EXPERIMENTS IN
ELECTION REFORM

BRUCE E. CAIN

TODD DONOVAN

CAROLINE J. TOLBERT

Editors

BROOKINGS INSTITUTION PRESS

Washington, D.C.

ABOUT BROOKINGS

The Brookings Institution is a private nonprofit organization devoted to research, education, and publication on important issues of domestic and foreign policy. Its principal purpose is to bring the highest quality independent research and analysis to bear on current and emerging policy problems. Interpretations or conclusions in Brookings publications should be understood to be solely those of the authors.

Copyright © 2008
THE BROOKINGS INSTITUTION
1775 Massachusetts Avenue, N.W., Washington, D.C. 20036
www.brookings.edu

All rights reserved. No part of this publication may be reproduced or transmitted in any form or by any means without permission in writing from the Brookings Institution Press.

Library of Congress Cataloging-in-Publication data

Democracy in the states : experiments in election reform / Bruce E. Cain, Todd Donovan, and Caroline J. Tolbert, editors.
    p.   cm.
    Includes bibliographical references and index.
    Summary: "Offers a twenty-first-century agenda for election reform based on lessons learned in the fifty states. Examines the impact of reforms intended to increase the integrity, fairness, and responsiveness of the electoral system. Topics include the relationship between early voting and turnout, hurdles for third-party candidates, and strategies for redistricting reform"—Provided by publisher.
    ISBN 978-0-8157-1336-4 (cloth : alk. paper) — ISBN 978-0-8157-1337-1 (pbk. : alk. paper)
    1. Elections—United States. 2. Voting—United States. 3. Democracy—United States. I. Cain, Bruce E. II. Donovan, Todd. III. Tolbert, Caroline J. IV. Title.
    JK1976.D46 2008
    324.60973—dc22   2008014076

9 8 7 6 5 4 3 2 1

The paper used in this publication meets minimum requirements of the American National Standard for Information Sciences—Permanence of Paper for Printed Library Materials: ANSI Z39.48-1992.

Typeset in Minion

Composition by Cynthia Stock
Silver Spring, Maryland

Printed by R. R. Donnelley
Harrisonburg, Virginia

Contents

Acknowledgments

Early versions of some of the chapters in this book were presented at a symposium hosted by the Department of Political Science at Kent State University titled "2008 and Beyond: The Future of Election and Ethics Reform in States" (January 16–17, 2007). Portions of several chapters also appeared previously in *PS: Political Science & Politics:* Barry C. Burden, "Ballot Regulations and Multiparty Politics in the States," *PS* 40: 4 (October 2007): 669–74; Todd Donovan, "A Goal for Reform: Make Elections Worth Stealing," *PS* 40: 4 (October 2007): 681–86; Thad Hall, J. Quin Monson, and Kelly D. Patterson, "Poll Workers and the Vitality of Democracy: An Early Assessment," *PS* 40: 4 (October 2007): 647–54; Michael McDonald, "Regulating Redistricting," *PS* 40: 4 (October 2007): 675–80; Paul Gronke, Eva Galanes-Rosenbaum, and Peter A. Miller, "Early Voting and Turnout," *PS* 40: 4 (October 2007): 539–646. This material is reused with permission of Cambridge University Press.

We would like to thank the Department of Political Science at Kent State University and Vernon Sykes (chair), Caroline Tolbert (co-chair), Erin O'Brien (co-chair), and Jamie Callender (co-chair) for sponsoring and organizing the symposium. We are also grateful to the University of Iowa for providing institutional support for this project.

CAROLINE TOLBERT, TODD DONOVAN,
AND BRUCE E. CAIN

1

The Promise of Election Reform

The quest to improve the processes of election and representation within the decentralized structure of American government has produced many reform experiments across the states. Some of these experiments have been intentional; others have not. Intentional experiments—particularly those promoted by citizen initiative—have tried to make elections less corrupt, more responsive, and fairer. State and federal courts have contributed to this intentional experimentation by forcing legislatures to change electoral practices that conflicted with constitutional principles and congressional mandates. The results have included experiments with term limits, redistricting practices, ballot access laws, campaign finance rules, and other aspects of election systems.

Unintentional experiments have also been conducted, notably in election administration. The decentralized structure of American elections produces tremendous variation in the ways registration records are kept, polling places are operated, and ballots are designed and counted. We can learn a lot from these natural experiments, even if they were not designed with this goal in mind.

Together these intentional and unintentional experiments have produced significant variation in the rules, institutions, and procedures governing elections across the United States. In this book we take advantage of this variation to evaluate the effects of different election reforms. Rather than focus on a single issue area such as campaign finance or legislative redistricting, we evaluate an array of election rules and practices.[1] The topics covered range from the mechanics of electoral administration to structural reforms such as term limits and redistricting. In each case the authors evaluate what does and does not work and summarize the results of their analysis in nonstatistical language, making them accessible to readers without experience in quantitative methods.

The American states offer a laboratory for experimenting with electoral reform. Too often scholarly discussion focuses on the need to set up new experiments. Too infrequently attention turns to evaluating the results of past efforts. In this book we do the latter. By leveraging subnational experiments— intentional and otherwise—we hope to learn important lessons about how to reform America's election system.

Why Election Reform? Why Now?

The forces of mass opinion motivating efforts to reform American elections are numerous, but a few stand out. These include the perception among the public that votes are counted improperly, that money dominates politics, and that elections have little effect on who governs and how. The proportion of Americans who believe that elections make the government pay "a good deal" of attention to what people think declined from 65 percent in 1964 to 37 percent in 1988.[2] Reflecting the same skepticism, in 1990 most respondents to the American National Election Study (ANES) said they did not care much about who won congressional elections.[3] Since then these numbers have improved. In 2004 the proportion of respondents who said they did not care much about the outcomes of congressional races was closer to one-third. Similarly, surveys conducted in the wake of the 2000 elections reveal increased belief in the importance of elections, with about one-half of respondents saying that elections made the government pay attention. Yet these figures still indicate considerable disillusionment within the electorate.

This disillusionment is often fueled by the uncompetitiveness of most congressional elections. Frustration with the slow pace of turnover in Congress played a major role in building enthusiasm for term limits in the early 1990s.[4] Roughly half the states passed ballot initiatives to restrict state legislative terms. Voters in some states also passed limits on congressional terms, but those measures were ruled unconstitutional. Partly as a result, many reformers have refocused their attention on campaign finance rules and redistricting practices. Both currently work largely in the favor of incumbents, who typically enjoy substantial fundraising advantages over challengers and tend to hail from safe, one-party districts.

Today reelection rates in the U.S. House of Representatives remain high— often more than 96 percent of incumbents are reelected—and significant cynicism about the utility of elections remains. Many incumbent legislators, at both state and federal levels, run for reelection without a challenge from a major party opponent. Most win in landslides.

The 2006 midterm elections that swung control of Congress from Republicans to Democrats demonstrate how few seats are competitive by traditional standards: only 28 of 435 seats were won by margins of 10 percent or less. But 2006 also proved that congressional elections could produce a change in party control of Congress. Some seats that switched party in 2006 had been held by incumbents previously elected by margins of greater than 10 percent. Although the alteration of party control of Congress produced by the 2006 election may have boosted the proportion of Americans who think elections "make government pay attention" (as it did after the change in party control after the 1994 election), public concern about the electoral insulation of incumbents will likely endure. Polls show that public support for congressional term limits remains high and that approval of Congress remains tepid.

A second major force driving contemporary election reform is public distrust of the role of money in politics. Although the "battleground" (that is, competitive states and districts) has been shrinking in recent decades, the amount of money spent on elections continues to increase. The 1971 and 1974 Federal Election Campaign Acts, which prohibit large political contributions, have gradually been weakened by court and administrative decisions, particularly those contributing to the rise of "soft money." Unregulated soft money, with no limits on individual contributions, became the dominant source of funding for the 1996 presidential election. Campaigning for reelection, President Bill Clinton pushed the 1974 law to its limits by encouraging affluent donors to fund Democratic Party "issue advocacy" efforts. The Republicans followed suit, and the Federal Election Commission allowed the practice.[5]

By the late 1990s the volume and sources of money in politics had become major issues. A 1997 survey by the Pew Research Center for the People and the Press found that 66 percent of Americans felt that "political contributions have too much influence on elections and government policy." A similar proportion agreed that campaign finance reform should be a top priority.[6] Nonetheless, nearly $500 million in unregulated soft money found its way into the 2000 presidential election—nearly double the amount in 1996. There was also an explosion of party-controlled soft money in the 2000 congressional races, which increased the spending advantages that incumbents enjoyed over challengers.[7] Public discontent associated with unregulated money in politics was met with passage of the Bipartisan Campaign Reform Act (BCRA, or "McCain-Feingold") of 2002 at the federal level, while efforts in several states led to experiments with new campaign finance regulations and, in a handful of states, with publicly financed elections. Yet concern about the influence of money on politics remained strong. In 2004 most Americans agreed that "government is pretty much run by a few big interests looking out for themselves."[8] Two years later a poll conducted by a group advocating election finance reforms showed that 75 percent of voters supported voluntary public financing of congressional elections.[9]

A third force behind contemporary reform efforts stems from the crisis of the 2000 presidential election in Florida and problems with election administration in subsequent contests. Events associated with the last two presidential elections shattered many voters' confidence in the integrity of the election system. The 2000 presidential contest was one of the closest in history, with a dispute over a narrow, 500-vote margin in Florida determining the winner. It was also an election in which the national popular vote winner, Vice President Al Gore, lost the election—yet that peculiar aspect of American elections generated less controversy than Florida's contentious recount methods, a confusing ballot design in one county, long lines at polling places, police roadblocks near polling places, and, before election day, illegal purges of eligible voters from registration records. The U.S. Civil Rights Commission estimates that thousands of voters were wrongly removed from the Florida voter rolls in November 2000.[10]

The events in Florida reveal that county-level decisions and local events at 190,000 polling places can have a tremendous effect on who wins the presidency. They also taught voters more than most had ever wanted to know about the mechanics of voting. Americans learned that among different voting machines—punch-card readers, lever machines, handwritten ballots, optical scanners, electronic voting machines—some had much higher error rates than others.[11] The problems associated with the punch-card voting machines used in some Florida counties stimulated a national debate about "hanging chads" and "pregnant chads."

Two weeks before the Supreme Court's five-to-four *Bush* v. *Gore* decision, most Americans disagreed that or did not know whether either presidential candidate had "legitimately won."[12] In the end, the vast majority of Americans (80 percent) accepted George W. Bush as the "legitimate president," but this sentiment reflected respect for the court and a desire to move forward much more than it reflected confidence in election administration.[13] A substantial number of voters, particularly among African Americans, remained unconvinced that their votes would be counted accurately in subsequent elections.[14]

The election administration crisis of 2000 prompted Congress to pass the Help America Vote Act (HAVA) in 2002. This law required local election administration officials to begin replacing older equipment with electronic voting machines and to provide provisional ballots to any voters whose names did not appear on polling place voter rolls. HAVA funneled billions of dollars to states for improving election administration and fueled innovation as states moved to meet new federal guidelines. It also generated controversy by promoting the use of electronic voting machines, which many citizens, particularly Democrats and African Americans, distrusted.[15]

Despite the implementation of HAVA, controversy over election administration continued through the 2004 election. Once again the outcome of the presidential contest depended on a close vote in a single state (Ohio), and media attention again focused on controversy over election administration. Election night produced long lines at polling places in heavily Democratic and urban areas, an undersupply of new electronic voting machines, new allegations of improper purging of voter rolls, and lockdown conditions for recounting votes in some precincts. Ohio also highlighted the prominent role that partisan officials play in elections. Ohio's Republican secretary of state, R. Kenneth Blackwell, presided over the administration of the election while running President Bush's reelection campaign in that state. Even before election night Blackwell generated controversy with rulings on issues such as whether provisional ballots could be counted if cast outside one's precinct and whether voter registration forms could be accepted if printed on paper of less than a certain weight. Confidence in the election was also damaged by controversy over the vendors selected to provide electronic voting machines. A private company, Diebold, designed many of Ohio's electronic voting machines. Before the 2004 election an e-mail from Diebold's chief executive officer that was leaked to the media promised to "help Ohio deliver its electoral votes to the President," undermining public confidence in the new computerized voting machines and prompting calls for a verified "paper trail."[16] The conclusion reached by most scholars—that for the most part computerized voting machines worked well in 2004—did little to allay these fears.[17]

Outside Ohio, another close election highlighted additional administrative problems. The final outcome of a three-round recount in Washington's 2004 gubernatorial race that placed Democrat Christine Gregoire in office depended in part on counting "misplaced" ballots found days after the election and on counting votes cast by ineligible voters. Disgruntled Republicans could be seen driving cars with bumper stickers reading She's Not My Governor on the same roads with cars sporting Re-Defeat Bush stickers.

The cumulative effect of these events on public confidence in the integrity of American elections cannot be understated. A 2006 Pew Research Center survey found 32 percent of unregistered voters reporting little or no confidence that their votes would be accurately counted if they were to vote in the November 2006 election.[18]

Table 1-1 puts Americans' perceptions of election administration in international perspective. In 2004 citizens in thirty-seven nations were asked, "Thinking of the last national election, how honest was it regarding counting and reporting the vote?" The United States was the only established democracy in which most people failed to believe that their recent national election was "very honest" or at least "somewhat honest." Only 39 percent of Americans replied that their election was at least "somewhat honest," in comparison with 96 percent of Danes and Finns, 80 percent of Canadians and New Zealanders, and 75 percent of Spanish and Japanese citizens. In the United States, Democrats, independent voters, African Americans, citizens with high levels of general political distrust, and the less educated were particularly suspicious of elections.[19] Only Russians were (slightly) more cynical than Americans about the honesty of their most recent election, which was a one-sided contest in 2004 that saw Vladimir Putin reelected with 71 percent of the vote. Even so, Americans were more likely than citizens of any other nation to reply that their election was "very dishonest."

The only nations with levels of cynicism about vote counting approaching that of the United States were the Philippines, Mexico, Taiwan, and Venezuela—all countries with weak democratic traditions. To take just one of these examples, the 2004 Venezuelan recall vote on Hugo Chavez was administered by a national election commission dominated by members of Chavez's ruling party, and the election was plagued by allegations of vote buying, voter-roll purges, flawed voter lists, unannounced closings of polling places in opposition neighborhoods, and the use of electronic voting machines provided by a Florida company with links to Chavez.[20] Yet only 18 percent of Venezuelans found that election to be "very dishonest," whereas 23 percent of Americans reached the same judgment about the 2000 presidential election.

The United States also performs poorly in voter turnout. According to the International Institute for Democracy and Electoral Assistance, when countries are ranked by their average turnout in all elections since 1945, the United States comes in 139th among 172 countries.[21] The 2004 presidential election was one of the most closely contested races of the past century, yet turnout of the voting-age population was just 55 percent, or 60 percent of all eligible voters.[22] In the 2006 midterm election, average nationwide turnout among the population of eligible voters was just 43 percent, with turnout varying considerably from state to state. In Minnesota 61 percent of eligible citizens voted in the 2006 election, in comparison with only 29 percent of Mississippi citizens (table 1-2).

Table 1-1. *Citizen Evaluations of Honesty of Elections, Thirty-Seven Nations, 2004*[a]

Percent

"Very honest or somewhat honest"		"Very honest"		"Very dishonest"	
Cyprus	99.0	Cyprus	95.4	United States	22.9
Denmark	96.3	Denmark	73.6	Venezuela	17.7
Finland	95.5	Finland	70.5	Taiwan	16.3
Netherlands	93.9	Netherlands	59.3	Mexico	12.8
Norway	92.5	Norway	59.2	Philippines	11.5
Austria	89.9	Switzerland	53.9	South Africa	8.1
Sweden	89.3	Sweden	51.3	Bulgaria	7.7
Switzerland	88.0	New Zealand	49.7	Uruguay	7.6
Belgium	86.4	France	49.5	Slovakia	6.7
Germany	82.9	Ireland	48.7	Chile	6.2
Ireland	81.8	South Africa	47.8	Russia	5.5
Portugal	81.1	Austria	47.0	Spain	3.6
New Zealand	80.2	Australia	45.9	Hungary	3.2
Canada	80.0	Spain	45.1	France	3.1
France	77.1	Canada	43.8	Israel	3.1
Australia	76.1	Germany	42.2	Slovenia	2.5
Poland	76.0	Belgium	41.1	Latvia	2.4
Spain	75.2	Uruguay	40.6	Ireland	2.3
Japan	75.0	Great Britain	39.5	Czech Republic	2.1
South Korea	74.3	Hungary	36.7	Belgium	1.5
Hungary	74.2	Chile	34.9	Australia	1.5
South Africa	73.8	Venezuela	33.5	Germany	1.3
Israel	73.4	Israel	32.6	Great Britain	1.3
Great Britain	71.8	South Korea	25.4	Portugal	0.9
Slovenia	69.3	Mexico	23.3	Poland	0.9
Chile	63.6	Taiwan	21.3	Japan	0.8
Uruguay	63.5	Slovakia	20.1	Sweden	0.8
Czech Republic	62.7	Slovenia	16.6	South Korea	0.7
Slovakia	62.1	Japan	16.3	Netherlands	0.6
Mexico	61.6	Czech Republic	15.1	Canada	0.6
Venezuela	60.6	United States	13.6	Finland	0.5
Latvia	54.2	Philippines	13.5	New Zealand	0.5
Taiwan	49.1	Portugal	13.3	Norway	0.4
Bulgaria	46.8	Poland	9.7	Austria	0.2
Philippines	44.5	Bulgaria	8.0	Denmark	0.2
United States	39.0	Latvia	7.6	Cyprus	0.0
Russia	38.5	Russia	2.5	Switzerland	0.0

Source: International Social Survey Program (www.issp.org). The U.S. survey was administered by NORC (www.norc.org/projects/general+social+survey.htm).

a. Respondents were asked: "Thinking of the last national election in [country], how honest was it regarding counting and reporting the vote? Very honest, somewhat honest, neither honest or dishonest, somewhat dishonest, very dishonest."

Table 1-2. *Indicators of Democratic Elections, American States, 2006–08*

Percent except where indicated

State	Turnout VEP[a,c]	Turnout VAP[a,c]	Competitive Senate race (winning margin)[b,d]	Competitive governor race (winning margin)[b,d]	Days before election to register[b,e]	Voting early (mail or in person)[a,t,g]	Reporting they had to show a photo ID to vote[f,h]	Reporting problems with their voter registration[f,i]	Waiting 30 minutes or more in line to vote[f,j]
Alabama	37.4	35.8	...	16	10	7.4	90.7	2.3	0.8
Alaska	50.8	48.1	...	8	30	13.4	66.7	1.4	0.4
Arizona	38.8	33.2	9	28	29	53.8	94.2	3.4	1.7
Arkansas	37.3	35.3	...	14	20	36.7	83.8	2.3	5.9
California	40.1	32.0	24	17	29	41.8	21.9	3.7	4.4
Colorado	47.1	43.1	...	15	29	57.1	93.8	2.8	24.0
Connecticut	45.7	42.2	10	28	14	6.0	96.8	3.5	1.0
Delaware	43.0	39.0	41	...	20	3.0	89.3	4.7	6.0
Florida[k]	39.9	34.0	22	7	29	38.5	97.3[l]	4.0	2.0
Georgia	34.5	30.4	...	20	29	19.7	84.4	3.6	5.8
Hawaii[k]	37.8	34.7	24	28	30	41.8	92.3[l]	4.6	2.4
Idaho	45.5	41.8	...	9	0	14.9	26.6	1.8	6.2
Illinois	40.6	36.1	...	10	29	12.6	33.5	4.0	1.1
Indiana[k]	36.2	35.0	74	...	29	13.0	99.3	4.5	2.2
Iowa	48.7	46.3	...	10	0	24.7	18.1	1.8	1.0
Kansas	43.5	41.1	...	17	14	21.9	17.6	1.0	2.8
Kentucky	40.7	39.0	...	...	28	6.3	72.7	2.9	4.2
Louisiana[k]	30.1	28.8	...	...	24	5.6	96.3	5.2	0.5
Maine	53.5	53.0	54	8	0	19.9	8.4	1.3	0.0
Maryland	46.7	41.8	10	7	29	14.5	21.3	3.3	12.2

Massachusetts	49.1	44.4	38	21	20	7.6	12.6	2.3	0.0
Michigan	52.2	49.9	16	14	30	13.8	19.2	2.1	4.0
Minnesota	60.8	56.3	20	1	0	9.7	34.8	3.4	2.3
Mississippi	29.3	28.5	29	...	30	8.5	22.3	5.1	0.5
Missouri	50.2	48.1	3	...	28	9.1	50.4	3.4	7.7
Montana	56.7	56.0	1	...	0	28.3	87.4	4.0	2.2
Nebraska	47.7	45.1	28	50	10	27.4	8.9	3.2	1.0
Nevada	35.7	30.9	14	4	30	57.5	30.3	4.7	1.4
New Hampshire	40.8	39.5	...	48	0	7.0	12.5	3.7	0.0
New Jersey	40.1	33.8	8	...	29	4.4	14.1	4.7	0.4
New Mexico	41.8	38.8	42	38	28	52.5	37.4	2.1	2.8
New York	34.5	30.3	36	40	25	5.3	19.1	3.2	0.8
North Carolina	31.4	28.7	...	...	0	28.9	23.0	4.0	2.4
North Dakota	45.7	44.7	39	...	0	24.3	98.6	2.1	1.5
Ohio	47.5	46.2	12	23	30	18.5	96.8	5.0	6.5
Oklahoma	36.1	34.5	...	34	24	12.3	15.6	3.7	0.3
Oregon	50.6	48.2	...	8	20	97.9	29.3	2.2	0.0
Pennsylvania	43.6	42.5	18	20	30	4.2	22.1	2.6	1.8
Rhode Island	52.1	46.4	6	2	30	3.8	13.9	4.1	0.8
South Carolina	35.2	33.1	...	10	30	11.4	57.8	3.9	6.9
South Dakota[k]	58.3	57.1	...	28	15	24.1	99.0	2.6	0.0
Tennessee	41.8	39.8	3	39	30	53.4	64.8	2.8	26.2
Texas	30.2	25.6	26	9	30	51.2	53.6	4.7	9.2
Utah	34.5	32.3	32	...	20	20.4	35.2	5.6	2.3
Vermont	54.9	53.6	33	16	10	16.8	11.6	4.7	0.0
Virginia	44.3	40.4	1	12	28	9.3	78.5	3.3	5.3
Washington	46.6	42.6	17	...	30	85.4	61.4	2.2	0.8
West Virginia	32.6	32.2	30	...	30	14.4	23.5	7.1	0.5

Table 1-2 (*continued*)

State	Turnout VEP[a,c]	Turnout VAP[a,c]	Competitive Senate race (winning margin)[b,d]	Competitive governor race (winning margin)[b,d]	Days before election to register[b,d]	Voting early (mail or in person)[a,f,g]	Reporting they had to show a photo ID to vote[f,h]	Reporting problems with their voter registration[f,i]	Waiting 30 minutes or more in line to vote[f,j]
Wisconsin	53.3	50.9	37	8	0	11.2	27.6	6.0	2.8
Wyoming	50.7	49.4	40	40	0	19.5	14.2	0.7	0.0
National average	43.0	40.4	24	19	21.5	25.9	48.9	3.05	3.5

Source: Multiple sources. See notes.

a. Higher values are better.

b. Lower values are better.

c. VEP = voter-eligible population (all eligible voters); VAP = voting-age population. Turnout rates are for the 2006 congressional elections. From Michael McDonald's website at George Mason University (http://elections.gmu.edu/voter_turnout.htm).

d. Data based on authors' calculations of the competitiveness of the Senate and gubernatorial races in the respondent's state. Values are winning vote margins, as percentages, between the winner of the race and the runner-up. Missing data indicate no election for this office in 2006.

e. Days before an election by which citizens must register to vote. Data current as of October 2008 from the Demos Foundation. States with 0 have either election day registration or no voter registration.

f. Data aggregated to the state level from survey responses in the 2006 Cooperative Comparative Election Study (CCES) of 30,000 respondents from all fifty states (www.polimetrix.com). State estimates calculated using Polimetrix survey weights.

g. Question wording: "Did you vote in person on election day at a precinct, in person before election day, or by mail (that is, absentee or vote by mail)?"

h. Question wording: "Were you asked to show picture identification, such as a driver's license, at the polling place this November?"

i. Question wording: "Was there a problem with your voter registration when you tried to vote?"

j. Question wording: "Approximately how long did you wait in line to vote on election day?"

k. States requiring photo identification to vote in 2006. South Carolina required photo identification in 2004 but in 2006 reverted to government identification or a voter registration card.

l. Anomaly: state without photo identification law and a high proportion of voters in this state showed voter identification to vote.

What are the reasons Americans give for not voting? The Pew Research Center's "Early October 2006 Turnout Survey" found that 40 percent of voters who had not registered or voted in the 2004 elections mentioned logistical issues, such as having just moved or being busy with work.[23] Another 30 percent said they did not care or had no confidence in politics. Most others were ineligible to vote. More than one-third of registered nonvoters mentioned dislike of candidates or disinterest as reasons for not voting in 2004. One-quarter said they were too busy or that voting was somehow too inconvenient. More than half of Americans (57 percent) completely or mostly agreed with the general statement, "I sometimes feel I don't know enough about the candidates to vote," indicating that a lack of knowledge or interest in politics was a widespread reason for disengagement in politics. These responses suggest that low participation in American elections has at least two major dimensions. The choices that elections present may fail to mobilize the interest of a substantial proportion of citizens, and the administration of elections presents another set of barriers.[24] The inconvenience associated with registration and voting and the lack of confidence in the honesty of the election system both undermine voting.

Table 1-2 shows how the fifty states rate on several indicators of election performance as of 2006–08. The table reveals substantial variation across the states in the competitiveness of candidate races in 2006. In Nebraska, for example, the race for governor was decided by a margin of 50 percentage points, whereas in Minnesota the winning margin was 1 percentage point. If voters believe that most elections are likely to be decided by large margins, they may be discouraged from voting by the belief that their votes do not matter.

The states' elections rules also vary considerably. For example, registration deadlines differ from state to state. In 2008 Iowa, Montana, and North Carolina began to allow voters to register on the day of the election, joining seven other states. Yet many states still require registration a full month before the election, significantly reducing turnout. Similarly, states vary in their approaches to making voting convenient through absentee voting, mail voting, and early voting, all of which may increase turnout. Nearly 98 percent of voters in Oregon participated in early voting (all-mail elections, no polling places), in comparison with 4 percent in Rhode Island (either in person at a polling place or by absentee voting). Identification requirements for voting vary considerably from state to state, as does the proportion of respondents saying they had to show some form of photo identification to vote. Surprisingly, some share of voters in every state reported that they had to show a picture ID, although not all states have such a requirement.

This last finding suggests that the actual conduct of an election can be as important as the rules. Among the challenges some voters confronted in 2006 were problems with their registration and long waiting lines at polling places. The percentage of citizens reporting problems with their registration at the polling booth ranged from a high of 7 percent in West Virginia to a low of about 1 percent in Wyoming and Kansas. At 4 percent and 5 percent, respectively, Florida and Ohio were not that far from the national average, despite the media attention devoted to their problems. Waiting times to vote varied across a broader range, with close to a quarter of Colorado and Tennessee voters reporting that they waited in line more than thirty minutes, in comparison with none in New Hampshire. Generally, in small and rural states, fewer voters reported waiting more than thirty minutes in line to vote.

The Goals of Election Reform

Since 2000 states have adopted myriad election administration reforms. Many of these sought to make the act of voting easier and the processes of registering voters, running polling places, and counting votes more accurate. Other efforts, including those focusing on campaign finance, term limits, and reform of districting practices, attempted to address issues of electoral competition. A common theme across these reform efforts is that "something" must be done to restore public confidence in elections.

In this book we consider these reforms in terms of their ability to promote three essential, interrelated goals: integrity, participation, and responsiveness. The *integrity* of an election system rests on a fair and impartial application of rules for registering voters, casting votes, and counting ballots. This means that the administration of elections must be efficient: voter rolls and vote counts must be accurate. In addition, the election system must be transparent: voters should understand where to vote, how to use voting machines, how to read the ballot, and whom to ask for help.

Second, the election system should encourage full *participation* so that the electorate is representative of the eligible voter population. Increased turnout is a goal that might be accomplished by making voting and registration easier and more convenient, by including citizens more directly in policy decisions, and by increasing electoral competition. Of course greater participation does not automatically lead to a more representative electorate. Therefore, policymakers must ensure that the rules governing registration and voting do not lead to systematic bias. They should not present different barriers for racial or ethnic minorities, the poor, the uneducated, the elderly, and the young.

Third, the rules governing elections should promote *responsiveness* to changes in citizen preferences. Elections, in other words, should offer voters meaningful choices. This goal can be promoted by making it easier for third-party candidates—or any candidates—to run for office and by drawing legislative district lines to maximize competition. These reforms can increase the likelihood that incumbents will face credible challengers.

Contemplating a counterfactual world with opposite goals can help underscore the importance of these broad ideals. The opposite of an election system with integrity is a corrupt system in which outcomes fail to reflect mass preferences. The opposite of a fully participatory election system is one based on a biased sample of the electorate. The opposite of a responsive election system is one that is excessively stable and unchanging in the face of shifts in public preferences.

An Overview of the Book

In considering recent attempts at election reform with these goals in mind, we organized the chapters in this volume into three parts. In part 1 we examine reforms aimed at improving the integrity of the election process. These reforms generally take the form of administrative and technological innovations within the existing structure of representation. In part 2 we assess some proposals that aim to increase participation and turnout. Such reforms typically focus on making voting and registration more convenient or on stimulating voter interest and participation in elections through the use of direct democracy. In part 3 we consider reforms that aim to improve the responsiveness of electoral outcomes. These include structural changes and rule changes that alter the mix of candidates, issues, and parties facing voters. These structural reforms may open up the process to more voters, create a more equitable division of districts, and ensure that women and minorities are represented in government.

In the concluding chapter, Bruce Cain summarizes the major findings of the book and discusses broader questions about the future of election reform in America. He focuses on the lessons learned from first-generation election reforms in the American states and on the promises that second-generation reforms may hold. His discussion ends with five guidelines for future election reformers.

The two chapters in part 1 are concerned with the integrity of the elections. Since the adoption of HAVA in 2002 the states have witnessed a massive shift toward computerized voting machines. In chapter 2 Lonna Rae Atkeson and

Kyle Saunders draw on survey data from the 2006 elections to explore the effects that election administration, particularly the use of electronic voting machines, has had on voter confidence in the election system. In chapter 3 Thad Hall, Quin Monson, and Kelly Patterson focus on poll workers to study the effects of training on election administration.

The chapters in part 2 examine election participation. Although most advanced industrialized nations have universal voter registration if not compulsory voting, and Europe has progressed rapidly with remote Internet voting, only a handful of states allow election day registration (Iowa, Montana, and North Carolina being the most recent adopters), and many states continue to require registration a month before the election. In chapter 4 Eric Gonzales Juenke and Julie Marie Shepard analyze the effects of new voting centers that allow Colorado voters to vote anywhere in their county of residence on election day. Another trend is the steady rise in early voting, discussed in chapter 5 by Paul Gronke, Eva Galanes-Rosenbaum, and Peter Miller. In chapter 6 Caroline Tolbert, Todd Donovan, Bridgett King, and Shaun Bowler compare the effects of convenience voting reforms and electoral competition on voter turnout in the states over time. While the current literature tends to focus on individual reforms in isolation, this chapter shows that convenience voting laws and electoral competition may combine to increase participation in elections. Caroline Tolbert and Daniel Bowen, in the final chapter in part 2, look at the use of direct democracy—ballot initiatives and referenda—to expand democratic participation by allowing voters to make policy choices directly, potentially justifying expansion of the process.

Part 3 focuses on improving the responsiveness and competitiveness of the election system. In the 2004 elections, just fourteen U.S. House seats were considered very competitive (vote margin of 5 percent or less), while in a typical election more than one-third of state legislative races are uncontested.[25] Thad Kousser, Christopher Cooper, Michael McDonald, and Barry Burden examine reforms that seek to reinvigorate the election system by offering voters new or more choices. In chapter 8 Kousser looks at term limits, concluding that although they increase turnover in state legislatures they do not increase electoral competition. In chapter 9 Cooper examines the effects of multimember districts in state legislatures, paying particular attention to their implications for third parties. In chapter 10 McDonald explores alternatives to the practice of legislative redistricting, which typically limits competition by protecting incumbents. And in chapter 11 Burden analyzes the relationship between ballot access regulations and the strength of third parties.

Unfortunately, legislators rarely have strong incentives to support reforms that may put their own seats at risk or otherwise weaken the advantages they enjoy over challengers. Therefore, reformers must often look for other avenues to promote change. In chapter 12 Daniel Smith discusses the role of ballot initiatives in promoting election and ethics reforms in the American states, and in chapter 13 Todd Donovan returns the discussion to the fundamentals by showing why electoral competition is so important and how it affects the representation of voter preferences, election turnout, and polarization within Congress. Increased competition, he concludes, is not just an important means to an end; it is itself a goal of democracy.

A Twenty-First-Century Reform Agenda

A hundred years ago Progressive Era reformers pressed for sweeping changes in government rules and institutions. The Progressives were largely concerned with combating the power of big business and corrupt urban political machines. The reforms they promoted, however, had the much larger effect of updating and modernizing government for the twentieth century. These reforms included measures aimed at improving the integrity of the election system, such as the secret ballot, the long ballot, and the civil service. The last of these placed most federal employees on the merit system and marked the end of the so-called spoils system, in which government jobs were provided in exchange for votes. They also encompassed structural election reforms intended to improve participation and responsiveness, such as women's suffrage, the direct election of U.S. senators, direct democracy (initiative, referendum, and recall), and the shift from ward district to at-large elections.

At the beginning of the twenty-first century we hear repeated calls for a new progressivism to reevaluate America's electoral institutions.[26] Once again, political elites have resisted attempts to change electoral institutions, evidenced by widespread partisan gerrymandering of state legislative and congressional districts.[27] To reduce the corruption of machine politics historical Progressives advocated reforms that changed representation from geographically based wards to at-large (citywide) districts.[28] Today a shift from single-member plurality districts to proportional representation for Congress and state legislatures may be the only way to end partisan gerrymandering.[29] A 2008 national survey finds that 62 percent of Americans support a proposal for proportional representation to elect Congress, which would increase the number of third parties.[30] Historical Progressives adopted the direct election of U.S. senators, and today there are calls to directly elect the president via a national popular vote and instant runoff voting. The 2008 survey finds that 58 percent of Americans support the direct election of the president and elimination of the Electoral College.[31]

While the Progressives advocated direct democracy at the subnational level, today a national referendum is being discussed. Even though the United States is one of the only nations in the world never to give voters a direct say in making laws at the national level, the referendum has popular support. The 2008 survey finds that 66 percent of Americans would support a proposal to create a national referendum whereby laws referred by Congress would be voted on.[32] (This percentage could be high: we know from studies of opinion that responses to such questions inflate positive responses over how voters would respond to a real-world choice.)[33]

Some research suggests that the states likely to update election laws and procedures in the period 2000–01 were those with legislative term limits (where lawmakers were more willing to take risks), swing states in the 2000 presidential election (which had higher voting error rates), and those in which statewide commissions recommended reforms.[34] Thus elections reforms, such as term limits, may beget additional reforms, and multiple factors (from election administration errors to competition) may combine to facilitate updating election rules. A modern version of the Progressive Era's leadership may be critical to the reform of America's election system today, but this is the very piece that may be missing.

In response to these calls for reform, we suggest that a successful election reform agenda in the United States requires the threefold strategy outlined above: reforms to improve the integrity of elections, reforms designed to increase political participation, and structural reforms of state election systems to improve responsiveness and electoral competition. These three components of America's reform agenda are represented by the three sections of this book.

Notes

1. Many of the chapters in this volume were presented as papers at a conference hosted by Kent State University's Department of Political Science, "2008 and Beyond: The Future of Election and Ethics Reform in the States," Columbus, Ohio, January 16–18, 2007 (http://dept.kent.edu/columbus/symposium/).

2. Center for Political Studies (2004).

3. Center for Political Studies (2004).

4. Benjamin and Malbin (1992).

5. Mann (2004).

6. See www.opensecrets.org/pubs/survey/s2.htm.

7. Ornstein, Mann, and Malbin (2000).

8. Center for Political Studies (2004).

9. Brennan Center, "Breaking Free with Fair Elections," 2007 (www.brennancenter. org/dynamic/subpages/download_file_48611.pdf).

10. A draft of the executive summary of the report can be found at www.washington post.com/wp-srv/onpolitics/transcripts/ccrdraft060401.htm.

11. Cal Tech–MIT Voting Technology Project, "Residual Votes Attributable to Technology," version 2, March 30, 2001 (www.hss.caltech.edu/~voting/CalTech_MIT_ Report_Version2.pdf).

12. Pew Research Center, "Many Question Bush or Gore as Legitimate Winner," survey report, December 1, 2000 (http://people-press.org/reports/display.php3?Report ID=22).

13. CNN poll, December 13, 2000 (http://archives.cnn.com/2000/allpolitics/ stories/12/13/cnn.poll/index.html).

14. Kohut (2006).

15. Carl Vinson Institute of Government (2003).

16. Melanie Warner, "Machine Politics in the Digital Age," *New York Times,* November 9, 2003.

17. Alvarez and Hall (2006).

18. See http://people-press.org/dataarchive/.

19. This was found via a multivariate model estimating Americans' responses to the International Social Survey Program question about honesty in elections. The model also included gender, political interest, and age. Results are available from the editors on request.

20. Smartmatic is based in Florida and owned largely by Venezuelan investors. It purchased Sequoia Voting Systems in 2005 (http://news.bbc.co.uk/2/hi/americas/ 6098256.stm).

21. "Turnout in the world—country by country performance" (www.idea.int/vt/ survey/voter_turnout_pop2.cfm). For more on the popular vote, see the National Popular Vote Plan at www.nationalpopularvote.com.

22. Michael McDonald, "United States Election Project," 2007 (http://elections. gmu.edu/voter_turnout.htm).

23. See http://people-press.org/dataarchive.

24. Donovan and Tolbert (2007).

25. Squire (2000).

26. Tolbert (2003).

27. McDonald and Samples (2006); Mann and Cain (2005); Butler and Cain (1992); and Cain (1985).

28. Historical Progressives also used at-large districts to circumvent the constituency of political machines, including ethnic immigrants and political parties more generally. Critics contend at-large elections disenfranchised ethnic immigrants and today hinder representation for racial minorities. Today there is a shift back to wards to improve geographically based minority representation or mixed representation; however, more than 60 percent of U.S. cities use at-large elections.

29. Barber (2000); Barber (1995); Donovan and Bowler (2004); Bowler, Donovan, and Brockington (2003).

30. University of Iowa Hawkeye Poll 2008 (www.uiowa.edu/election/news-events/index.html#hawkeyepoll) questioned a nationwide sample of 856 adult registered voters between February 1 and February 5, 2008, using telephone surveying and random digit dialing. Question wording: "Some people suggest we should use proportional representation to elect Congress. This would probably mean that three or more parties would be represented in Congress. Would you support such a proposal?"

31. Question wording: "When it comes to electing the President, some suggest we get rid of the Electoral College and simply elect the candidate who most people voted for. States with large populations could have more influence over who wins. Would you support or oppose such a proposal?" For more on the popular vote, see the National Popular Vote Plan at www.nationalpopularvote.com.

32. Question wording: "There is a proposal for a national referendum to permit people to vote directly to approve or reject some federal laws. Would you support this proposal to give voters a direct say in making laws?"

33. Bowler and Donovan (2007).

34. Palazzolo and Moscardelli (2006).

PART I

Promoting Integrity

LONNA RAE ATKESON AND KYLE L. SAUNDERS

2

Election Administration
and Voter Confidence

The 2000 presidential election was a wake-up call to elected leaders, public officials, and election scholars. The electoral fiasco—most prominent in Florida but also in states such as New Mexico and Ohio—revealed deficiencies in voting equipment. In addition, registration mix-ups and problems with absentee ballots may have led to the loss of as many as 6 million votes.[1] Confusing ballot designs, such as the butterfly ballot in Florida's Dade County, were found to have led voters to vote incorrectly.[2] Although such election administration problems have no doubt existed for a long time, the closeness of the 2000 presidential race and the fact that the lost votes could have changed the election outcome brought these problems to the policymaking forefront.

In response, Congress passed the Help America Vote Act (HAVA) on October 29, 2002. It was the first ever comprehensive federal law on electoral administration, which has traditionally been the purview of the fifty states and literally thousands of local administrators. Before this the federal government had only dabbled with election oversight in states covered by the Voting Rights Act and by motor voter legislation. HAVA provided $3.9 billion to upgrade

This chapter originally appeared as Lonna Rae Atkeson and Kyle L. Saunders, "The Effect of Election Administration on Voter Confidence: A Local Matter?" *PS: Political Science and Politics* 40, no. 4 (October 2007): 655–60. Copyright © 2007 by the American Political Science Association. Reprinted with permission of Cambridge University Press. All rights reserved.

Data were collected with the generous support of the University of New Mexico's Research Allocation Committee. We thank Luciana Zilberman, Lisa Bryant, Alex Adams, former New Mexico secretary of state Rebecca Vigil-Giron, former Colorado secretary of state Gigi Dennis, David Magleby, and the Center for the Study of Elections and Democracy at Brigham Young University for their assistance with this project. Any errors are our own.

election equipment, especially punch-card systems, and established the Election Assistance Commission and minimum election administration standards for the states and for the local officials who are mostly responsible for administering elections.

Despite the implementation of HAVA requirements in the 2004 presidential election, including the change in many states to electronic touch-screen voting, problems continued. This time the focus was on Ohio, but controversies erupted elsewhere as well. Problems arose with the new electronic machines, including overcounting votes. Precincts in many urban areas lacked enough voting equipment, which led to long waiting lines, especially in minority areas. Exit polls in key battleground states showed large discrepancies from actual vote outcomes, raising additional questions about the accuracy and fairness of the election process. Such concerns led Robert F. Kennedy Jr. to publish an article in *Rolling Stone* in June 2006 titled, "Was the 2004 Election Stolen?" Although election scholars could find no evidence of systematic fraud, media coverage of apparent problems continued to raise doubts about the nation's election system.[3]

Voter confidence in the U.S. election system is crucial, because elections are the link between citizens and their elected officials. In a representative democracy it is the ballot box that allows voters to send their elected leaders mandates for policies and to hold them accountable. If voters lack confidence that their votes are counted correctly, then the most fundamental aspect of representative democracy is in doubt.[4] Perhaps the report "Building Confidence in U.S. Elections," by the Commission on Federal Election Reform, says it best: "The vigor of American democracy rests on the vote of each citizen. Only when citizens can freely and privately exercise their right to vote and have their vote recorded correctly can they hold their leaders accountable. Democracy is endangered when people believe that their votes do not matter or are not counted correctly."[5]

The reforms discussed in this chapter aim to improve the integrity of elections by improving voter confidence in election administration. We conducted a postelection survey after the 2006 elections in two congressional districts, one in New Mexico and one in Colorado, that provides the data for the discussion. (For details on the model, see the appendix to this chapter.)

Theoretical Background

Voter confidence in elections is a specific measure of a functional democracy. It is one of an array of measures, which includes political efficacy and trust in government. Political scientists have watched these last measures since the 1950s, when regime support was high in the United States.[6] Since then scholars have noted a large erosion in confidence in government in the United States and in Europe.[7] This change is disconcerting because measurements of regime support capture the public's commitment to their system of governance: theoretically, greater levels of political efficacy and trust in government lead to democratic stability and economic security, whereas lower levels have the potential to destabilize a government and create economic insecurity.

One problem with studies of confidence in government is that they have focused on broad measures of regime support. When researchers ask standard questions about "people in the government" or "people running government," they pay little attention to the object or experience of the evaluation.[8] Moreover, these broad measures likely stem from respondents' specific experiences.

We believe that it is voters' specific experiences with government, such as election administration, that need to be measured, since these measures can lead to accurate assessments of where voters' distrust of government can be repaired.[9] Trust in elections leads to trust in the institutions of government and to individual attachment to the political system. By measuring citizens' attitudes toward the institutions of government, we may miss citizens' connections to the governing process, and those may be critical in assessing and understanding the changing nature of citizens' satisfaction with government. In addition, using confidence in the election process as a measure enables us to focus on the procedures of democracy as opposed to its institutions, providing an alternative referent for assessing the health of the democracy. Further, voter confidence seems to be related to voter turnout, so understanding the dynamics of voter confidence may be helpful in building an active citizenry.[10]

Background

Our research focused on a fundamental measure of voter satisfaction: whether a voter believes his or her vote was counted as intended. In our study, the term *voter confidence* refers to this measure. Our data came from an Internet and mail survey we conducted immediately following the 2006 midterm elections in two congressional districts, New Mexico's first and Colorado's seventh. We chose these districts in part because their congressional contests were highly competitive and therefore more likely to have seen increased voter interest and activity and to have experienced greater problems at the polls.

Perhaps more important for the question of voter confidence, both Colorado and New Mexico had recently undergone myriad reforms in their voting laws in response to interest group pressure to create fair, accurate, and voter-verifiable election administration systems. New Mexico, for example, was the first state to move from a predominantly electronic voting system to statewide, mandated paper ballots designed for optical scanning of "bubbles," or circles, that voters filled in by hand to indicate their choices. The intent was to provide a paper trail so that elections could be audited for accuracy. Further, New Mexico passed legislation to implement a statewide audit of 2 percent of the machines beginning in 2007 to ensure the accuracy and fairness of election outcomes.

Meanwhile, Colorado was the frontrunner in the implementation of many innovative changes, including vote centers. Recent changes to state law mandated a paper trail to ensure voter integrity. In the 2006 cycle, some Colorado voters had the option of choosing touch-screen systems with voter-verifiable paper rolls or optical scan ballots. In addition, both states were among the first adopters of early voting and absentee voting, resulting in many voters' choosing to cast their ballots before election day. In New Mexico, about one in five voters took advantage of early voting, and about one in five voted absentee, leaving just more than half of voters voting on election day. In Colorado, about half of voters voted absentee, and a little more than one in ten voted early, with the remainder voting on election day. Thus our sample provides interesting variation in voters' interactions with the electoral process to assist in evaluating voter confidence.

Method

We sent 4,050 letters to a random sample of registered voters in both congressional districts so that they would arrive on or immediately following Election Day and requested their participation in our election administration survey.[11] The letter explained the survey and directed recipients to a website where they could take part in the survey.[12] The website provided respondents' frequently asked questions (FAQs) and internal review board (IRB) policies. The letter also explained that respondents could request a mail survey.

Voters in the sample who did not respond were contacted three more times with a postcard reminding them of the study, the URL, their ability to request a mail survey, and their identification number for the survey. The response rate for the sample was about 14 percent (New Mexico 15.3 percent, Colorado 12.1 percent; $N = 870$).[13] More than five out of six respondents (83.5 percent) chose the Internet option, and not quite one in six (16.5 percent) chose the mail option. Analysis of the sample shows that it accurately reflects many sample population characteristics and the election outcome, suggesting that the response rate did not produce a biased sample.[14]

Survey questions asked respondents about their election experience (voter confidence, voting problems, method of voting, experience with poll workers, voter satisfaction); it took measures of confidence in the election process (including the ability of the machines to provide paper audits), attitudes toward fraud, voter access, and voter identification; and it asked for evaluations of the president, the congressional candidates, and local and state election administrators. Several questions related to the congressional race (for example, vote choice, political activity) and demography.[15]

For the purposes of this chapter, we look at responses to a single question: "How confident are you that your vote in the November 2006 election will be counted as you intended?" Respondents could choose from the answers, "Not at all confident," "Not too confident," "Somewhat confident," and "Very confident."

Our primary independent variables were three sets of conceptual factors likely related to voter confidence. The first set is related to the voting experience itself. When voters have problems voting—for example, because the ballot is confusing or too long or because poll workers are unhelpful—they are likely to feel less confident that their votes will be counted.[16] Conversely, the more enjoyable their voting experience, the more likely they are to feel that their votes will be counted.[17] We hypothesized that the quality of a voter's experience with the voting process would be directly and positively related to his or her confidence in the process. Another factor in the set is the way the voter executes his or her vote. A national study found that absentee voters had significantly lower voter confidence than people who voted on election day.[18] We included in our model dummies for both early voters and absentee voters, making election day voting the category of reference.

Our second set of conceptual factors relates to the attitudes that voters bring to the process. One is their attitude regarding the machine they use to cast their ballots and whether it offers a verifiable record of their vote. In New Mexico both early voters and election day voters used identical optical scan paper ballots, whereas in Colorado most early and election day voters used touch-screen ballots, and some had the choice of optical scan paper ballots or touch-screen ballots. Therefore, we asked voters how strongly they agreed or disagreed with the following statement: "The bubble paper ballot [or the touch-screen ballot] method provides for a paper receipt that can validate the election results." We then matched voters' attitudes toward the machines to their voting method, creating a scale indicating how confident they felt in the technology they used.[19]

We also asked voters about their attitudes toward their election official—in both cases, the county clerk. We hypothesized that the more confidence voters have in the job their county election official is doing, the more likely they are to feel confident that their votes will be counted. We asked, "We are interested in whether you strongly approve, approve, disapprove, or strongly disapprove of how your county election official has handled her job."

The last attitude we looked at was the perceptual lens that voters brought to the voting booth through their party identification. Earlier research had shown that partisanship played an important role in structuring attitudes, including trust in government, and we suspect that it plays a role in voter confidence as well.[20] Voting administration problems and alleged partisan politics, whether in Florida with former secretary of state Katherine Harris or in Ohio with former secretary of state J. Kenneth Blackwell, appear to have favored Republican political outcomes over Democratic ones. Therefore, we expected Democrats to have less voter confidence than Republicans.

Finally, we considered a variety of demographic variables, including gender, age, education, income, the respondent's state, and race.[21] Previous research suggested that political resources, including education and income, increased political efficacy and trust, so we expected they would have a similar effect on voter confidence. Previous research also suggested that African Americans were likely to be less trusting of government and to have significantly less voter confidence than whites.[22] Therefore, we expected to find a similar relationship between race and voter confidence. There were no a priori reasons to hypothesize that either gender or age influenced voter confidence, but we included them as part of our standard model.

Results

Confidence in the process of voting, as measured by our survey of voters in two congressional districts, was generally high with 42 percent of respondents reporting that they were very confident (table 2-1). However, this percentage is 16 percentage points lower than that found in a national poll conducted before the 2006 elections by the Pew Research Center, which shows 58 percent of respondents being very confident.

Although this discrepancy might suggest that important differences exist between preelection and postelection environments, it might also suggest that local context matters a great deal in measuring voter confidence. National data do provide an important overall look at voter confidence, but localized studies may be necessary to control for the myriad differences in voter rules

Table 2-1. *Voter Confidence in the Election Process, Local and National Surveys*
Percent except as indicated

Confidence level	Local survey[a]	National survey[b]
Very confident	42	58
Somewhat confident	42	29
Not too confident	10	9
Not at all confident	4	3
Don't know, not sure	2	1
N	835	1,503

Source: See appendix 2A for particulars on the local survey; for the national survey see Pew Research Center for the People and the Press, "Democrats Hold Enthusiasm, Engagement Advantage; November Turnout May Be High," news release, October 11, 2006 (http:people-press. org/reports/).
a. Survey of voters in two New Mexico and Colorado congressional districts. Voters were asked, "How confident are you that your vote in the November 2006 election will be counted as you intended?"
b. Pew 2006 survey. Voters were asked, "How confident are you that your vote will be accurately counted in the upcoming election?"

(for example, rules governing absentee voter and voter registration), election administration (for example, availability of vote centers, voting machines used, history of voting problems in the area or state, and the competence of election officials and poll workers), and contexts of the races (for example, competitiveness, media coverage, and the negativity of campaign).

Our findings demonstrate that voters' direct experiences with the voting process have a significant influence on their confidence in it. The more helpful the poll workers were and the more voters were satisfied with the voting method, the more confident they were that their votes were counted. A confusing ballot, however, lowers confidence. Voting absentee or early also resulted in lower confidence, especially for absentee voting. This last finding is extremely important because states are increasingly providing voters with these alternative ways to vote. Absentee voting and early voting probably reduce voter confidence because they disconnect voters from election day activities. When people vote absentee, for example, they may be unsure whether their ballot arrived in time to be counted or fear that they filled out the form incorrectly. Early voters may feel it more likely that their ballot will be lost or destroyed when machines are turned on and off over the course of early voting.

We also find support for our argument that voters' attitudes are important to their confidence in the process. When voters use a voting machine that they believe produces verifiable results, they are more confident in the election process. When they have a positive evaluation of their county election official, they are also more confident in the election process.

The perceptual lens of party identification is also important. In the survey, the stronger a voter's identification with the Republican Party, the greater was his or her voter confidence. The election dramas of the last few years, outcomes of which have favored Republicans, have affected voters' confidence in the process. This last finding is particularly troubling, because the election process should not be partisan.

Demographic variables show some expected and some unexpected effects. Income was positively related to voter confidence, as expected, but education was not. Gender, age, and the state dummy had no relationship to voter confidence, also as expected. The survey's race variable showed that race has no relationship to voter confidence: because race in this study overwhelmingly represents Hispanics, not African Americans, this finding may represent a key difference between minority groups. African Americans have a long history of being denied their civil and voting rights, but there is no evidence that the Latino voters' experience is markedly different from the white experience.

Implications for Reform

On the basis of these results, we make the following recommendations for policymakers and election administrators, including county clerks and secretaries of state across the nation. County election administrators must work to produce a positive voter experience. Poll workers must be well trained. And ballots must be unambiguous and easy to use. For example, in the New Mexico survey open-ended questions about why voters rated their overall voting experience as fair or poor revealed that the bubbles on the ballot were too small and difficult for many voters to color in—a problem that could easily be remedied by using larger fonts.

More generally, when voters use a method of voting they enjoy, they are more confident in their voting experience. Allowing voters choices among voting methods may therefore be key to greater confidence. In New Mexico many people disliked the new bubble paper ballots, but they were used for the only machines available to voters. In Colorado, on the other hand, voters in some counties could choose between a bubble paper ballot and a touch-screen machine. Such options produce greater voter confidence. However, offering different options may be too costly and inefficient for many jurisdictions.

The attitudes that voters bring to the voting process are also important. First, machines that produce verifiable results increase voter confidence. Second, voters' confidence in their county election officials is also key. In our study, nearly two in five voters (37 percent) could not evaluate this official, even though this is an elected position. We believe that a more visible role for the local election official could be a factor in increasing voter confidence. The county official needs to appear competent, nonpartisan, and helpful. Overt or perceived partisanship can reduce voter confidence, as shown by the party identification variable, and therefore the local official needs to pay attention to helping all constituents in the election process. In New Mexico, for example, several heavily Republican precincts ran out of ballots on election day. Although such accidents happen, administrators must work to prevent them, because they undermine administrators' integrity, potentially increase disapproval with their job performance, and hence decrease voter confidence. Equally important, it also likely has the direct effect of preventing citizens from voting. Voter education through public service announcements would assist in connecting voters to their vote administrator and help to create a more positive voter experience and consequently greater voter confidence.

The results also suggest that it is important to look closely at why early and absentee voting produces less confidence. States are increasingly offering these options to their voters, yet the survey suggest that such options may be problematic for voter confidence. Therefore, we cannot recommend these policies. It is unclear, however, what underlying mechanism produces this difference, so we are cautious in interpreting the implications of these findings.

In conclusion, we urge more scholarly interest in questions of voter confidence and voter satisfaction. The process by which Americans elect their leaders is at least as important as the trust they place in them once they take office. Many of our conclusions assist in directing efforts toward remedying the problems voters face when they cast their ballots and ultimately toward improving voter confidence. Yet much work remains to be done, and many questions remain to be answered. Ours is only a first step in this important area of research.

Appendix 2A

Table 2A-1 presents the variables used in the survey. Table 2A-2 presents the results of the ordered probit model of voter confidence. Table 2A-3 presents the first differences in probabilities derived from our ordered probit model. It provides detailed information about the raw probability change estimates of respondents in a particular response option when each independent variable is varied from its minimum to maximum and all of the other variables in the model are set to their medians.

Table 2A-1. *Descriptive Statistics*

Variable	Median	Mean	Minimum	Maximum
Voter confidence (dependent variable)	3	3.25	1	4
Early voting (dummy, early = 1)	0	0.24	0	1
Absentee voting (dummy, absentee = 1)	0	0.41	0	1
Race (dummy, white = 1)	1	0.76	0	1
Gender (dummy, 1 = female)	1	0.54	0	1
Chronological age	56	54.94	18	91
Education (high school or less, some college, college, advanced degree)	3	2.73	1	4
Income (16-category ordered measure)	7	7.52	1	16
Party identification (strong Democrat to strong Republican)	3	3.80	1	7
Ever had problems at the polls (yes = 1)	0	0.18	0	1
How confusing was your ballot (not at all to very)	1	1.51	1	4
Respondent thought ballot was too long (strongly disagree to strongly agree)	2	2.33	1	5
Respondent enjoyed method of voting (strongly disagree to strongly agree)	4	3.75	1	5
Respondent has a positive opinion of county election official (strongly disapprove to strongly approve)	3	2.80	1	5
Agreed voting method used produced verifiable results	4	3.88	1	5
State (dummy, New Mexico = 1)	1	0.54	0	1

Table 2A-2. *Predicting Voter Confidence in the Election,*
Ordered Probit Model[a]

Variable	Probit coefficient	Standard error	Model summary[b]
Voting experience			
Voting problems	−.202	.129	NS
Poll workers helpful	.355***	.084	+++
Confusing ballot	−.281***	.060	+++
Long ballot	−.066	.043	NS
Enjoyed voting method	.199***	.054	+++
Voted absentee	−.392***	.118	− −
Voted early	−.199*	.119	−
Voter attitudes			
Voting method produces verifiable results	.115**	.054	++
County election officer's job evaluation	.259***	.039	+++
Party identification	.097***	.022	++
Demographics			
Age	.0001	.003	NS
Gender (female)	−.030	.090	NS
Education	.073	.047	NS
Race (white)	.114	.116	NS
Income	.035***	.014	++
State (New Mexico)	.131	.123	NS
Cut 1	.915	.489	
Cut 2	1.820	.489	
Cut 3	3.370	.499	
Chi square	140.95***		
N	672		

*p < .10   **p < .05   ***p < .01

NS = not significant.

+++ = change of probability > .30.

++ or − − = change of probability between .15 and .30.

+ or − = change of probability between 0 and .15.

a. The software program Clarify and the software Stata 9.0 were used. The dependent variable was measured on a scale from 1 (not at all confident) to 4 (very confident). Direction of relationship is denoted by a plus or a minus.

b. The number of pluses or minuses denotes comparative change in probability from option 3 (somewhat confident) to option 4 (very confident) when varying each independent variable from its minimum to its maximum and holding all other variables at their medians. The modeled probability with all variables at their medians is .57 for the very confident category.

Table 2A-3. *First Differences Resulting from Ordered Probit Model of Voter Confidence*[a]

Variable	Significance level	Not at all confident	Not too confident	Somewhat confident	Very confident
Initial model					
Change in probability for					
Voter experience		.005	.036	.389	.570
Voting problems	NS	−.003	−.018	−.059	.081
Poll worker helpfulness	***	−.060	−.151	−.164	.375
Confusing ballot	***	.035	.110	.169	−.315
It took to long to vote with the ballot I used	NS	−.002	−.016	−.081	.100
Enjoyed voting with method used	***	−.020	−.080	−.206	.306
Voted absentee	***	.008	.039	.108	−.156
Voted early	*	.004	.017	.058	−.079
Voter attitudes					
Voting method produces verifiable results	**	−.010	−.043	−.127	.179
County election officer's job evaluation	***	−.018	−.081	−.288	.387
Party identification	***	−.007	−.038	−.176	.220
Demographics					
Age	NS	−.001	−.003	−.015	.019
Gender	NS	.000	.002	.009	−.011
Education	NS	−.003	−.018	−.069	.092
Race	NS	.002	.009	.029	−.039
Income	***	−.006	−.035	−.155	.197
State (New Mexico)	NS	−.002	−.010	−.037	.049

$*p < .10$ $**p < .05$ $***p < .01$
NS = not significant.
a. The dependent variable was measured on a scale from 1 (not at all confident) to 4 (very confident). The numbers represent the comparative change in probability of being in each category when varying each independent variable from its minimum to its maximum while holding all other variables at their medians.

Notes

1. Caltech/MIT Voting Technology Project, "Voting: What Is, What Could Be," 2001 (http://vote.caltech.edu).

2. Wand and others (2001).

3. Manual Roig-Franzia and Dan Keating, "Latest Conspiracy Theory—Kerry Won—Hits the Ether," *Washington Post*, November 11, 2004, p. A02.

4. Scholars have also asked whether changes in support for government represent a maturation of the public and indicate a healthy, critical electorate (Norris 1999).

5. See www.american.edu/ia/cfer/.

6. Center for Political Studies (2007).

7. Dalton (1999).

8. See, for example, Hill (1981).

9. Rahn, Brehm, and Carlson (1999); Price and Romantan (2004).

10. Alvarez, Hall, and Llewellyn (2006).

11. The former New Mexico secretary of state Rebecca Vigil-Giron and the former Colorado secretary of state Gigi Dennis were kind enough to provide us with the voter registration files, updated through the last day of registration activities in 2006, for the congressional districts.

12. The URLs were votenewmexico.unm.edu and votecolorado.unm.edu.

13. We calculated the response rate by dividing the number of surveys returned to us, either online or by USPS, by the total number of eligible respondents. The response rate is the maximum response rate as defined by the American Association for Public Opinion Research (2000). Because of the poor quality of both states' voter registration files, more than 22 percent of our sample was unreachable.

14. Atkeson and others (2007).

15. For a summary of our findings, a more in-depth discussion of our sample, and a frequency report of our questions, see http://vote2006.unm.edu/ea2006.htm.

16. Reported problems in voting include the voter's name being absent from the voter list, the voter's having to vote provisionally, the voter's having a difficult time finding his or her polling place, someone else's having voted under the voter's name, lack of proper voter identification, and absentee ballots that arrived late or not at all. Regarding ballot confusion, we asked, "How confusing did you find your ballot? Very confusing, somewhat confusing, not too confusing, or not confusing at all?" We also asked, "How long did you wait in line at your polling place in minutes?" and "How helpful were the poll workers at your voting location? Very helpful, somewhat helpful, not too helpful, or not helpful at all?"

17. We asked respondents to strongly agree, agree, neither agree nor disagree, disagree, or strongly disagree with the statement "I enjoyed voting with the method I used."

18. Alvarez, Hall, and Llewellyn (2006).

19. The question used a Likert-type scale. Absentee voters were given the mean score to prevent listwise deletion in the regression equation.

20. Bowler and Donovan (2002); Brewer and Sigelman (2002); Bullock, Hood, and Clark (2005); Cook and Gronke (2005); Alvarez, Hall, and Llewellyn (2006).

21. Summary statistics for all the variables used in this study are given in the appendix to the chapter. Self-identified nonwhite voters in our sample were largely Hispanic; they were 12.3 percent of the total sample. African Americans were 2.1 percent; Asians, 1.5 percent; and American Indians, 1 percent. In New Mexico, Hispanics were 19 percent of the sample.

22. Abramson (1983); Brewer and Sigelman (2002); Bullock, Hood, and Clark (2005); Alvarez, Hall, and Llewellyn (2006); Pew Research Center for the People and the Press, "Democrats Hold Enthusiasm, Engagement Advantage; November Turnout May Be High," news release, October 11, 2006 (http://peoplepress.org/reports/).

THAD HALL, J. QUIN MONSON,
AND KELLY D. PATTERSON

3

Poll Workers' Job Satisfaction and Confidence

The aftermath of the 2000 election process has been one of constant learning in regard to election administration in the United States. The initial focus of both scholars and policymakers after the election was on voting technologies in order to discover which technologies most accurately recorded votes. More recently, however, scholars have come to recognize the critical role that poll workers play in shaping voters' perceptions of the fairness of the democratic process as well as their confidence that ballots are counted accurately.[1] Consequently, in this chapter we focus on understanding who these poll workers are, what motivates them, and what type of training poll workers receive.

Poll workers are crucial intermediaries between voters and voting technology. In previous work, we described them as "street-level bureaucrats" who powerfully affect the experience that voters have on election day.[2] Even seemingly simple things, such as setting up and closing down voting machines and determining when to check a voter's identification or when to allow a voter to cast a provisional ballot, can affect voters' experiences with the voting process and even election outcomes. For example, when poll workers in an Indiana precinct in the 2006 general election could not set up the voting

Authors are listed alphabetically. Data collection in Cuyahoga County, Ohio, was funded by the Election Science Institute (ESI) through a contract with the Cuyahoga County Commission. We are grateful to Steven Hertzberg of ESI for his assistance in the data collection. The Utah poll worker survey was funded by the Institute of Public and International Affairs at the University of Utah. Steven Snell of the Center for the Study of Elections and Democracy at Brigham Young University provided valuable research assistance for this project.

machines in their precinct, it created delays in the opening of the polls and also may have undermined some voters' confidence in the electoral process.[3]

In this chapter we seek to expand our understanding of poll workers based on the results of two surveys conducted in the 2006 primary elections in Cuyahoga County, Ohio, and in Utah's Third Congressional District. These two jurisdictions faced similar challenges. Not only did they both have competitive primary elections but they also both had adopted the same electronic voting technology—Diebold TSX with a voter verified paper audit trail. However, as the survey results show, the poll workers in both jurisdictions were demographically different from each other, were motivated by different forces, and had dramatically different experiences in interacting with the voting technology. This last difference, we argue, can likely be traced to differences in poll worker training between the two jurisdictions.

Survey Methodology

We used slightly different methods for sampling poll workers in Ohio and in Utah. In both jurisdictions the poll worker surveys were conducted in conjunction with exit polling. All poll workers in the exit polling locations were contacted with a request to participate in the survey. In Utah the survey was conducted with poll workers at thirty randomly selected exit polling locations in the congressional district.[4] In Ohio the survey was conducted with poll workers at fifty randomly selected exit polling locations and then supplemented by an additional random sample of poll workers from other polling locations throughout the county. In Ohio the survey was conducted by telephone; in Utah the survey was conducted by mail.

The surveys used generally accepted methods for telephone and mail surveys.[5] Full survey questionnaires and other methodological details are available from the authors upon request. The Ohio survey had a response rate of 54 percent ($N = 527$); the Utah survey had a response rate of 91 percent ($N = 131$).

The response rate for the Ohio survey is defined as the proportion of eligible respondents who participated. The cooperation rate, defined as the proportion of eligible respondents successfully contacted who agreed to participate, was 85 percent. Telephone interviews lasted an average of nineteen minutes and were conducted by Promark Research Corporation of Houston, Texas.

The Utah survey was a joint effort of the Center for the Study of Elections and Democracy at Brigham Young University and the Institute of Public and International Affairs (IPIA) at the University of Utah, with the fieldwork conducted by IPIA. The response rate of 91 percent for the mail survey is defined as the proportion of eligible respondents who participated.

To simplify the presentation we pooled the two surveys to produce the estimates for tables 3-6 and 3-7. To control for the differences between the two jurisdictions (evident in earlier tables), a dummy variable was included in the model for the survey location. The models were estimated in Stata, with robust standard errors. When the models for each location were estimated separately (not shown), the Ohio models in table 3-6 and both Ohio and Utah models in table 3-7 produced substantively similar results. The separate models in table 3-6 would not converge for the Utah data, likely due to the small sample size.

Given that there is no literature on surveying poll workers, the questions included in the survey were based on discussions with election administrators, academics, and other experts and on a review of general survey literature in political science. The basic folk wisdom about poll workers holds that they are women, that they are older than the general population, and that they are not technically savvy. We sought to test these assumptions. We were also interested in identifying the benefits to poll workers of training, hypothesizing that poll workers who receive more hands-on training are more likely to have positive attitudes about the training. In addition, we expected positive training experiences to increase poll workers' confidence in the electoral process and reduce the likelihood of problems at the polls. Finally, we expected certain demographic factors, such as age, education, and technological savvy, to affect both reactions to training and election day performance. Better educated poll workers and those with more technological savvy were hypothesized to handle the transition to electronic voting better, while older poll workers were more likely to have concerns about the training and the new technology.

Demographics of Poll Workers

Our survey data show that, as assumed, poll workers in both jurisdictions were mostly female and older (table 3-1). However, there were important demographic differences between the two jurisdictions we surveyed. Approximately 69 percent of poll workers in the Ohio sample were female, compared with 79 percent of poll workers in the Utah sample. In Cuyahoga County, the mean age was sixty-five and 27 percent were seventy-five or older. By contrast, the average age of a poll worker in the Third Congressional District was fifty-nine, and only 18 percent were seventy-five or older. In fact, almost 40 percent of poll workers in Utah were under age fifty-five, compared to 24 percent in Ohio.

Table 3-1. *Characteristics of Poll Workers*
Percent

Characteristic	Ohio	Utah
Female	68.9	79.1
Male	31.1	20.9
Ages 18–24	2.5	2.3
Ages 25–34	1.5	3.1
Ages 35–44	5.9	9.9
Ages 45–54	14.0	24.4
Ages 55–64	17.6	24.4
Ages 65–74	30.9	17.6
Ages 75–84	24.3	15.3
Ages 85 and older	3.2	3.1
High school or less	40.1	16.8
College	48.7	67.9
Postgraduate	11.3	15.3
White	66.1	96.2
Black	30.5	0.8
Other	2.9	3.1
Democrat	65.4	17.2
Independent	6.0	3.1
Republican	28.6	79.7
Not employed full time	86.9	81.7
Employed full time	13.3	18.3
"Very" comfortable using computer	44.0	46.2
Uses Internet daily	36.6	46.2

In both jurisdictions approximately 45 percent of poll workers claimed that they were very comfortable using computers. In Utah approximately the same percentage claimed to use the Internet daily; roughly 37 percent of the Ohio poll workers said the same. Not surprisingly, these usage rates are age dependent. Among poll workers under age fifty-five, almost 66 percent of those in Ohio and more than 70 percent of those in Utah said that they were very comfortable using computers. In contrast, among poll workers age seventy-five and older, only 27 percent of those in Ohio and 9 percent of those in Utah claimed to be very comfortable using computers. These data suggest that the technological savvy of poll workers will change as younger poll workers replace older ones.

Poll workers in Utah were more likely to have some college education than those in Ohio. However, this is another factor in which age is an important control variable: older poll workers were less likely to have some college education in both jurisdictions, so replacement over time of older poll workers with younger ones will likely change this measure. Regarding race and party affiliation, poll workers again reflected their broader communities: Utah poll workers were generally white and Republicans; those in Ohio were more racially diverse and tended to be Democrats.

Motivating and Recruiting Poll Workers

Given the older age of poll workers, one key question is how more poll workers can be recruited and retained. In the surveys, the question "How were you first recruited as a poll worker?" was asked slightly differently in each state, to accommodate requests by government officials involved with one of the surveys (table 3-2). Nonetheless, we can draw some conclusions across the two jurisdictions. Poll workers and political parties were critical recruitment mechanisms. In Ohio party leaders at the local level were often quite involved in nominating and approving poll workers. In Utah local party leaders played a much smaller role, but party-sponsored precinct caucus meetings were actively used to recruit poll workers. More than half of poll workers in both jurisdictions were recruited through these two channels. By contrast, initiatives by local election officials, such as job postings and advertisements in the media, attracted between 4 percent and 10 percent of poll workers.

We also asked poll workers about factors that influenced their decision to serve in this capacity. More than half of workers in both jurisdictions were motivated by either a sense of duty as a citizen or a sense of being the type of person who does his or her fair share. Few respondents reported doing it under pressure (not wanting to say no to someone); similarly, just being asked by a party official was not a very important reason to serve. Several items were judged "very important" by one-third of respondents in Ohio and one-quarter of respondents in Utah: making money and being with people who share their ideals.

When we examine these items by subgroupings, we find several interesting results. There were no differences across self-reported party identification; all partisans were similarly motivated. African Americans, lower income individuals (under $50,000 income), and less educated individuals (high school graduates or less) were more likely to respond that a sense of duty was a very important reason for being a poll worker, compared to white, higher

Table 3-2. *Recruitment and Motivation of Poll Workers*
Percent

	Ohio	Utah
Recruiting agent:		
Political party official	19.4	10.9
Precinct caucus	**	40.3
Booth or poll worker	36.7	20.9
Advertisement in local media	4.6	1.6
Teacher or professor	1.2	**
Official job posting by county	6.0	2.3
Self, seeking position	**	14.0
Other	32.1	10.1
"Very" important reason for becoming a poll worker:		
I am the kind of person who does my share.	81.2	60.9
I think it is my duty as a citizen.	73.8	69.8
I can be with people I enjoy.	54.3	33.9
I found it exciting.	39.3	24.4
I received recognition from people I respect.	38.9	12.7
I wanted to make some extra money.	38.3	26.6
I like to be with people who share my ideals.	38.1	29.1
I wanted to learn about politics and government.	32.3	30.7
I was asked by someone in my political party.	29.0	11.6
I did not want to say no to someone who asked.	18.8	3.9

$**p < .05$

income, and better educated individuals. We find similar results on the education variable for being motivated by the desire to do their share. The very young (eighteen to twenty-four-year-olds) were not likely to stipulate civic duty as a motivation; instead, they were most likely to say they were doing it for the money.

Poll Worker Training

Election administration is a relatively unique activity because the frontline workers do not do the job on a regular basis. In addition, they typically work without supervision.[6] This means that effective preelection training is critical. If polling places are to operate smoothly, workers need to understand how to accomplish certain tasks and how to address any problems that may arise.

The following discussion of training frontline employees demonstrates the challenges involved:

> Training for employee development is typically focused on improving the performance of continuing employees in their particular job knowledge and skills. On-the-job training is frequently used to demonstrate job functions and classroom sessions are used to convey general information. Supervisory development involves new and continuing *frontline managers* and develops skills such as delegation, the building of employee motivation, interpersonal communications, and how to work with small groups. Supervisors are often taught by a "tell-show-do" method where supervisory practices are discussed, demonstrated, and the trainees practice each of the skills. A debriefing session is often conducted after practicing the skill in question to answer any questions and clarify supervisory practices.[7]

Notice how little of this passage can be applied to poll workers. The recommendation to train supervisors using the tell-show-do method can be implemented to train precinct poll managers. But poll workers cannot easily be taught through on-the-job training, especially because their job is so episodic in nature. (The one-day nature of the job may also limit benefits from peer-to-peer learning in the workplace.)[8] Poll workers can be taught through classroom sessions, but these sessions must by the nature of the work cover both job function and general information. Finally, the cost of elections and the ongoing nature of postelection work, which can last up to one month after the election, mean that debriefing sessions for poll workers are likely to be rare.

The failure to debrief poll workers makes it difficult for election officials to create a culture of learning that allows the organization to "make use of institutional knowledge, and benefit from past experience."[9] Election officials, like any organization, need to have a built-in mechanism that allows them to learn based on previous experience and then use this experience to plan for the future. However, in the public sector, training is often underfunded, largely because of the lack of centrality of training in an organization's mission and the difficulty of immediately measuring the benefit of employee training on organizational outcomes.

When selecting training methods, it is obvious that one size does not fit all; different people have different learning styles. However, for individuals who are doing a job for the first time and need to hit the ground running, training using role playing and simulations, coupled with case studies and small group discussions, is generally an effective use of multimethod instruction. By contrast, the lack of interactivity associated with both lecture-only and self-study training methods, such as videotapes and training manuals, can make these methods less effective.[10]

Variations in training were evident between Utah and Ohio. Training for the Ohio sample followed a traditional model. Three-hour training sessions were conducted lecture style before groups of at least thirty poll workers; sometimes the number of trainees exceeded forty. This training was hampered by problems with training materials and with problems with the training sessions for the trainers. The county elected to write its own training manual for poll workers, and the manual was revised several times during the training period to eliminate errors. The training was largely facilitated using trainers hired by the county elections staff.[11]

By contrast, training in most Utah counties was implemented jointly by the counties and Diebold, in cooperation with a vendor specializing in information technology training. The latter conducted the training sessions. The training materials were much more consistent with election day procedures, the training sessions were quite small (usually fourteen to sixteen people per class), and they provided substantial hands-on practice with the new equipment. Salt Lake County, the largest county in the state and a substantial portion of the Third Congressional District, implemented a program called Practice Makes Perfect, which allowed poll workers to come back as often as they desired in the days leading up to the election. More than half of the poll workers in Salt Lake County took advantage of this program.[12]

In addition to these differences, the survey uncovered several important issues with training (table 3-3). First, poll worker training, especially with equipment being rolled out for the first time, is complex and difficult to understand. A minority of poll workers in both jurisdictions strongly agreed with the statement that the training was easy to understand, with poll workers in Utah somewhat more likely to agree. Older poll workers in both jurisdictions were significantly more likely to view the training as being difficult to understand, compared to younger poll workers. Second, poll workers in Utah were more likely to think that the training prepared them well for election day; there was no difference among age cohorts regarding the percentage who felt they were well prepared by the training. However, in Ohio older poll workers were less likely to think that the training prepared them well. Third, poll workers in Ohio were much more likely to say that they saw differences between the way voting machines operated during training and the way they operated on election day. This was true across all age cohorts in Ohio. Those

Table 3-3. *Training of Poll Workers*
Percent

Comments, questions, answers	Ohio	Utah
Attended zero or one training sessions	68.8	50.0
"Strongly" agree that I was able to spend enough time practicing on the voting machine	16.0	18.6
"Strongly" agree that training sessions were too long	8.1	5.6
"Strongly" agree that training sessions were boring	6.2	2.4
"Strongly" agree that training was easy to understand	16.1	24.8
"Strongly" agree that training prepared me well for election day	14.1	24.0
There were differences between how I learned to operate the voting machine in training and how the it operated on election day	41.1	13.2
Training differed from the actual procedures "a lot"	28.2	6.3
Training differed from the actual procedures "somewhat"	46.4	50.0
Training differed from the actual procedures "a little bit"	25.4	43.8

who saw a difference were likely to say that their training and election day experiences were "somewhat" or "a lot" different.

Differences in poll workers' perceptions reflect differences in the training procedures outlined above. The hands-on training and smaller classes used in Utah left poll workers feeling confident in their ability to do their job; further, once they were on the job, the Utah workers found fewer differences between their training and election day activities. By contrast, the lecture format of training and the content in Ohio left poll workers feeling less well prepared than those in Utah and more likely to see differences between training and election day.

Not surprisingly, the survey results show that training affects polling place operations as well. Poll workers who did not perceive the training as preparing them very well were also more likely to have problems in setting up or closing down the voting machines. Likewise, poll workers who noticed differences between the way voting machines worked during training and the way they worked on election day were more likely to agree that there were problems at the polls setting up or closing down the machines.

There are, however, some interesting counterintuitive findings as well. Technological savvy, measured by Internet use and by comfort using computers, did not have the expected effect on poll workers' propensity to report starting-up and closing-down problems. On average, the more technologically savvy poll workers were virtually indistinguishable from their counterparts in terms of their likelihood to report problems. While it is possible that training with the voting machines mitigated the technological divide among poll workers, it is also possible that skills with regular computers and the Internet did not translate well to voting machine use. It is also notable that attending additional trainings did not decrease Ohio poll workers' propensity of reporting problems with setting up or closing down voting machines (table 3-4). Because additional trainings did affect Utah's poll workers in the expected way, this variation might further highlight a weakness in Ohio's training methods.

Three key outcome variables can be discerned in studying election administration: satisfaction, confidence, and comparisons of voting technologies (table 3-5). Responses are the proportions of poll workers who were very satisfied with their job as a poll worker, were very confident that the ballots in the election were counted accurately, and agreed strongly that the touch-screen machines were better than the punch-card equipment used in previous elections. Across the two jurisdictions, Utah poll workers had much more positive assessments across the three questions. Such differences probably reflect differences between Ohio and Utah in the competitiveness of elections and the overall partisan environment. Even so, the descriptive data suggest that the three training variables included in the analysis have an important impact on these three outcome variables. In every case, a more positive training experience led to more confidence, satisfaction, and a higher opinion of the touch-screen equipment. Party affiliation also mattered: Democrats were less confident than Republicans that the ballots were counted accurately, a finding echoed in surveys of voters.[13]

Problems and Confidence

A multivariate analysis examined the factors that led poll workers to report being very satisfied with their job and very confident that the ballots in the election were tabulated accurately. Ordered logit models show that poll worker training and the frequency of the poll worker's use of the Internet played a key role in predicting satisfaction and confidence. In addition, poll workers in Utah had more confidence and satisfaction than their counterparts in Ohio (tables 3-6 and 3-7).

Examining the job satisfaction model first, we see that all of the variables have the expected sign. Perceptions of training as well as the election day experience affected poll workers' job satisfaction. Poll workers who felt that their training prepared them well for election day were more likely to be

Table 3-4. *Poll Workers Problems with Voting Machines*

Percent agree

Characteristic	Problems setting up voting machines		Problems closing down voting machines and reporting results	
	Ohio	Utah	Ohio	Utah
Female	55.1	18.2	54.7	15.7
Male	57.5	22.2	60.5	7.4
Ages 18–24	38.5	0.0	38.5	0.0
Ages 25–34	62.5	25.0	71.5	0.0
Ages 35–44	44.8	7.7	41.4	15.4
Ages 45–54	52.8	21.9	55.6	18.8
Ages 55–64	56.5	19.4	51.1	9.4
Ages 65–74	61.4	31.8	69.2	26.1
Ages 75–84	54.8	10.5	50.4	0.0
Ages 85 and older	50.0	0.0	46.7	25.0
High school or less	57.2	23.8	51.0	9.1
College	52.8	19.5	60.3	13.5
Postgraduate	63.8	10.0	60.3	20.0
White	59.6	18.9	59.9	13.6
Black	48.3	0.0	50.7	0.0
Other	46.7	25.0	46.7	25.0
Democrat	55.2	4.5	56.9	18.2
Independent	57.1	0.0	63.0	0.0
Republican	58.5	22.0	59.3	13.7
Not employed full time	54.2	19.2	57.0	13.1
Employed full time	63.8	16.7	55.1	16.7
Less than "very" comfortable using computer	55.3	19.4	56.9	12.9
"Very" comfortable using computer	54.9	18.3	57.1	15.0
Does not use Internet daily	55.7	23.9	55.7	12.9
Uses Internet daily	55.3	13.3	57.5	15.0
Noticed difference in voting machine during training and on election day	65.1	43.8	66.0	23.5
Did not notice difference in voting machine during training and on election day	48.8	15.5	49.3	12.5
Training "somewhat" or "just a little" different from election day	65.5	50.0	60.7	26.7
Training "a lot" different from election day	64.4	0.0	78.0	0.0
"Strongly" agree that training was easy to understand	44.3	3.1	43.8	18.8
Less than "strongly" agree that training was easy to understand	58.0	24.5	59.5	12.4
Less than "strongly" agree that training prepared me for election day	55.8	23.2	58.7	15.3
"Strongly" agree that training prepared me for election day	39.1	6.2	44.3	9.7
Attended zero or one training session	56.7	22.2	55.1	20.0
Attended more than one training session	54.3	14.1	59.2	7.7

Table 3-5. *Poll Workers' Job Satisfaction, Confidence,*
and Voting Machine Assessment

Percent

Characteristic	Very satisfied with job as poll worker		Very confident ballots counted accurately		Touch-screen voting better than old system	
	Ohio	Utah	Ohio	Utah	Ohio	Utah
Female	41.2	73.5	40.4	79.2	63.9	79.4
Male	43.3	65.4	53.8	88.5	62.5	69.2
Ages 18–24	38.5	100.0	53.8	100.0	53.8	100.0
Ages 25–34	25.0	100.0	25.0	100.0	75.0	100.0
Ages 35–44	45.2	61.5	33.3	76.9	77.4	69.2
Ages 45–54	45.8	67.7	43.8	83.9	71.8	87.1
Ages 55–64	42.4	78.1	48.9	80.6	64.4	68.8
Ages 65–74	39.1	69.6	42.3	73.9	67.1	78.3
Ages 75–84	40.2	65.0	44.1	85.0	52.0	70.0
Ages 85 and older	64.7	100.0	73.3	66.7	50.0	100.0
High school or less	46.4	77.3	46.1	81.8	63.7	81.8
College	37.1	71.3	40.6	80.2	64.1	78.2
Postgraduate	44.8	70.0	56.1	85.0	61.4	70.0
White	40.0	72.4	48.5	80.3	58.0	77.2
Black	45.5	100.0	37.0	100.0	73.9	100.0
Other	53.3	50.0	40.0	100.0	78.6	75.0
Democrat	42.4	71.4	38.5	76.2	66.8	66.7
Independent	41.4	25.0	50.0	75.0	70.4	75.0
Republican	39.0	75.2	55.2	83.0	60.3	80.2
Not employed full time	41.3	71.7	45.7	79.0	62.2	76.4
Employed full time	45.5	73.9	39.1	91.3	71.0	82.6
Less than "very" comfortable using computer	41.2	71.0	40.7	77.9	56.8	76.8
"Very" comfortable using computer	43.5	73.3	48.9	85.0	71.4	78.3
Does not use Internet daily	39.0	69.0	39.4	79.4	61.3	73.9
Uses Internet daily	47.4	73.3	53.2	83.3	67.5	81.7
Training "somewhat" or "just a little" different from election day	33.8	71.5	40.9	86.7	56.8	66.7
Training "a lot" different from election day	31.0	0.0	29.8	100.0	48.2	0.0
Less than "strongly" agree that training was hands-on	38.2	68.2	41.8	79.6	61.5	75.0
"Strongly" agree that training was hands-on	60.2	83.3	60.0	95.7	74.7	95.7
Less than "strongly" agree that training prepared me forelection day	36.2	67.0	41.7	79.2	61.1	76.3
"Strongly" agree that training prepared me for election day	71.8	83.9	61.6	93.3	80.3	86.7

Table 3-6. *Factors Affecting Confidence and Satisfaction (Ordered Logit Model)*

Variable	Satisfied with job as poll worker		Confidence in accurate vote count	
	Coefficient	SE	Coefficient	SE
High school or less	−0.030	0.286	−0.266	0.301
College or some college	−0.321	0.266	−0.524	0.276*
Democrat	−0.100	0.248	−0.363	0.271
Republican	0.107	0.276	0.346	0.295
White	−0.014	0.403	0.109	0.357
Black	0.248	0.434	−0.220	0.386
Ages 18–24	−1.014	0.829	−1.088	0.858
Ages 25–34	−1.002	0.836	−1.983	0.911**
Ages 35–44	−1.030	0.749	−1.815	0.682***
Ages 45–54	−0.773	0.714	−1.181	0.634*
Ages 55–64	−0.982	0.713	−1.109	0.627*
Ages 65–74	−0.984	0.705	−1.335	0.606**
Ages 75–84	−0.900	0.703	−1.163	0.605*
"Very" comfortable using computer	−0.085	0.213	0.190	0.193
Uses Internet daily	0.382	0.215*	0.334	0.200*
Problems setting up voting machine	−0.305	0.229	−0.045	0.223
Problems closing down voting machine	−0.727	0.207***	−0.778	0.227***
Training "very" different from election day	−0.349	0.301	−0.384	0.271
"Very" prepared on election day	1.406	0.254***	0.996	0.263***
State (Utah = 1)	1.093	0.251***	1.049	0.287***
Cut point 1	−4.113	0.831	−5.352	0.792
Cut point 2	−2.554	0.795	−4.010	0.757
Cut point 3	−0.659	0.777	−1.394	0.742
Pseudo R^2	0.0869		0.108	
Log likelihood	−666.686		−555.281	
N	650		642	

*$p < .10$ **$p < .05$ ***$p < .01$
SE = standard error.

satisfied. The negative sign for poll workers who saw differences between the training and actual experiences on election day is in the expected direction but does not achieve statistical significance. Poll workers were less likely to be satisfied if there were problems closing down the voting machines. The effect of problems with setup is in the expected direction but not statistically significant. Daily Internet use positively influenced job satisfaction as well. While not

Table 3-7. *Factors Affecting Problems with Voting Machines (Ordered Logit Model)*

Variable	Starting-up problems		Shutting-down problems	
	Coefficient	SE	Coefficient	SE
High school or less	0.071	0.250	−0.399	0.243*
College or some college	−0.165	0.227	−0.070	0.228
Democrat	0.026	0.244	0.324	0.244
Republican	0.200	0.255	0.482	0.257*
White	0.139	0.335	0.214	0.318
Black	−0.205	0.380	−0.075	0.358
Ages 18–24	−0.045	0.635	0.008	0.683
Ages 25–34	1.134	0.599*	1.067	0.664
Ages 35–44	0.098	0.428	0.394	0.571
Ages 45–54	0.624	0.385	0.662	0.516
Ages 55–64	0.737	0.372**	0.563	0.502
Ages 65–74	0.594	0.353*	1.191	0.491**
Ages 75–84	0.299	0.364	0.506	0.497
"Very" comfortable using computer	0.090	0.180	0.027	0.178
Uses Internet daily	−0.240	0.176	−0.198	0.189
Training "very" different from election day	0.409	0.284	1.304	0.272
"Very" prepared on election day	−1.213	0.264***	−0.816	0.257***
State (Utah = 1)	−1.312	0.198***	−1.331	0.203***
Cut point 1	−1.547	0.496	−1.153	0.604
Cut point 2	0.096	0.498	0.618	0.611
Cut point 3	0.201	0.498	0.757	0.613
Cut point 4	1.755	0.503	2.031	0.622
Pseudo R^2	0.0578		0.071	
Log likelihood	−868.684		−863.14628	
N	642		639	

*$p < .10$ **$p < .05$ ***$p < .01$
SE = standard error.

statistically significant, the coefficients for age and education have the expected sign compared to the reference group (eighty-five years old or older and postgraduates).

When we examine confidence that ballots were counted accurately, we see that, again, Utah poll workers were more confident. When we consider demographic groups, we find that the oldest and youngest poll workers were most confident that ballots were tabulated accurately. Education also played a role; the best educated were more confident than the less well educated. We also see a difference between daily Internet use and self-reported comfort level with computers; both are in the same direction, but only Internet use achieves statistical significance.

Again, training and election day experiences clearly influenced poll workers' confidence that the ballots were counted accurately. Poll workers who thought that the training prepared them well for election day were very likely to think that ballots were counted accurately. Conversely, problems closing down the machine—when the voting machines have ballots in them—negatively affected confidence that ballots were counted accurately. Problems setting up the voting machines had no discernable effect on confidence in ballot tabulation.

Training was the critical factor in both models that predict problems setting up and closing down the voting machines. Poll workers who felt that they were very well prepared by the training were less likely to agree that there were problems in these areas. Poll workers who saw major differences between election day voting and the training were more likely to say that there were problems shutting down. Again, although the difference is not statistically significant, poll workers who used the Internet daily were less likely to agree that there were problems starting up the voting machines. Poll workers in Utah were also less likely to agree that there were problems starting up and closing down the voting machines.

Implications for Reform

Poll workers are critical players in the election process because they affect the confidence voters have in the election process and generally serve as mediators between the voter and the ballot. The poll worker is the face of the election for voters who vote in a precinct on election day, which remains the most common method of voting in the United States.

In our work, we bring new data on the demographics of poll workers and the factors that make poll workers confident that ballots are counted accurately and make them satisfied with their job. We see that there is no one type of poll worker and that they vary both within and across jurisdictions. The Utah Third Congressional District poll workers were younger and better educated than the poll workers in Cuyahoga County, Ohio. We also see that many of these poll workers were not technological neophytes: a sizable percentage used both computers and the Internet daily. This bodes well for the future of elections in the United States, since newer poll workers are likely to be more technologically adept.

Training also varies across jurisdictions. Poll workers in Utah were more likely to agree strongly that their training was easy to understand and prepared them well for election day. They were also much less likely to agree that there were differences between how they were taught to use the voting machines and how the machines actually operated on election day. Moreover, among those who did report differences between the training and their election day experiences, most did not think the differences were very large. In contrast, in Ohio more than one-quarter of workers thought that their training and election day experiences differed.

The two jurisdictions obviously had very different experiences with the voting machines on election day. Ohio had more problems setting up and closing down the machines. These problems were reported by poll workers in all demographic groups. However, poll workers who found the training prepared them well for election day were less likely to have problems setting up the machines or closing them down. Not surprisingly, poll workers in Utah were more confident that ballots were counted accurately, more satisfied with their jobs as poll workers, and more likely to say that touch-screen voting was better than the older system.

Finally, multivariate analyses of confidence and satisfaction show that Utah poll workers were more confident and satisfied. Having problems shutting down the polls lowered confidence that ballots were counted accurately. Conversely, having good hands-on training increased confidence that ballots were counted accurately. Further, technological competence, as measured by daily computer and Internet use, affected satisfaction.

Given their importance to the confidence that voters have in the system, there is clearly a need for more study of poll workers. Several data collection efforts have been undertaken since the 2006 elections, and these should shed more light on the factors that affect voters' and poll workers' confidence and satisfaction in the electoral process. Given that the 2008 election is likely to be highly competitive, understanding these links is important for both academics and election officials.

Notes

1. Hall, Monson, and Patterson (2006); Atkeson and Saunders (2007).
2. Hall, Monson, and Patterson (2006).
3. Other examples of such occurrences can be found at http://electionupdates. caltech.edu/2006_11_05_archive.html.

4. Because Utah uses primary elections only when party conventions fail to select a candidate for office, the Third Congressional District race was the only competitive, high-turnout election in the state for the primary. We surveyed all poll workers in the precincts selected for the exit poll.

5. Lavrakas (1993); Dillman (2000).

6. Alvarez and Hall (2006).

7. Patton and others (2002, p. 327).

8. See, for example, Argyris and others (1994); Patton and others (2002).

9. Patton and others (2002, p. 332); see also Senge (1990).

10. Kenneth C. Green, "High Tech vs. High Touch: The Potential Promise and Probable Limits of Technology-Based Education and Training on Campuses" (www.ed.gov/pubs/competence/section4.html [March 14, 2008]); Patton and others (2002, pp. 332–34).

11. Information on training in Cuyahoga County comes from an author interview with Dane Thomas, Jacqueline Maiden, and Rosie Grier, Cuyahoga County Board of Elections staff, May 11, 2006, Cleveland, Ohio. See also Election Science Institute, "DRE Analysis for May 2006 Primary," Cuyahoga County, Ohio, August 2006 (http://bocc.cuyahogacounty.us/gsc/pdf/esi_cuyahoga_final.pdf [February 6, 2007]); and Cuyahoga Election Review Panel, "Final Report," Cuyahoga County, Ohio, July 20, 2006 (www.cuyahogavoting.org/cerp_final_report_20060720.pdf [February 6, 2007]).

12. Information on training in Utah is from multiple author interviews with Lieutenant Governor Gary Herbert; his chief of staff, Joseph Demma; and his deputy director, Michael Cragun. Salt Lake County clerk Sherrie Swenson and Salt Lake County Elections director Julio Garcia were also interviewed on July 20, 2006.

13. Alvarez, Hall, and Llewellyn (2006); Hall, Monson, and Patterson (2006).

PART II

Promoting Participation

ERIC GONZALEZ JUENKE AND JULIEMARIE SHEPHERD

4

Vote Centers and Voter Turnout

Scholars, candidates, local bureaucrats, party organizations, and even Congress have considered numerous electoral reforms that might improve voter turnout. The most recent and common changes include vote by mail (VBM), early voting, and absentee voting. In this chapter we examine the impact of vote centers, a reform that was introduced in many Colorado counties in the 2006 general election. Vote centers change how votes are cast on election day by reducing the number of polling places available to voters, while allowing anyone in the county to vote at the most convenient location (doing away with precinct-based polling completely).[1] This reform, it is thought, influences late deciders most directly, thus potentially increasing not only the overall turnout but also the demographics of the voting pool.[2]

We combine two theoretical stories to explain when and how electoral rules might affect voter turnout. First, electoral competition, which has been shown consistently to affect turnout, creates an environment in which elites must pay attention to procedural changes like vote centers and adjust their strategies accordingly. Thus convenience voting should increase overall turnout in competitive areas where elites provide information and incentives for voters to use the new technology. Second, when particular elites find the new procedure to be strategically advantageous, we should see a change in the demographics of the voting pool. That is, if a new procedure encourages elites to mobilize different types of nonvoters, then new types of voters will be observed at the polls. This is an elite-based theory of turnout, but it does not conflict with the rational voter theory.[3] Rather, this is a slightly nuanced way to understand the conditions under which elites provide mobilizing incentives to individuals and how procedural changes influence this relationship.

Vote Centers

Vote centers are polling places situated throughout a county that allow any registered voter to vote at any location. Thus someone could vote on the way home from work, downtown on their lunch break, or wherever might be more convenient. A countywide electronic database of voter information is available at each voting center, allowing election officials to verify voters' information and registration status.[4] The intent is to lower the cost connected with traveling to and from a specific location, especially for late deciders.[5] Under the vote center system, there are significantly fewer physical locations at which to vote, but voters have dozens more location options from which to choose.

Vote centers were the brainchild of the Larimer County (Colorado) clerk and recorder Scott Doyle, who asked in the wake of the 2000 election, "We don't live like we did two hundred years ago, so why are we voting like we did two hundred years ago?"[6] They were used for the first time in Larimer County during the 2003 election. At that time, according to Colorado's election law, precincts could be combined in off-year elections, which is essentially what vote centers accomplished. However, Doyle had approached Secretary of State Donnetta Davidson and asked for her support in bringing the vote center idea before the state legislature if it proved successful in Larimer in 2003. The 2003 election in Larimer County was a success, and Doyle moved forward with the support of State Senator Steve Johnson (and State Representative Bob McCluskey) to change Colorado statutes to allow vote centers to be used in any election in the state.

The resulting law, SB04-153, defines vote centers as a "polling place at which any registered elector in the political subdivision holding the election may vote, regardless of the precinct in which the elector resides."[7] The law also grants the ability to combine precincts in any election. With the approval and backing of the Colorado legislature, Larimer County has now had six successful elections using vote centers. Other counties in Colorado—and more recently, outside of Colorado—have begun to test similar programs. (Indiana, Nevada, and California are all implementing some form of vote center in some counties.)

Mesa County was the second county in Colorado to use vote centers in a general election. In 2005 the Mesa County clerk and recorder, Janice Rich, formed a task force that included both party chairs as well as other citizens.[8] This group was charged with studying the projected influence of vote centers on the county, determining where the centers should be located, and educating the public about the changes. In deciding where to establish vote centers, the task force looked at where voters tended to vote early, as early voting could be done at several locations instead of a single precinct. A unique strategy they used was to place as many vote centers as possible at locations that were previously precinct-polling locations; it was their intention to keep the voting process as similar as possible to that of previous years. In addition to Mesa County, Denver County and Douglas County attempted to use vote centers in the 2006 general election; they had less success, in large part due to the lack of preparation ahead of time and computer disasters on election day.

Research on vote centers is limited due to their recent implementation on a wide scale.[9] Robert Stein and Greg Vonnahme have done a few individual-level studies that examine the role of vote centers in generating increased turnout.[10] Their initial findings in Larimer County suggest that vote centers did, in fact, increase voter turnout in 2003, but it remains to be seen if these effects were related to their novelty and media coverage or if they will sustain themselves over time. Stein and Vonnahme's study of the 2006 general election expands the number of counties observed and finds that vote centers have a modestly negative effect on turnout.[11] The result however might be due to the inclusion of Denver and Douglas counties in the sample, both of which experienced major election day problems that were not necessarily caused by the switch to vote centers. Thus the early evidence concerning vote centers and turnout is in development. The present study contributes to this development by taking a different theoretical and empirical approach.

Elites Matter

We are interested in the role elites play in advancing and using electoral reforms. While there is limited literature that looks at this specific elite causal story, Gary Cox forwards the idea that changes in "party systems" or the rules governing elections affect both electoral outcomes and "parties' mobilizational incentives."[12] Along these same lines, Samuel Patterson and Gregory Caldeira, Stephen Rosenstone and John Hansen, and Robert Stein, Christopher Owens, and Jan Leighley consider the primary role of elites in using procedural changes to mobilize voters.[13] For example, in their study of early voting, Stein, Owens, and Leighley note that electoral reforms in general "are not self-actuating" and must be accompanied by "agents . . . to intervene between the opportunities created . . . and eligible voters."[14]

An elite-based theory of turnout may explain why procedural changes typically have modest effects on turnout. Elites do not have incentives to take advantage of procedural changes most of the time; they are interested in winning an election, not in getting people to turn out to vote per se. For example, if an incumbent is running unopposed, no one (except perhaps the government) has an incentive to spend resources on informing voters of new voting procedures or new voting sites. In contrast, in competitive elections, where information and mobilization are at a premium, we should observe increased turnout due to changes in vote procedures.[15]

Similarly, an elite-based theory of turnout suggests that differences in vote procedure should rarely be expected to change the demographics of the electorate. If, however, a particular procedural change might provide a strategic electoral advantage, we would expect to see changes to the demographic makeup of the electorate. For example, if African American voters were uniquely eligible for a small monetary reward for voting, we would expect to see Democrats use this procedure change to their advantage, and we would expect to see increased turnout among African Americans, mostly in competitive areas.[16] While this example is exaggerated, it is not hard to envision more legitimate types of vote changes differentially affecting one group over another. Stein, Owens, and Leighley find that Democrats in Texas were singularly advantaged by early voting reforms in 2002 because party elites found a way to increase turnout among their supporters in a way that Republicans could not.[17]

This begs the question of whether partisan elites are responsible for some of the changes to procedure we observe. In the case of Colorado's vote centers, it appears that the decision to change was a bureaucratic one made in response to the federal Help America Vote Act, not as a way to advantage one party or the other. In spite of this, vote centers could still influence the voter pool demographics if Republicans or Democrats realize that the new procedure could provide them the upper hand in a close election. One of the main concerns in Denver before the 2006 election was how older and lower-resource voters would handle the changes to some polling locations. We would expect the Democratic Party to be more concerned about these voters and thus to expend more resources and time educating and mobilizing than their Republican counterparts, all else equal.

Elite Interviews: Did Vote Centers Change Mobilization Strategy?

To examine the role political leaders played in implementing and utilizing vote centers, we conducted interviews with a variety of Colorado elites. For the purposes of this study, elites included candidates and members of governing organizations. The majority of the elites contacted were from the Denver metro area, in addition to those from the Western Slope (the city of Grand Junction) and Larimer County. To better understand the role of elites in the election process, specifically their relation to electoral reforms such as vote centers, we asked questions regarding elites' knowledge of vote centers, efforts to alter the electoral process by switching to vote centers, and mobilization strategies. These interviews provided us with insight into how elites responded—and in many cases, did not respond—to the changing electoral rules.

The majority of state representatives we interviewed in Denver County had become aware of vote centers in 2004, when SB04-153 (the bill that amended the state statute to allow vote centers) was first heard in the Local Government House Committee. All of the representatives remember hearing the bill and the testimony of the Larimer County clerk and recorder, Scott Doyle. Representative Joel Judd stated, "Mr. Doyle made [vote centers] sound like a smart idea," leading him to wonder why this idea had not been developed sooner.[18] Most of the legislators interviewed indicated they voted for the bill in committee and on the House floor, because there was no compelling reason to vote against it. It was evident that this group of elites did not support the change in statute because of a perceived partisan advantage but simply because it was presented as a good idea with a proven track record in Larimer County.

When looking for a correlation between the presence of vote centers in the 2006 election and elite behavior, we noted a few minor relationships. Several factors made it difficult to observe elites' behavior for the majority of the Denver County races. Many of the races, for instance, were uncompetitive because candidates were running unopposed for "safe" Democratic seats or because the candidate was a long-term incumbent. Due to such low competition, many of the candidates admitted they did not engage in significant campaigning or mobilization activity. Two specific races, however, demonstrated higher levels of competition and mobilization.

In the city of Grand Junction, Colorado Senate District 7 was an open seat in the 2006 election. State Representative Joshua Penry and former State Representative Matt Smith were the two Republicans seeking the nomination in the August primary. Both Penry and Smith were active in Mesa County politics, and both were well liked and widely known.

Penry was first made aware of the new electoral rules approximately a year prior to his primary.[19] To ensure that his potential voters were informed, Penry prepared a walking list, targeting registered Republicans for the primary, and did door-to-door drops containing flyers that listed the ten most convenient locations where voters could cast their ballots. Penry also sent out multiple mailers in which he included absentee ballot applications and self-addressed stamped envelopes so voters could vote ahead of time and avoid any confusion on election day. Penry explained that this was a way to "count his votes before election day." He would do "ballot chasing" and get weekly reports from the county clerk's office detailing who had cast ballots in that week, compare it to his master list of targeted voters, and then follow up with those who had not yet voted or requested an application. Penry used similar methods for both the primary and the general election. He believes that the flyers listing vote center locations were one of the most effective tools in his campaign.

House District 1, in the Denver metro area, was another competitive race in 2006. The Democratic candidate Jeanne Labuda ran a fairly aggressive campaign, benefiting from the efforts of candidates from nearby House districts who had less competitive races. Campaign tactics for this race centered on informing voters of the new vote centers. According to Representative Michael Cerbo, who was involved in Labuda's campaign, "Vote centers played a critical role in [the] race; we had to allocate a significant amount of resources to educating the electorate."[20] Due to the unique geographical composition of Colorado House District 1, cutting into three counties, only one of which used vote centers (Denver), the campaign had to make additional targeted efforts. Instead of sending out a general mailer, Labuda sent two versions of her campaign information, one for Denver County voters and the other with general information to non-Denver voters.[21]

In State House District 3 (in Denver) Representative Anne McGihon also responded aggressively to the introduction of vote centers in Denver County, fearing that they would present a "large scale catastrophe."[22] When she learned of the impending reform, McGihon arranged meetings with other members of the state legislature and even the Denver mayor's office to discuss concerns about the transition. To prevent possible problems with vote centers, McGihon worked actively ahead of time to inform her voters about the changing election system and encourage them to vote early or vote absentee to avoid the polls on election day. McGihon's campaign used mailers and robo-dial automated calls to remind voters to cast ballots ahead of election day. Indeed, on election day, McGihon's district had some of the longest wait lines in the city. Despite the long lines and her concerns, McGihon easily won her race; she attributes her success to voters who cast ballots early and by mail.

In the interviews, all of the elites indicated they would actively change their mobilization tactics in the face of electoral reforms, such as vote centers. Nonetheless, with the exception of Penry, Labuda, and McGihon, candidates in 2006 seemed to be largely unconcerned or unaware of the potential effects of vote centers and thus did not alter their mobilization behavior.

Quantitative Evidence: 2006 County-Level Turnout

The 2006 election provides a good test of the elite-based theory because it was the first time that many counties in Colorado used vote centers in a general election, and the election itself was salient across the state due to a competitive governor's race, a number of nationally significant House races, and a large number of ballot issues ranging from gay rights to government ethics reform. The data are at the county level.[23] There are obvious limitations to this aggregate approach, but in the absence of statewide survey data the county information should provide suggestive evidence.[24]

The elite-based theory described above suggests three hypotheses:

—Hypothesis one: Vote centers have no relationship with turnout in less competitive counties, all else equal.

—Hypothesis two: Vote centers are positively related to turnout in competitive counties, all else equal.

—Hypothesis three: In counties that do not use vote centers, increasing competition will create higher turnout, all else equal.

Table 4A-1 displays the descriptive statistics for the small data set. These are 2006 electoral data for sixty-one of Colorado's sixty-four counties, supplemented with 2000 census information to gain demographic leverage in our models. Aside from Latinos and (to a lesser extent) Native Americans, there is not much in the way of racial or ethnic diversity in Colorado. Unless we specifically look at Denver County over time, we will not be able to test the broader question of how procedural variation affects voting pool demographics.[25] Nonetheless, it is important to control for the demographic makeup of the counties to separate race and ethnicity effects from the structural variables of interest.

Voter turnout in 2006 in Colorado was relatively high, averaging 58 percent across all counties, and ranged from 47 percent to 73 percent.[26] Twenty-nine percent of the counties in the sample used vote centers, thus we have a good deal of variation with which to work.[27] Other controls include the population of the county, the percentage of Democratic, Republican, and Independent (unaffiliated) voters in each county, as well as measures of education and poverty.[28]

Measuring elite mobilization is an extremely difficult task without specific information from the candidates or parties. We instead use party competition as a very rough indicator of mobilization. It is reasonable to suspect that the more competitive counties experienced more mobilization efforts by both parties. The most important statewide race was for governor; thus the vote gap in each county between the Republican and Democratic gubernatorial candidates serves as a measure of party competition. The competition measure was created by subtracting the number of Beauprez (Republican) votes from the number of Ritter (Democrat) votes, taking their absolute value, and dividing by the total number of votes cast for these two gubernatorial candidates.[29] For example, if a county cast 100 votes for Bueaprez and 100 for Ritter, the measure would be: ABS(100–100)/200, or 0. If the county was split 50 votes for Bueaprez and 150 votes for Ritter (or vice versa), the observation would be ABS(50–150)/200, or .50 (50 percent vote gap). The variable can theoretically range from 0 to 100 percent, but the data for Colorado show this range to be confined between a 0 and 59 percent vote difference between the two. Thus an increase in this measure indicates a decrease in the level of party competition in the gubernatorial election in 2006 (a wider gap between the candidates). Finally, the interaction of vote center usage and "competition" is included as a direct test of the hypotheses above. The theory suggests that competition boosts the use of vote centers as a mobilizing device and that vote centers increase turnout in competitive areas.

Table 4A-2 displays three regression models of aggregate voter turnout, using total turnout (number of votes cast divided by number of registered voters in the county) as the dependent variable. The main differences in the models are based on the inclusion/exclusion of the vote center dummy, the competition measure, and the interaction of the two. Models 1 and 2 incorporate the gubernatorial competition measure and the interaction term separately, while model 3 simply examines the independent effect of vote centers on overall turnout levels (an intercept effect). All three models also include a baseline control for county turnout during the last statewide governor's race (in 2002). Controlling for turnout in 2002 provides the best look at differences between turnout in similar elections. That is, instead of trying to explain overall turnout, these models explore the factors influencing the remaining variation after turnout history is taken into account. While these models are very restrictive, we should still expect to see significant effects for competition and vote center usage.[30]

The main results can be summarized briefly. First, counties using vote centers are not associated with an increase in turnout in any of the models.[31] In fact, when there is a significant relationship between vote centers and turnout (model 2) it is negative (although the substantive effect is marginal). Second, the competition measure is not statistically related to turnout in either models 1 or 2. This is probably a function of the measure itself, as it is unlikely that competition had little effect on turnout in Colorado in 2006. Third, the interaction of vote centers and electoral competition is not statistically significant.[32] That is, not only does party competition have little relationship with turnout, but the combination of vote centers and competition is also a nonfactor. The hypothesis that vote centers only affect turnout in competitive areas finds no support. These generally null findings might surprise proponents of vote centers, but they are consistent with most of the procedural change literature and also with some initial individual-level findings for the same election in Colorado.[33]

All three models demonstrate that county-by-county turnout is a function of historical voting patterns and involves relatively few "new" factors, including procedural changes. As expected, turnout in the 2002 election is the most significant and influential factor in explaining turnout in 2006. Also, the proportion of Latinos and Native Americans in a county are both associated with lower turnout in 2006, and the proportion of registered Democrats in a county (compared to registered Republicans) is positively and significantly associated with higher turnout. The latter result may be evidence of a larger Democratic trend in the state over the last few elections, as the state House and Senate as well as the governor's office are now all controlled by Democrats. Finally, the proportion of independent voters in a county is negatively related to turnout (again, compared to Republicans), verifying the importance of partisanship in mobilizing voters.

Implications for Reform

Vote centers are sold to the public as a convenience, but we find little quantitative evidence that vote centers, on their own, do anything to influence overall turnout in a county—and when they do, the effect is slightly negative. Indeed, this may be why vote centers will be coming soon to counties and cities all across the United States; they benefit bureaucrats without harming elites. If vote centers have a negligible effect on election day turnout, possibly convenience habitual voters, and lower costs for bureaucrats who are adjusting to the Help America Vote Act, they may be a magic elixir for policymakers.

To the extent that vote centers convenience habitual voters and voters with disabilities, they appear to be a positive change. Also, in the long run, vote centers may increase turnout over time, as new voters find them more convenient than precinct voting and as more people become habitual voters.[34] Unless party and campaign elites find vote centers to be strategically advantageous, however, we should not expect them to change the demographics of the voting population.[35] Currently, this "new thing" in election day voting appears to be a lot like every other procedural change before it. It is different, unique, and convenient, but at the end of the day it appears to do little to change the size and makeup of the voting population.

Appendix 4A

There are sixty-four counties in Colorado. Denver and Douglas counties are excluded from the analyses because of well-published computer and machine problems during the 2006 election (both used vote centers). Broomfield County is excluded because it did not exist during the 2000 census (it did not use vote centers in 2006).

Table 4A-1. *Descriptive Statistics of Colorado Counties, General Election 2006*
Percent unless otherwise indicated

Dependent variable	Mean	Deviation	Minimum	Maximum
Voter turnout	58	6	47	73
Population (number)	58,538	124,985	558	527,056
Used vote center	29	Dummy	0	1
Governor vote gap	21	15	0	59
Black	1	2	0	9
Latino	15	14	1	65
Asian	1	1	0	4
American Indian	1	1	0	9
Noncitizen	4	3	0	15
Democrat	29	12	13	73
Republican	42	13	14	70
Older than 25 with HS degree	85	7	68	96
Household in poverty	12	5	4	30
Turnout in 2002[a]	56	10	34	81
N	61	61	61	61

a. This year marked the last comparable statewide governor's race.

In the table 4A-2, separate models use a measure that resembles the voting-eligible population as the dependent variable, using census 2000 voting-age population and noncitizen figures (there are no data at the county level for 2006), and generate results not substantially different from those presented (vote centers remain insignificant and insubstantial). This is not an unreasonable approach: our elite-driven framework indicates that vote centers might have both preelection mobilization effects and election day turnout effects, but here the results do not change, and for the most part the vote center research is interested in how vote centers affect election day turnout of registered voters, which is why we present these models.

What about county population size? Including controls for population size does not change the results. These controls include (separately) county population, logged county population, and a regression model using weighted county observations by population. Vote centers are never significantly associated with turnout in any of these models.

Variance inflation factor (VIF) diagnostics for the first model indicate little correlation between the independent variables. The only potential correlation occurs between the percentage of Latino voting-age population (VAP) and measures of county education levels and poverty levels (tolerance level [1/VIF] = .187). Models that exclude high school degree and households in poverty do not alter the overall conclusions.

Table 4A-2. *Explaining County Turnout in Colorado in the 2006*
General Election, Three Models

Percent country turnout

Dependent variable	Model 1		Model 2		Model 3	
Used vote center	−.006	(.017)	−.020	(.010)*	−.018	(.010)+
Governor vote gap	.008	(.067)	−.016	(.055)	. . .	
Vote center/vote gap	−.064	(.067)	. . .	. . .		
Black VAP	−.091	(.324)	−.137	(.316)	−.114	(.317)
Latino VAP	−.223	(.088)**	−.227	(.086)**	−.233	(.085)**
Asian VAP	−.606	(.614)	−.610	(.605)	−.608	(.612)
American Indian VAP	−.929	(.284)**	−.991	(.268)**	−.954	(.261)**
Democrat	.246	(.089)**	.240	(.088)**	.229	(.077)**
Independent	−.185	(.092)*	.183	(.093)*	−.187	(.086)*
Households in poverty	.177	(.193)	.197	(.191)	.194	(.189)
Older than 25 with HS degree	.033	(.109)	.044	(.112)	.027	(.108)
2002 turnout	.319	(.081)**	.301	(.086)**	.302	(.085)**
Constant	.387	(.117)**	.393	(.121)**	.408	(.104)**
R^2	.72		.71		.71	
F statistic	14.96**		16.58**		18.56**	
Root MSE	.037		.037		.037	
N	61		61		61	

$+ p < .10$ $^* p < .05$ $^{**} p < .01$ (two-tailed test)

a. OLS coefficients and robust standard errors are reported. Models excluding the lagged dependent variable do not change the substantive results, although the coefficient for vote centers is significant (95 percent) and remains negative.

Notes

1. This is entirely different from precinct "consolidation," which still assigns voters to a predetermined polling place.

2. Stein and Vonnahme (2006, 2007).

3. Aldrich (1993); Downs (1957); Leighley (2001).

4. Stein and Vonnahme (2006).

5. Dyck and Gimpel (2005); Stein and Vonnahme (2006).

6. Scott Doyle, interview with the authors, 2007.

7. Colorado General Assembly, *Local Government Committee Report* (www.leg.state.co.us/clics2004a/csl.nsf/).

8. Mesa County Vote Center Task Force, 2005, *Summary Report* (www.mesacounty dems.com).

9. Vote centers are important beyond Colorado precisely because they are becoming very popular among election officials and will be coming soon to counties and cities across the country.

10. Stein and Vonnahme (2006, 2007).

11. Stein and Vonnahme (2007).

12. Cox (1999, p. 387).

13. Patterson and Caldeira (1993); Rosenstone and Hansen (1993); Stein, Owens, and Leighley (2003).

14. Stein, Owens, and Leighley (2003, p. 7).

15. Rosenstone and Hansen (1993); Stein, Owens, and Leighley (2003).

16. Of course, Republicans and others would fight this hypothetical change tooth and nail, thus explaining why we rarely see partisan-advantaged changes in the first place.

17. Stein, Owens, and Leighley (2003). Republican voters were already very likely to vote, regardless of procedure, thus Republican Party leaders had a hard time increasing the size of their electorate.

18. Joel Judd, interview with authors, 2007.

19. Joshua Penry, interview with authors, 2007.

20. Michael Cerbo, interview with authors, 2007.

21. Judd, interview with authors, 2007.

22. Anne McGihon, interview with authors, 2007. McGihon's race ended up being uncompetitive, but she is one of the few elites we spoke to who changed tactics specifically in response to vote centers; it is unclear if the two are related.

23. We were able to construct a data set by calling county clerks and recorders directly and asking for the total number of ballots cast. Turnout was calculated by dividing the number of votes cast by the number of registered voters in each county in November 2006. See the appendix to this chapter.

24. See table 4A-2 for a note regarding empirical checks on this aggregate approach.

25. These data are being processed and are not available for this analysis.

26. Colorado's official turnout figures are artificially high, as the state now uses a category called "active voters" in their turnout numerator. This group only includes voters who voted in the last general election or notified the state that they were indeed still active. For academic studies of turnout, the inactive group of voters is exactly the group in which we are interested. We use overall turnout figures here.

27. Vote center usage was tabulated using information from the secretary of state via Bob Stein (fairvotecolorado.org) and direct phone calls to county clerks and recorders.

28. All of the models were run with the exclusion of Denver and Douglas counties to see if these two counties were driving the results, since both of them experienced unfortunate problems with computers and voting machines on election day, depressing turnout. The results do not change significantly, and the two counties are excluded in the results presented in tables 4A-1 and 4A-2. The partisan figures are from the Colorado secretary of state's office and reflect the number of registered members of each group in November 2006. The demographic information comes from the 2000 census and measures the proportion of each racial and ethnic group as a share of the voting-age population.

29. One could also just take the absolute value of the difference in vote percentages for each candidate. The absolute value is needed because we are interested in the distance, not the direction of the distance, between the two candidates' votes.

30. Precisely because vote centers are supposed to alter turnout differences across counties *and* over time, this is the best way to test this without individual-level vote history data (see Stein and Vonnahme 2007, and below, for a discussion of their findings).

31. This matches some basic statistics regarding which counties chose to make the switch to vote centers. Counties using vote centers had lower overall turnout in both 1998 (62 percent) and 2002 (53 percent) compared to counties that used traditional precincts (66 percent and 58 percent, respectively). Thus the causal direction of this relationship remains unclear.

32. We did estimate the appropriate coefficients and standard errors for the interaction term separately, using the estimator described in Brambor, Clark, and Golder (2006). We find a significant effect (95 percent confidence) for the interaction of "competition" and "vote centers" when electoral competition is measured between .20 and .40. Again, however, the substantive effect is marginal to negligible (0–2.5 percent) and generally supports the null findings reported here.

33. Berinsky, Burns, and Traugott (2001); Berinsky (2005); Giammo and Brox (2007); Karp and Banducci (2000); Southwell and Burchett (2000); Stein and Vonnahme (2007).

34. Stein and Vonnahme (2007).

35. Future work (during the 2008 general election) will combine individual-level elite and mass data to tease out the joint effects of mobilization and vote centers in altering voting behavior. We will also test for any demographic changes to the voting population, as we do not know if vote centers differentially affect older or lower-resource voters, as feared by some.

PAUL GRONKE, EVA GALANES-ROSENBAUM,
AND PETER A. MILLER

5

Early Voting and Voter Turnout

Early or convenience voting—understood in this context to be relaxed administrative rules and procedures through which citizens can cast a ballot at a time and place other than the precinct on election day—is a popular watchword among election reformers. Early voting is attractive because of claims that increased convenience reduces the costs of voting, resulting in higher turnout and higher-quality voter decisions. For this reason, states have experimented extensively with early voting laws. Yet the empirical literature finds mixed results, with some studies suggesting a turnout increase as large as 10 percent, while others find that voting convenience has little or no impact on turnout. The literature, to put it simply, is unsettled.

Our goals in this chapter are fourfold. First, we provide a map of the states in which early voting reforms have been adopted (figure 5-1); the figure also notes how frequently voters have taken advantage of these balloting methods. Second, we recapitulate the arguments supporting these types of reform. Third, we summarize previous scholarly research regarding the impact of convenience voting methods on voter turnout. Finally, we present our own findings regarding the impact of early voting on turnout.

Only one early voting reform—voting by mail—has had a positive impact on turnout, and that only in presidential elections. Most other reforms have a negligible, and in some cases negative, impact on turnout. Referenda and initiatives on the ballot interact with convenience voting methods, implying a complex interplay between these two types of ballot change, and these cannot be easily disentangled. The growing length of ballots as a consequence of an increasing use of initiatives and referenda may have led to the adoption of

Figure 5-1. *Early Voting Rates, by State, November 2004 General Election*

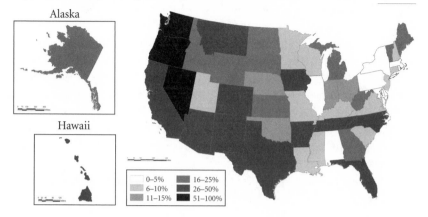

early voting as well as an increase in the educative function of elections. Our findings correspond with much of the literature, which argues that parties and campaign organizations, via the avenue of mobilization, are the primary engines that drive turnout in the United States.[1] Ballot reforms have, at best, a marginal effect and are unlikely to solve the challenge of low voter participation.

An Introduction to Early Voting

For the purposes of this chapter, *early voting, convenience voting,* and *non-precinct voting* are blanket terms we use to describe any system in which voters can cast their ballots before election day and at a place other than the polling station (although often it is a county office).[2] This definition covers a bewildering array of electoral systems. In some localities absentee balloting can be done in person and may be referred to as *early voting;* or it can be done by mail and may be referred to as *vote by mail.* In Sweden *postal voting* describes in-person voting in the post office. The following list summarizes the terms and their usage:

—*No-excuse absentee voting (vote by mail; absentee vote by mail):* Voters apply for an absentee ballot without any requirement for a reason. They receive the ballots as early as forty-five days before the election and must return it by the date of the election. In some localities, it must bear a postmark dated on or before the election. This method is in wide use.

No-excuse absentee voting allows voters to request an absentee ballot without providing a reason, such as travel or hospitalization. In some states, notably California, a voter can also request "permanent" absentee status, essentially becoming a regular vote-by-mail voter. Unrestricted access to an absentee ballot contrasts with the former norm of absentee eligibility: casting your ballot before election day because you are infirm, out of the country (in the military or living overseas), away at college, or otherwise unable to make it to the polls (nonetheless, restricted access to absentee ballots is still current law for sixteen states in the Northeast and South). This traditional form of absentee balloting has historically been quite restrictive, and the proportion of ballots cast via this method is very low. Use of no-excuse absentee balloting, in contrast, has increased dramatically over time in many states and localities.

—*In-person early voting (in-person absentee balloting):* Voters have the option of casting a vote early at a satellite location or at the county elections office. In most localities the voter simply shows up. Texas adopted this method early, followed by Georgia, Tennessee, and Iowa. Many more states have now adopted it.

—*Vote by mail (postal voting):* Voters receive ballots in the mail approximately two weeks before the election. Ballots can be returned by mail or dropped off at satellite locations. Oregon and New Zealand have adopted this method, as has the United Kingdom for local elections.

At the time of this writing, thirty-one states allowed early in-person voting—either alone or in conjunction with absentee by-mail voting—whereby voters can cast early ballots just as they would do on election day, commonly at the local elections office but increasingly at satellite locations such as community centers, churches, and even grocery stores. The important distinction between early in-person and other early voting systems is the requirement that individuals show up in person to cast a ballot. If we accept that getting to the polls imposes a significant barrier to participation, then in-person systems only partially relieve this burden; in addition, the convenience factor varies among systems, depending upon where voters can cast ballots.

Finally, in the vote-by-mail (VBM) system all voters receive and cast their ballots via regular mail. It has been used by the state of Oregon for all elections since 1998 (the first statewide election conducted in this manner was a 1993 special election, and vote by mail was used in two special Senate elections in 1995 and 1996 and in a 1996 presidential preference primary). VBM has been used in some local elections in California. During the 2006 general election, thirty-four of thirty-nine counties in Washington State conducted their elections entirely by mail; it is likely that VBM will become the statewide elections system for Washington in the next few years. Typically, the voter receives a voter's guide approximately three weeks before election day, followed by the ballot, which is generally mailed eighteen days before the election. The voter may return the ballot any time after it is received, usually fifteen days or closer to election day, continuing up to and including election day.

The Where and How of Convenience Voting Reforms

The first voting reforms aimed squarely at convenience took place in the 1980s, when absentee and early in-person voting were opened to a wider electorate, rather than simply to voters who were sick, elderly, disabled, in college, or traveling. No-excuse absentee balloting, in particular, became a popular method for anyone inconvenienced by going to the polls, regardless of the reason. Currently, twenty-eight states have no-excuse absentee laws. In addition, many states allow voters to cast a ballot at the county clerk's office or elections office before election day if they are going to be out of town or need assistance (in-person early voting). By the late 1990s twenty states had at least one type of convenience voting on the books, and some had two: Washington and California allowed voters to apply for permanent absentee status; six states allowed both no-excuse absentee voting and early in-person and absentee voting.

The advance of nonprecinct voting methods began before the 1980s: by January 1980 forty-seven states had adopted traditional absentee voting. Although this number dropped to forty-five states by January 1990 and to twenty-seven by January 2000, several nontraditional nonprecinct voting methods had been adopted by 2008:

—No-excuse absentee voting had been adopted by twenty-eight states.

—No-excuse absentee voting and permanent absentee status had been adopted by four states.

—In-person early voting (but not no-excuse absentee balloting) had been adopted by six states.

—No-excuse absentee voting and in-person early voting has been adopted by twenty-five states.

—By-mail voting had been adopted by one state.[3]

The myriad scandals and debacles uncovered during the 2000 presidential election, even though mainly technological and clerical in nature, gave momentum to a national movement toward more widespread nonprecinct voting methods. In the wake of the election, many states expanded their election systems to include convenience options on the premise that reducing the administrative pressures on election day would reduce the likelihood of a

Table 5-1. *Early Voting as Percentage of Total Turnout in General Election, Top Fifteen States, 2004 and 2006*

State	2004	2006
Oregon	82.25	71.87
Washington	68.48	84.86
Nevada	52.28	49.86
New Mexico	50.61	61.11
Tennessee	47.30	46.25
Colorado	47.13	54.38
Arizona	40.77	46.97
Arkansas	36.93	22.66
Florida	36.19	27.73
California	32.61	26.15
Texas	32.56	24.43
Montana	31.56	29.03
North Carolina	31.17	20.67
Hawaii	30.92	27.15
Iowa	30.10	21.95

Source: Authors.

snafu, be it minor or major. After the adoption of the Help America Vote Act in 2002, additional pressures on election officials made the administrative and technological benefits of early voting systems much more appealing. Other motivations included cost and concerns that there would not be enough new machines to process all the ballots cast in person on election day. Finally, public and legislative calls for voting machines that provided voter-verifiable paper audit trails after 2004—necessitating, in some cases, costly repurchasing of election equipment—further ramped up the pressure to move voters out of the precincts. After all, the traditional pen and paper absentee ballot provides a familiar method to keep a paper record.

Geographically, nonprecinct voting reforms throughout the last twenty-five years have occurred outside the Northeast. The West Coast and Southwest, in particular, began instituting postal methods early. Texas has become the most prominent state using early, in-person (EIP) voting, with seven other states following Texas's lead. This trend is quite clear in the rates of early voting in the 2004 general election (see map). While not uniformly the case, high numbers of early voters primarily appear in states with a high percentage of rural population and in those that are geographically large. All but one of the fifteen states with the highest early voting rates in 2004 fit these descriptions (table 5-1). In previous work, we found those individual voters who face long commutes or who live in rural areas were more likely to cast their ballots earlier rather than holding them until election day.[4] State legislatures and election officials recognize the burdens that voting can place on some voters and, as a result, adopt reforms that make it easier for these voters to cast a ballot.

Those states that adopted nonprecinct voting systems early in the observed time period also have the highest current rates of early voters. Eleven of the top fifteen early voting states in 2004 had instituted some type of liberalized early voting by the 1990s. Only eight of the remaining twenty-five had liberalized by that point. What is apparent from figure 5-1 and table 5-1 is the rapid increase in early voting once states adopt these reforms. A significant proportion of voters clearly prefer to be able to vote other than at the precinct place and earlier than on election day. In some states, this proportion seems to peak at 30–40 percent of the electorate, but in other states there seems to be no upper bound. For example, 85 percent of Washington voters cast their ballots absentee in 2006, and Washington State will be nearly fully vote by mail in the 2008 election.[5]

Election officials are often strong advocates of early voting reforms. The Oregon secretary of state, Bill Bradbury, is a primary example. Bradbury argues that voting by mail has four positive effects on the election process: it increases turnout and results in more citizens having a stake in their government; it results in more thoughtful voting, enhancing the democratic process; it offers greater procedural integrity; and finally, it saves taxpayer dollars.[6] Similar arguments have been made in favor of early in-person and relaxed absentee voting. The two primary national organizations that deal with election administration, the National Conference of State Legislatures and the National Association of Secretaries of State, issued reports after the 2000 elections, and again after the passage of the Help America Vote Act, that urge states to consider reforms that would allow early voting.[7] Many reformers hope that early voting may help reengage Americans in the electoral process.[8] But do these claims stand up to empirical scrutiny?

Convenience Voting and Turnout: The Literature

The empirical evidence to date supports election officials in one respect— early voting is associated with higher quality election administration. Early in-person voting, absentee balloting, and vote by mail have all been found to result in a more accurate count.[9] The verdict on cost savings, however, is less clear. The state of Oregon estimates savings of nearly 17 percent of the cost of

holding elections by adopting VBM, while EIP and liberalized absentee balloting do not clearly result in cost savings.[10]

The evidence regarding turnout is much weaker, although positive. Nonprecinct methods should increase turnout, theoretically, by easing the resource
demands of voting, primarily by eliminating the need to go to the polling
booth or by providing more convenient times to vote.[11] Empirical evidence
weakly supports this expectation. Liberalized absentee balloting leads to a
small but significant growth in turnout.[12] Early in-person voting also slightly
stimulates participation.[13] Finally, most evidence suggests that VBM increases
turnout, perhaps by as much as 10 percent.[14] Recent work has questioned the
generalizability of the 10 percent turnout effect. There is some evidence that
this spike in turnout is due to a novelty effect and is not sustained beyond the
first three elections using VBM. There is, however, a significant turnout effect
by vote by mail of about 5 percent in Washington State over the 1960–2006
period.[15] A turnout effect of about 4.1 percent is also found in Swiss elections
from 1970 to 2005.[16] Last, and contrary to theoretical expectations, one study
finds a negative turnout effect associated with VBM.[17]

The performance of electoral reforms on changing who votes is more
mixed. "What has not been widely recognized," says one researcher, "is that this
wave of reforms has exacerbated the socioeconomic biases of the electorate."[18]
This claim is sustained in compositional studies of all three systems. Politically
active segments of the population often take advantage of these liberalized
voting systems. VBM increases turnout by retaining likely voters in less intense
campaigns (for example, midterm and local elections) rather than by recruiting new voters into the system.[19] The two studies of absentee balloting indicate that rates of absentee voting vary positively with levels of partisan
mobilization: candidates harvest absentee voters in localities where party
organizations are strong, benefiting Republican candidates.[20] A study of early
in-person voting in Harris County, Texas, shows that that there were significantly larger numbers of Democrats and strong partisans among the "early
voters" than among election day voters.[21] A pattern of partisan advantage is
not clear from the literature on early voting, but it is clear that partisans on
either end of the political spectrum vote early at a higher rate than moderate
voters, in part due to party mobilization efforts.[22]

These studies, while helpful, are hampered by limitations in research design
and methodology that affect their applicability to the past decade of reforms.
Some studies have considered only the first three VBM contests.[23] One pio-
neering work considered only municipal elections in three Western states in

the early 1980s.[24] Some studies of in-person early voting are based on single elections and in a state where rates of early voting have increased dramatically in the past fifteen years.[25] A 1996 study is based on one county and relies on self-reports of turnout.[26] Finally, the two studies of absentee balloting rely on absentee ballot rates that are less than half of what they are today.[27] In the next section of this chapter, we address these shortcomings by providing a new and comprehensive look at the turnout effects of convenience voting reforms.

Turnout and Convenience Voting Reforms

In this section, we estimate the impact of convenience voting on turnout over a longer period than in previous work, considering all varieties of such reforms and with a larger geographic scope.

We relied upon an established model to assess the effects of the presence and number of initiatives on turnout.[28] These authors argue that ballot initiatives, far from making the election too complicated and thereby discouraging turnout, do the opposite: they increase turnout, primarily by increasing the salience of the election. Here we are less interested in replicating their findings for the effects of initiatives than we are in seeing whether early voting similarly increases turnout not by educating the electorate but by lowering at least one barrier to ballot access.

The data set of the established model contains a rich set of other correlates of turnout, including region, election type, institutional provisions, and the demographic characteristics of the state (racial diversity, educational attainment, and per capita income).[29] To this data set we added a measure of early voting reforms collected from archival sources. We coded reforms into six categories: traditional absentee balloting, no-excuse absentee balloting, no-excuse absentee balloting with permanent absentee status, in-person early voting, no-excuse absentee plus in-person early voting, and voting by mail. These six categories were then collapsed into dummy variables, with traditional absentee balloting as the excluded category, and added to the turnout model.[30]

A complete regression is included in the appendix to this chapter, but in the interests of clarity we focus here on the most salient results of the five models. The first model replicates the established model, following its lead with respect to methodology.[31] Our model has, however, two important differences: first, we exclude the measure of the number of initiatives in order to test the impact of early voting reforms independent of any ballot modifications; and second, we do not estimate separate models for midterm and for presidential contests. In the second model, we add the "number of initiatives" variable to see how it changes the estimated impact of convenience voting reforms. The third, fourth, and fifth columns essentially replicate the established model but add voting reform measures as well as a broader set of regional dummies to capture any remaining regional differences in balloting technology and turnout. The theoretical reasons behind these modeling decisions are elaborated below.

—Ballot initiatives are associated with an increase in turnout of about 0.476 percent in midterm elections.

—No-excuse absentee voting has no discernible effect on turnout.

—No-excuse absentee voting with permanent status is associated with about a 4 percent decrease in turnout in midterm elections.

—Early in-person voting has no discernible effect on turnout.

—Voting by mail is associated with an increase in turnout of about 6.8 percent in presidential elections.

—Turnout in the Northeast is 3.4 percent higher than that in the South across presidential and midterm elections.

—Turnout in the Midwest is 5.8 percent higher than that in the South across presidential and midterm elections.

—Turnout in the West is 5.6 percent than that in the South across presidential and midterm elections.

These results are puzzling: Why would convenience voting reforms reduce turnout? Our first intuition was to control for the number of initiatives on the ballot, under the assumption that there may be an interaction between the appearance of initiatives and voter turnout. Once we control for the number of initiatives on the ballot, the impact of all reforms save VBM disappear. The effect of VBM declines from about 6.1 percent to about 2.1 percent, and is no longer statistically significant. The sign of no-excuse absentee switches to a negative effect, though it and the other reforms remain insignificant.

In the next set of analyses, we consider two additional possibilities. First, we were intrigued by the finding that including initiatives in our turnout model altered so substantially the impact of voting reforms. One possibility, we speculate, is that states with high numbers of initiatives are much more likely to adopt convenience voting methods. After all, in states with long, complex ballots, the argument to provide voters more time to navigate the ballot and more leisure to consider complex initiatives is much more compelling. We took a first pass at controlling for these effects by adding additional regional dummy variables to our model.

Second, we wanted to consider the argument that the impact of initiatives and referenda as "educative" mechanisms only operates in midterm contests, when voter information and interest are relatively lower.[32] Thus we reestimated our model three ways: for presidential contests, midterm contests, and pooled (presidential and midterm contests together).

To turn to the second hypothesis—that there are important differences between presidential and midterm contests—we found additional support for our claim that voting reforms have no clear positive impact on turnout. First, the impact of voting by mail is now restricted solely to presidential contests; and second, no-excuse absentee voting with a permanent status option is associated with a decline in turnout. In the pooled model, only no-excuse absentee voting with permanent status retains explanatory power; the rest of the voting reforms show statistically insignificant relationships with voter turnout.

Is it possible that prior estimates of the impact of early voting reforms on turnout were all misspecified because they failed to take into account the number of initiatives and referenda on the ballot? We considered this possibility and present some intriguing graphics in figure 5-2. This figure contains two graphics. The top displays the number of initiatives, over time, in states that had some convenience voting (including no-excuse absentee balloting, the most common convenience voting method). There is little evidence of a trend in these data. However, the picture changes rather dramatically once we control for most liberal early voting provisions (eliminating those states that only allow no-excuse absentee balloting). Here we see a clear trend—the states that liberalized their voting laws after 1994 were the same states that experienced a rise in "citizen government" via the initiative process.

This seems to us a completely reasonable result, but it raises an important question of causality. Did states liberalize their voting provisions because they were experiencing an onslaught of initiatives? Some argue that states such as California, Oregon, and Washington have been forced to expand early voting because the ballot is long and complex to the point that precinct place voting is unrealistic. For example, the 2006 election in California was so long that the ballot guide was 192 pages long, while the Oregon Voter's Pamphlet was distributed in two volumes, ranging from 196 to 228 pages, depending on particular county elections. It even took two stamps to return an absentee ballot in California, a requirement that was not expected by either election officials or voters. There may be state political culture accounts that help explain both initiatives and ballot reforms, but we have not considered these here. The empirical result is clear, however: the number of initiatives and early voting

Figure 5-2. *Trends in Initiatives among States with Early Voting*

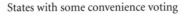

States with some convenience voting

Total number of initiatives

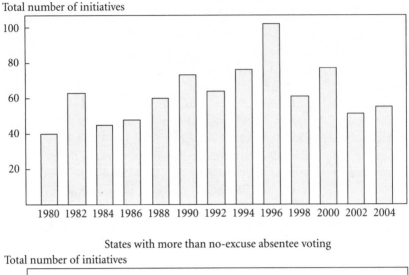

States with more than no-excuse absentee voting

Total number of initiatives

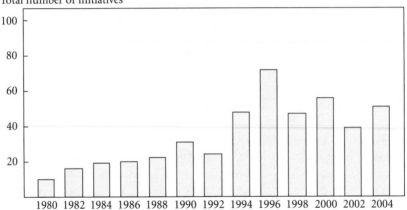

Source: Authors' calculations; Tolbert, Grummel, and Smith (2001); Tolbert and Smith (2005).

reforms are correlated, and when both are included in a regression, the impact of early voting reforms on turnout loses statistical significance.

Implications for Reform

Our findings support much of the literature that has found, at best, a modest impact of voting reforms on turnout. Our results are also consistent with theoretical presentations of the paradox of turnout. John Aldrich, in his masterful challenge to those who describe turnout as the "major example of the failure of rational choice theory," argues that turnout is a decision made at the margin, and thus is a decision that is responsive to very small changes in costs or benefits.[33] Voting, by this standard, is more an act of consumption than a complex bundle of costs and benefit calculations.

Early voting and convenience voting are just such minor changes, ones that make voting more convenient to be sure but that pale in significance to feelings of citizen empowerment, interest in and concern about the election, and political mobilization by parties, candidates, and other political organizations.[34] The impact of early voting, while measurable, is likely to be no larger than the modest changes in turnout that are popularly (and accurately) associated with bad weather.[35] And ironically, the compositional effects of these reforms seem to be quite analogous to the Republicanizing impact of rain.

These results lead us to be skeptical of those who advocate in favor of early voting reforms primarily on the basis of increased turnout. We are not arguing that these reforms are ineffective; much to the contrary, both previous research and our study find that reducing barriers to ballot access increases turnout. And there may be other good reasons to adopt such reforms. Ballot counting is more accurate; it leads to higher levels of public confidence in electoral outcomes, and it may ultimately lend greater legitimacy to our elective bodies. These reforms can save administrative costs and avoid headaches. In the post-2000 electoral environment, being an election official is a thankless task, and if such reforms improve our ability to recruit and retain high-quality election officials, then such reforms can be a useful bureaucratic tool. Finally, voters express a high level of satisfaction with the system. Perhaps these reforms will counter growing public unhappiness and skepticism about American electoral institutions.

However, if election officials and ballot reformers press for early voting in the interests of substantially boosting turnout and empowering traditionally disempowered groups, they are likely to be disappointed. The findings with respect to referenda and initiatives, in particular, point out the complex and interdependent nature of ballot reform. Changing one part of the ballot— such as reducing barriers to citizen initiatives—may create such a long and complex ballot that voter fatigue becomes a major issue, necessitating adjustments in other aspects of the balloting process.

There are no magic bullets for resolving long-standing inequities in American electoral politics. Early voting reforms, far from equalizing past inequities, instead show some signs of reinforcing them, encouraging turnout among habitual voters but failing to draw new voters into the system.

Table 5A-1. *Full Model, Turnout Effects of Convenience Voting Reforms, 1980–2004*

	Model without initiatives and regions	Model without regions	Full model		
			Presidential election	Midterm election	Pooled data set
Number of initiatives		0.415***	0.010	0.476***	0.244***
		(0.104)	(0.115)	(−0.108)	(0.870)
Percent high school	0.249**	0.221**	0.077	−0.005	0.050
graduates	(1.025)	(0.101)	(0.183)	(0.115)	(0.117)
Racial diversity	−20.445***	−20.925***	−17.564***	−17.234***	−17.223***
	(2.348)	(2.345)	(3.362)	(2.473)	(2.294)
Per capita income	0.000	0.000	0.000	0.000	0.000
	(0.000)	(0.000)	(0.000)	(0.000)	(0.000)
Closing date for registration	−0.157***	−0.169***	−0.181***	−0.213***	−0.192***
	(0.019)	(0.190)	(0.026)	(0.022)	(0.183)
No-excuse absentee by mail	1.023	−0.302	0.062	−1.818	−0.829
	(1.037)	(1.054)	(0.937)	(1.604)	(0.945)
No-excuse absentee by mail	−0.059	−1.098	0.578	−3.985***	−1.994*
with permanent status	(1.039)	(1.157)	(1.227)	(1.394)	(1.116)
option					
In-person early voting	−3.323**	−3.278**	−2.226	−1.402	−1.814
	(1.418)	(1.399)	(1.714)	(1.80)	(1.233)
In-person early voting and	1.839	1.513	1.376	0.258	0.961
no-excuse absentee by	(1.339)	(1.309)	(1.560)	(0.769)	(1.146)
mail					
Voting by mail	6.137***	2.067	6.839**	−1.862	2.147
	(2.20)	(2.692)	(2.734)	(2.252)	(2.552)
Western states			2.093	9.925***	5.599***
			(1.967)	(1.918)	(1.714)
Midwestern states			4.209***	7.686***	5.768***
			(1.167)	(1.181)	(0.961)
Northeastern states			2.570*	4.367***	3.404***
			(1.362)	(1.207)	(0.999)
Presidential election	16.264***	16.227***			16.088***
	(1.623)	(1.624)			(1.476)
Senatorial election	0.861**	1.068**	0.996	1.913**	1.393***
	(0.397)	(0.417)	(0.666)	(0.862)	(0.532)
Constant	27.213***	28.423***	50.822***	38.754***	35.687***
	(7.095)	(7.038)	(11.137)	(7.411)	(7.417)
R^2	0.725	0.731	0.549	0.567	0.758
Number of observations	649	649	350	299	649
Number of states	50	50	50	50	50

a. Data set made available by Tolbert and Smith, with additional variables coded by the authors. Dependent variable is percent turnout, as a percentage of voting-eligible population, and runs from 0 to 100. All voting reform variables are dummy variables, with traditional absentee balloting as the excluded category. All estimates are pairwise OLS with panel-corrected standard errors in parentheses.

* significant at 10 percent   ** significant at 5 percent   *** significant at 1 percent

Notes

1. Rosenstone and Hansen (1993).

2. In most of the methods considered here, the ballot must be cast before election day and is not cast at a precinct. For example, we do not consider voting centers in this chapter (Stein and Vonnahme 2006), even though they are arguably more convenient than many precinct places. Of the methods we examine, in a very few instances an "early" vote can be cast on election day. In Oregon, for example, as many as 25 percent of the ballots are hand delivered to the county office on election day (Gronke 2004).

3. The one state is Oregon.

4. Gronke (2004).

5. King County and Pierce County have not yet gone fully vote by mail.

6. Bill Bradbury, "The Voting Booth at the Kitchen Table," *New York Times,* August 21, 2001, p. A17.

7. National Association of Secretaries of State, "Election Reform: State-by-State Best Practices," 2001, and "New Millennium Best Practices Survey," 2003 (www.nass. org); National Conference of State Legislatures, "Voting in America: Final Report of the NCSL Elections Reform Task Force," 2001 (www.nscl.org).

8. Administration and Cost of Elections Project, Stockholm, 2004 (www.ace project.org); Adam Nagourney, "Early Voting Puts Many Candidates in Early Over-drive," *New York Times,* October 14, 2002, p. A1; Magleby (1987).

9. Alvarez and Hall (2003); Hanmer and Traugott (2004); Traugott (2003).

10. Hansen (2001). According to most election officials to whom we've spoken, the reason is that mixed systems (those with large numbers of nonprecinct voters and election day voters) have to manage the costs of both systems.

11. McDonald and Popkin (2001); Rosenstone and Hansen (1993).

12. Oliver (1996); Dubin and Kaslow (1996).

13. Neeley and Richardson (2001); Stein (1998); Stein and Garcia-Monet (1997).

14. See Berinsky, Burns, and Traugott (2001); and Karp and Banducci (2000) for increased turnout. Southwell and Burchett (2000) and Magleby (1987) estimate a 19 percent increase among voters using voting by mail, based on a study of local elections in California, Oregon, and Washington. This figure is dramatically higher than that obtained in other studies. However, all studies find a pattern of increasing turnout effects in lower profile contests, so it may be that this figure is accurate.

15. Gronke and Miller (2007).

16. Luechinger, Rosinger, and Stutzer (2007).

17. Thad Kousser and Megan Mullin find that VBM is associated with a 2.6–2.8 percent decline in turnout in California counties in the 2000 and 2002 general elections. See "Does Voting by Mail Increase Participation? Using Matching to Analyze a Natural Experiment," *Political Analysis,* July 13, 2007 (doi:10.1093/pan/mpm014).

18. Berinsky (2004, p. 1).

19. Berinsky, Burns, and Traugott (2001); Southwell and Burchett (2000); Southwell (1998).

20. Patterson and Caldeira (1985); Oliver (1996).

21. Stein (1998).

22. Stein, Owens, and Leighley (2003).

23. Karp and Banducci (2000); Southwell and Burchett (2000).

24. Magleby (1987).

25. Stein (1998).

26. Neeley and Richardson (2001).

27. Patterson and Caldeira (1985); Oliver (1996).

28. Tolbert, Grummel, and Smith (2001); Tolbert and Smith (2005).

29. Tolbert and Smith (2005). We do not describe or justify the inclusion of these variables here. Interested readers should go to Tolbert and Smith (2005) for this information.

30. We should note one important difference between our estimates and those of Tolbert and Smith (2005): rather than estimating separate models for presidential and midterm years, as they did, we choose to report a pooled model, which includes a dummy variable for the presidential election and an interaction term for the impact of initiatives during presidential contests. While we were able to replicate the tables presented in Tolbert and Smith exactly, we preferred this simpler specification. The bulk of the important results are the same.

31. Tolbert and Smith (2005).

32. Tolbert and Smith (2005).

33. Aldrich (1993, p. 246).

34. Stein, Owens, and Leighley (2003); Rosenstone and Hansen (1993).

35. Gomez, Hansford, and Krause (2007).

CAROLINE TOLBERT, TODD DONOVAN,
BRIDGETT KING, AND SHAUN BOWLER

6

Election Day Registration, Competition, and Voter Turnout

The challenge of increasing voter participation can be met in a variety of ways. In this chapter, we compare the effects of convenience voting reforms such as early voting, voting by mail, election day registration, and absentee voting laws to another key factor known to affect voter participation: electoral competition. We assess how the competitiveness of presidential races at the state level, congressional races, governor's races, and ballot measures affect turnout. Uncompetitive elections result from a series of factors, including gerrymandered or incumbent-protected legislative districts (see chapter 10), lopsided campaign financing, and single-member district elections.[1] Although state laws governing the voting process *and* the competitiveness of a state's election environment matter in understanding overall turnout levels, few studies have compared the effects of these head to head. We ask whether reforms of the voting process or structural reforms aimed at increasing electoral competition are more important for political participation in the American states over the past quarter century.

A number of scholars have focused on the practical consequences of state election reforms, but most examine these laws in isolation rather than together. For example, the important effect of state voter registration laws on turnout is well known.[2] Election day registration boosts turnout, especially among the young and more mobile, but racial minorities and the economically disadvantaged may not turn out in greater numbers.[3] State experimentation with motor voter registration, before the passage of the National Voter Registration Act, has been shown to increase overall turnout.[4] Some research has found that voting by mail increases participation.[5] Internet voting, although rarely used, has also been studied in terms of its relationship with turnout.[6] Administrative reforms, such as providing voting guides with sample ballots and polling place information, have been shown to increase turnout, especially of the young and the less educated.[7]

More recent research, however, suggests that many convenience reforms have had disappointing effects. Based on aggregate state-level data over time, a 2005 study concludes that simply making the voting process easier will not result in the mobilization of more voters.[8] In a similar spirit, others have argued that eliminating barriers to voting (such as easier registration, voting by mail) largely increases turnout among people demographically quite similar to those who already vote—those who are better educated, wealthier, and older.[9] To mobilize new and underrepresented voters, reform should not just be about making voting easier, but it should be about making it more rewarding as well. These studies do not, however, discuss electoral competition.

At the same time, a growing literature has focused on the lack of electoral competition in American congressional and state legislative races.[10] A few studies identify positive effects of electoral competition on turnout.[11] The campaigns and media effects associated with contested elections, as well as salient ballot measures (see chapter 5), appear to increase turnout in the U.S. and other nations.[12] Competitive contests may stimulate political interest and participation. Other research suggests that competitive elections not only increase turnout but also increase turnout of the young and the less educated, thus reducing the socioeconomic bias of state electorates.[13] Without the stimulating effects of competitive elections, voters with low levels of political interest may be less likely to develop into habitual voters.[14]

Most existing research, however, does not compare the benefits of increased electoral competition to the effects of state laws intended to make voting easier or more convenient.[15] Nor does it test any possible interactions between convenience voting reforms and stimulation from elite political activity in the form of electoral competition. This chapter does both and provides a more comprehensive evaluation of the effectiveness of convenience voting reforms in increasing turnout.

State Voting Laws

Although federal laws (civil rights legislation, motor voter legislation, and the Help America Vote Act) limit states' ability to regulate access to voting, there remains tremendous variation in state laws governing participation in elections (see table 6A-1; also see table 1-2 in chapter 1). For example, some states

require that voters register as many as thirty days before the election, imposing a severe cost on some potential voters. Others have begun to require voters to show government-issued photo identification, in response to concerns
about voting by illegal immigrants largely of Latino descent.[16] States also regulate where, when, and how individuals vote and register to vote. As of
November 2008, nine states will allow election day voter registration at the
polling place, and a tenth (North Dakota) does not require voters to register.
A growing number of states have created school or statewide holidays for voting, reducing costs for busy voters.

Measuring State Voting Reforms

In this study we pool data from the fifty states over a twenty-six-year period
(1980–2006) to model the potential effects of state voting laws and electoral
competition on turnout rates in presidential and midterm elections. Our
dependent variable is state-level voter-eligible population turnout by year,
for elections held between 1980 and 2006.[17] This variable subtracts ineligible
voters (felons and noncitizens) from the voting-age population to create a
more accurate measure of turnout in the states.

The primary variables used to predict turnout are eight state laws regulating voting: mail voting, photo identification requirements, election day holidays, regulations on felons, statewide computer registration database,
in-person early voting, election day registration, and no-excuse absentee voting (see table 6A-1). If a state had a particular law in effect in a given year in
the time series it was coded one, and if it did not it was coded zero for each
year. The table notes some state reforms going into effect for the 2008 election,
but these laws are not included in the statistical analysis. Since North Dakota
does not require registration to vote it is counted as an election day registration state. These data were collected from a variety of reputable government
and nonprofit sources, and represents one of the most comprehensive lists of
state voting laws that we are aware of, covering a quarter of a century.[18]

States with mail voting are those that allow local or state elections to be
conducted exclusively through the mail. Although Oregon and most of Washington have abolished traditional polling places in favor of mail voting, a
number of other states allow exclusive mail voting for off-year and local elections.[19] States' photo identification laws require voters to show picture identification before voting.[20] States with no-excuse absentee voting are those that
allow any registered voter to request a mail absentee ballot, and early voting
states permit in-person voting before election day at public locations.[21]

Although permanent absentee voting, early voting at the polls, and all-mail elections can overlap to allow all voting to occur before election day, in this study they are measured as separate laws. Election day registration allows voters to register to vote the day of the election.[22] Election day holidays, both school and statewide, are provisions that close schools used for polling places and public agencies on election day.[23] Statewide electronic voter registration databases are required by the Help America Vote Act (HAVA) but were adopted by states at different times; some states still do not have electronic voter registration databases as of 2007. These databases include registration for all voters and could reduce election day error and registration problems.[24] The felon regulation variable is coded so that states with more lenient provisions are given higher values. States coded as three do not disenfranchise felons and allow them to vote while in prison (Maine and Vermont), and states coded two restore felons' voting rights after the completion of prison or parole and probation. States coded as one permanently disenfranchise felons unless the government approves individual rights' restoration.[25]

We expect close elections to have higher campaign expenditures and thus generate interest and stimulate turnout. Our models of turnout take into consideration the competitiveness of state elections, as well as the eight state laws discussed above. We include the annual presidential margin of victory in a state to predict state-level turnout in presidential years. This variable is highly correlated with alternative measures of total campaign expenditures in presidential elections. The gubernatorial margin of victory, the senatorial margin of victory, as well as the percentage of uncontested U.S. House elections in a state at the time of an election are also used to predict midterm and presidential year turnout. The House election variable is used as a measure of uncompetitive races.[26] Higher values on the margin of victory variables are coded to indicate more competitive elections.[27] To control for the potential that ballot measures increase interest and turnout, the number of initiatives appearing on state ballots in each election year is also included.[28]

Demographic and economic factors are known to have important influences on turnout.[29] Since race has long been intertwined with state-level barriers to voting, we measure the size of each state's African American, Latino, and Asian populations with data from the 1980, 1990, and 2000 U.S. census.[30] We control for socioeconomic status by measuring state per capita income as reported by the U.S. Census (following earlier researchers).[31] Socioeconomic conditions are accounted for by including the percentage of each state's population with at least a high school degree and the median age of a state's population (by decade). The full statistical models include year dummy variables to control for change over time.[32]

Table 6-1. *What Predicts Turnout in Presidential Elections?*

Summary of findings from table 6A-1, columns 1 and 3

Competitive presidential race in state	Competitive governor's race in state	Competitive Senate race in state	Competitive congressional races in state	Initiatives on ballot
✓ (+)	...	...	✓ (+)	✓ (+)
Election day registration	Early voting	No-excuse absentee voting	Liberal felon voting rights	Mail voting
✓ (+)	...	...	✓ (+)	...
Election day registration interacting with a competitive presidential race	Early voting interacting with a competitive presidential race	No-excuse absentee voting interacting with a competitive presidential race		
...	✓ (–)	...		

✓ = statistically significant predictor of turnout with a 95 percent confidence interval.
+ = positive relationship.
– = negative relationship.

Findings: Turnout

The data are analyzed in the appendix to this chapter, using cross-sectional time-series analysis with panel-corrected standard errors, controlling for variation between states over time.[33] The results for presidential and midterm elections are reported in tables 6-1 and 6-2.

Presidential Elections

The effects of state voting laws on turnout in presidential elections over the past quarter of a century are reported in the appendix to this chapter (table 6A-2, model 1, and table 6-1). Of the eight laws included in the analysis, only two have any statistically significant association with turnout in presidential elections. Felon voting laws and election day registration are found to be associated with higher statewide voter turnout across time and place, holding all other factors constant. In presidential elections, turnout was 4.5 percentage points higher, on average, in states with election day registration than in states without election day registration. This is the only convenience voting reform to have a large and substantively significant association with higher political participation over the twenty-six-year period. Similarly, turnout was 1.8 percentage points higher, all things being equal, in states with modest regulations on felons voting than in states with the most restrictions, and 3.6 percentage points higher in the handful of states allowing full voting privileges for felons.

Notable is that states with early voting, no-excuse absentee voting, or mail voting were not associated with higher turnout rates. This could be due to measurement issues. If these three forms of early voting were considered as a package, as in chapter 5, the results may be different.

Although election day registration was found to be important, competitive elections were also associated with higher levels of turnout. Each 10 percentage point increase in the competitiveness of a presidential election corresponded with an increase of 1 percentage point in turnout, on average. For example, based on our model, in the 2004 presidential election, turnout in the swing state of Ohio should have exceeded turnout in Utah, the least competitive state, by more than 3 percentage points. Similarly, each initiative appearing on state ballots was associated with a 0.3 percentage point increase in turnout. Five ballot initiatives would thus correspond with a 1.5 percentage point increase in state turnout. Higher numbers of uncompetitive U.S. House races (measured by the proportion of races that were uncontested) corresponded with lower turnout. These effects may be additive. A close presidential election in a state, initiatives on the statewide ballot, and contested congressional races may combine to increase turnout. This suggests that engaging citizens in politics via electoral competition may be as important for turnout as making it easier to register to vote.

Midterm Elections

Midterm elections are characterized by lower information environments and significantly lower turnout than presidential elections (see table 6A-2, model 2, and table 6-2). We would thus expect the effects of information stimuli (such as active candidate campaigns) to have a larger effect in these off-year elections. The results of our analysis suggest that the same voting laws associated with higher turnout in presidential elections are also associated with higher turnout in midterms. Turnout was 2 percentage points higher, on average, in states with election day registration than in other states. Liberal felon voting rules were associated with an almost 2 percentage point increase in turnout, and full enfranchisement for felons (as in Vermont and Maine) was associated with an additional 2 percentage point increase. The positive

Table 6-2. *What Predicts Higher Turnout in Midterm Elections?*

Summary of findings from table 6A-1, columns 2 and 4

Competitive governor's race in state	Competitive Senate race in state	Competitive congressional races in state	Initiatives on ballot
✓ (+)	✓ (+)	✓ (+)	✓ (+)
Election day registration	Early voting	No-excuse absentee voting	Liberal felon voting rights
✓ (+)	. . .	. . .	✓ (+)
Election day registration interacting with a competitive governor's race	Early voting interacting with a competitive governor's race	No-excuse absentee voting interacting with a competitive governor's race	Mail voting
✓ (+)	. . .	. . .	. . .

✓ = statistically significant predictor of turnout with a 95 percent confidence interval.
+ = positive relationship.
– = negative relationship.

association between election day registration and turnout is consistent with earlier work, but the turnout level identified here is slightly larger.[34]

Early voting laws however, appear to be associated with slightly less turnout. Other state voting laws designed to make voting more convenient, such as no-excuse absentee voting, mail voting, a school holiday to vote, and computerized databases for registration have no measurable association with turnout in midterm elections across the fifty states. Notably, consistent with some new research, state laws requiring photo identification do not appear to decrease participation in either midterm or presidential elections.[35]

Competitive state elections clearly matter and are associated with substantially more citizen engagement with elections. A 10 percentage point increase in the competitiveness of the governor's race corresponded, on average, with a 0.56 percentage point increase in turnout. A 10 percentage point increase in the competitiveness of a U.S. Senate race corresponded with a 0.36 percentage point increase in state turnout. A smaller number of uncontested U.S. House races in the state also corresponded with greater turnout (with a 90 percent confidence interval). These effects of electoral competition were additive. Furthermore, each initiative on a statewide ballot increased turnout by half of a percentage point.

No-excuse absentee voting does not correspond with higher participation, nor does early voting. The lack of an association between turnout rates and many efforts designed to make voting more convenient has been noted in previous research.[36] All of this suggests that larger, structural factors affecting electoral competition may need to change for participation to increase substantially. If higher turnout is a goal of reform, reformers may want to focus on changes that increase the competitiveness of elections, on election day registration, and on allowing felons to vote.

Voting Reforms in the Context of Competitive Elections

A relatively unexplored question is whether the effects of election reforms such as election day registration (EDR) are conditional on a state's electoral context. That is, does increased convenience in voting have a more pronounced effect in a context where campaigns are working to attract attention and mobilize voters? In table 6A-2, model 3, we interact EDR with the competitiveness of presidential races in a state to estimate presidential-year turnout. In model 4 we test for the interaction between EDR and the competitiveness of state gubernatorial races to estimate midterm turnout. In separate models (analysis not shown) we did the same for early voting and no-excuse absentee voting.

We do not find that higher turnout in presidential election years had a significant association with the use of EDR in states where presidential elections were competitive—although the coefficient for the interaction term is positive and substantial. We do find that midterm election turnout was higher where EDR was used in the context of competitive gubernatorial races—higher than electoral competition alone or EDR alone would predict. States with EDR used in conjunction with competitive governor's races had significantly higher turnout than states with just EDR or just competitive governor's races (see table 6A-2, model 4). In the relatively low information environments of midterm elections, the stimulus of electoral competition may combine with easier voter registration rules to increase turnout in elections. The 1998 Minnesota gubernatorial race is an anecdote consistent with this result. Turnout may have increased that year because of the dynamic three-party contest for governor that featured Jesse Ventura and because unregistered citizens who were mobilized by the gubernatorial election were able to register at their polling places on the day of the vote.

We also identify an interaction between the presence of early voting laws and competitive presidential races (analysis not shown), but the effect was negative. The interaction between early voting and electoral competition had no effect on turnout in midterm elections. Similarly, no-excuse absentee voting laws did not interact with competition to increase turnout.

Implications for Reform

In exploring whether state voting reforms are associated with turnout in the states, we found mixed results. If we infer from the patterns of association we observe here, liberalizing felon voting rights and election day registration may end up having positive effects on increasing turnout. Other efforts, such as mail voting, early voting, and absentee voting, may not. We find evidence that competitive elections and ballot measures are associated with higher turnout in the states and that uncompetitive U.S. House races correspond with lower state turnout. Most important, we find evidence suggesting that electoral competition may interact with election day registration to increase turnout in midterm elections. Our models of turnout provide support for the idea that electoral competition may be necessary to engage citizens and increase political participation.[37] (See chapter 13.)

Many of the election reform efforts in the United States focus on changing state rules to ease voter registration and make voting more convenient. Yet if elections are not competitive—or worse uncontested—there will be fewer active campaigns and less political information. Citizens will have fewer choices at the ballot box and less incentive to learn about politics, to become informed and knowledgeable, and to vote. The analysis here suggests both election reform efforts and structural reforms of state election systems that increase the competitiveness of elections such as nonpartisan redistricting, legislative term limits, campaign finance reform, public financing of elections, free air time for ballot-qualified candidates, instant runoff voting, and forms of proportional representation may be necessary to produce major changes in turnout in American elections.[38] Reformers need to focus on making voting rewarding in order to more fully mobilize the electorate. Political scientists and policymakers seek higher turnout not only to increase turnout but also to lessen the biases in the participating electorate.[39] If we fail to acknowledge the important role of electoral competition while focusing extensively on convenience voting reforms, we may fail to reduce the underrepresentation of the poor and the young in the pool of voters.

Appendix 6A

State election reforms, their effects, and summary of results are detailed in the following two tables.

Table 6A-1. *Year of Adoption, Eight Election Reforms by State, 1980–2006*

State	Vote by mail	Photo ID to vote	Election day school holiday	Felon vote restoration	State-wide computer database	Early voting	Election day registra-tion	No-excuse absentee voting
Alabama	...	...	...	2003	...	...	...	1996
Alaska	...	...	...	...	1986	...	...	...
Arizona	...	...	...	...	2004	1994	...	1992
Arkansas	...	...	...	...	2006	1996	...	1980
California	1980	...	...	...	2006	1998	...	1980
Colorado	2000	...	...	1993, 1997	2002	1992	...	1992
Connecticut	...	...	...	2001, 2006	2006	...	...	...
Delaware	...	...	2000	2000	1990	...	...	...
Florida	...	2004	...	1990, 2004, 2006, 2007[a]	2006	...	...	1988
Georgia	...	...	...	1983	2002	...	...	1988
Hawaii	...	2004	1980	2006	2004	1980	...	1980
Idaho	...	...	...	...	2006	1980	1994	1980
Illinois	...	...	1998	...	...	...	...	...
Indiana	...	2004	...	...	2006	...	...	2004
Iowa	...	...	...	2005	...	1992	1998[a]	1992
Kansas	...	...	...	2002	2006	2002	...	1996
Kentucky	...	...	1992	2001	1980	...	...	...
Louisiana	...	2004	2000	...	1988	...	...	...
Maine	...	...	...	...	2006	...	1980	2000
Maryland	...	...	2000	2002, 2007[a]	2006	...	...	...
Massachusetts	...	...	...	2000	2006	...	...	...
Michigan	...	...	...	...	1998	...	...	...
Minnesota	...	...	...	...	2004	...	1980	...
Mississippi	...	...	...	...	2006	...	...	...
Missouri	...	...	...	...	2006	...	...	1998
Montana	...	...	2000	...	...	...	1998[a]	...
Nebraska	...	...	...	1993, 2006	2006	...	...	1994
Nevada	...	...	...	2001, 2003	2006	1994	...	1980
New Hampshire	...	...	...	1998, 2000	2006	...	1994	...
New Jersey	...	...	2000	...	...	...	...	...
New Mexico	...	...	...	2001, 2005	2004	1994	...	1994
New York	...	...	...	...	2006	...	...	...
North Carolina	...	...	...	...	...	2000	1998[a]	2000
North Dakota	...	...	...	...	...	...	2006	2000

State	Vote by mail	Photo ID to vote	Election day school holiday	Felon vote restoration	State-wide computer database	Early voting	Election day registra-tion	No-excuse absentee voting
Ohio	...	...	...	...	2006	...	...	2008[a]
Oklahoma	...	...	...	...	2004	...	...	1992
Oregon	1998	...	...	1999	2006	...	1980–88	1984
Pennsylvania	...	...	...	1995, 2000	2006	...	...	...
Rhode Island	...	...	2000	2006	2006	...	...	...
South Carolina	...	...	...	1981	1980	...	...	...
South Dakota	...	2004	...	...	2002	...	...	2004
Tennessee	...	...	...	1986, 1996, 2006	2006	1994	...	...
Texas	...	...	...	1983, 1997	...	1992	...	...
Utah	...	...	...	1998, 2006	2006	...	...	2004
Vermont	...	...	...	...	2006	1994	...	1994
Virginia	...	...	...	2000, 2002	2006	...	...	...
Washington	1994	...	...	1984	2006	...	...	1980
West Virginia	...	...	2000	...	2004	...	...	...
Wisconsin	...	...	...	...	2006	...	1980	2000
Wyoming	...	...	...	2003	2006	...	1994	2000

a. Laws adopted after 2006 are not included in the statistical analysis in table 6-2.

Table 6A-2. *Effects of State Voting Laws on Election Turnout, 1980–2006*[a]

	Model 1 presidential elections coef. (SE)	Model 2 midterm elections coef. (SE)	Model 3 presidential elections coef. (SE)	Model 4 midterm elections coef. (SE)
Electoral rules				
Early voting	−0.274	−01.095**	−0.199	−1.023**
	(0.841)	(0.462)	(0.862)	(0.468)
Election day registration	4.474***	1.977**	−1.164	−4.099
	(.671)	(.771)	(3.880)	(3.290)
Election day registration × competitive presidential race	...	...	6.351 (4.464)	...
Election day registration × competitive governor's race	...	...	...	7.902** (4.303)
Felon vote restoration	1.862***	1.866***	1.813***	1.817***
	(0.249)	(0.471)	(0.274)	(0.466)
Mail voting	−0.686	−0.903	−0.698	−0.932
	(0.889)	(0.757)	(0.878)	(0.777)
No-excuse absentee voting	−1.115*	−.363	−1.082*	−.493
	(0.652)	(0.500)	(0.645)	(0.500)
Photo identification to vote	−1.608	−1.097	−1.616	−.856
	(1.117)	(1.070)	(1.105)	(1.092)
Election day school holiday	−0.030	1.289	−0.067	1.082
	(1.408)	(1.167)	(1.449)	(1.071)
Statewide computer database for registration	0.106	0.578	0.107	0.461
	(0.891)	(0.933)	(0.889)	(0.899)
Electoral competitiveness				
Uncontested U.S. House races (percent)	−0.027*	−0.028	−0.028**	−0.029*
	(0.014)	(0.017)	(0.014)	(0.017)
Presidential race (1-vote margin)	10.478***	...	9.406***	...
	(2.799)	...	(2.978)	...
Senate race (1-vote margin)	0.933	3.630***	0.891	3.575***
	(0.606)	(0.555)	(0.611)	(0.518)
Governor's race (1-vote margin)	−0.877*	5.665***	−0.873*	5.240***
	(0.488)	(0.423)	(0.486)	(0.477)
Initiatives on ballot	0.357***	0.519***	0.359***	0.516***
	(0.078)	(0.076)	(0.079)	(0.077)

	Model 1 presidential elections coef. (SE)	Model 2 midterm elections coef. (SE)	Model 3 presidential elections coef. (SE)	Model 4 midterm elections coef. (SE)
State demographics				
Per capita income	0.002e-1**	0-.002e-1	0.002e-1**	0-.002e-1
	(0.007e-2)	(0.002e-1)	(0.007e-2)	(0.002-1)
High school graduates (%)	0.379***	0.476***	0.375***	0.465***
	(0.062)	(0.086)	(0.063)	(0.081)
Median age	−.264*	−.028	−.247*	−.034
	(0.135)	(0.255)	(0.134)	(0.257)
Black (%)	−0.179***	−0.236***	−0.179***	−0.243***
	(0.042)	(0.037)	(0.042)	(0.035)
Latino (%)	−0.235***	−0.267***	−0.233***	−0.264***
	(0.028)	(0.033)	(0.028)	(0.033)
Asian (%)	−0.222***	−0.013	−0.222***	−0.012
	(0.025)	(0.031)	(0.026)	(0.031)
Constant	25.693***	10.268	26.482***	11.064
	(7.775)	(12.096)	(7.618)	(11.849)
Wald chi square	81883.96***	19870.08***	81373.15***	15662.02***
R^2	.72	.62	.72	.63
N	350	349	350	349

*p < .1   **p < .05   ***p < .01

a. Pooled cross-sectional time-series model using fifty-state data. Dummy variables for years are excluded from this table. Dummy variables not incorporated into the model are presidential election year 1980 and midterm election year 1982. Unstandardized regression coefficients, with panel-corrected standard errors in parentheses. Significance levels based on two-tailed test. Data on the turnout of the voter eligible population for Louisiana in 1982 are missing. See Michael McDonald, United States Election Project (http://elections.gmu.edu/voter_turnout.htm).

Models 1 and 3 include all presidential elections between 1980 and 2006. Models 2 and 4 include all midterm elections between 1980 and 2006. Models 3 and 4 include an interaction term, which is whether the state has election day registration multiplied by how competitive the governor's race was. The × sign indicates multiplied by.

Notes

1. See Donovan and Bowler (2004).

2. Wolfinger and Rosenstone (1980); Squire, Wolfinger, and Glass (1987); Highton (2004).

3. Highton (1997); Fitzgerald (2005); Knack and White (2000); Brians and Grofman (2001).

4. Highton and Wolfinger (1998); Fitzgerald (2005); but see Martinez and Hill (1999).

5. Berinsky, Burns, and Traugott (2001); Karp and Banducci (2000); Southwell and Burchett (2000).

6. McNeal and Tolbert (2004); Alvarez and Hall (2004); Alvarez and Nagler (2001).

7. Wolfinger, Highton, and Mullin (2005); see also Primo, Jacobsmeier, and Milyo (2007) for a replication.

8. Fitzgerald (2005) uses aggregate fifty-state data over time, as we do here, but includes a somewhat different set of election reforms, including early adoption of motor voter laws.

9. Berinsky (2005).

10. See McDonald and Samples (2006); Squire (2000); Schickler, Citrin, and Sides (2003); Hogan (2004).

11. Patterson and Caldeira (1983); Cox and Munger (1989); Jackson (1997).

12. See, for example, Mark Smith (2001); Lacey (2005); Tolbert, Grummel, and Smith (2001); Smith and Tolbert (2004).

13. Donovan and Tolbert (2007).

14. Bowler and Donovan (2006).

15. Bowler and Donovan (2006) do this, but they examine a much shorter range of time than we consider in this chapter, and they measure competition in a presidential election, not in multiple electoral contests in a state. Oliver (1996) interacts party mobilization efforts (with a rough proxy of open primaries in a state) with liberal absentee voting rules. Oliver finds that no-excuse absentee voting alone does not increase turnout; rather, party mobilization in combination with liberal absentee voting rules increased overall turnout in the 1992 election. Oliver does not measure electoral competition, nor does he examine turnout in more than one election. He is one of the few to suggest that stimulation from political elites (a by-product of electoral competition) may interact with convenience voting reforms.

16. Alvarez, Bailey, and Katz (2007).

17. McDonald and Popkin (2001); Michael McDonald, United States Election Project (http://elections.gmu.edu/voter_turnout.htm).

18. See Fitzgerald (2005) for voting laws over time—but a somewhat different set of laws, including early state adoption of motor voter laws and mail-in voter registration.

19. The data for mail voting come from the National Conference of State Legislatures (www.ncsl.org) and the Council of State Governments, *Book of the States* (www.csg.org).

20. South Carolina required photo identification at the polls for just one election (2004) but eliminated the photo requirement for 2006.

21. Karp and Banducci (2001).

22. Data for these four variables over the twenty-six-year period are from the National Conference of State Legislatures (www.ncsl.org), electionline (www.election line.org), and the Council of State Governments, *Book of the States,* various years (www.csg.org).

23. The data for election day school holidays come from the Election Assistance Commission (www.eac.gov) and the Council of State Governments, *Book of the States,* various years (www.csg.org).

24. See table 1-2 in chapter 1. The data for statewide voter registration databases are from electionline (www.electionline.org).

25. The data for felon voting restoration laws are from the Sentencing Project (www.sentencingproject.org) and Right to Vote (www.righttovote.org) and are current as of 2006.

26. The percentage of uncontested U.S. House races in a state over time is from FairVote (www.fairvote.org); the presidential margin of victory measures are from President Elect (www.presidentelect.org); the gubernatorial margin of victory and the senatorial margin of victory are from Michael Barone and his various co-editors, *The Almanac of American Politics* (various years).

27. For each margin of victory, the difference between the percentage of votes for the winner and the percentage for the loser is turned into decimals by placing the difference in the formula 1-(percent for winner minus percent for the runner-up). States without a gubernatorial and Senate race are coded zero.

28. Smith and Tolbert (2004).

29. Leighley and Nagler (1992).

30. As Key (1949) has shown, racial considerations motivated the adoption of election rules that excluded African Americans and poor whites from political participation for decades, especially but not exclusively in the South. And even after the passage of landmark civil rights legislation in the 1960s, race continued to shape turnout. Hill and Leighley (1999) found that state racial diversity was a powerful predictor of turnout and barriers to voting (registration requirements) into the 1990s, not only in southern states but also nationwide. States with higher racial diversity had more restrictive voter registration requirements, measured by the closing date to register to vote.

31. Hill and Leighley (1999).

32. The use of year fixed effects and time-series analysis creates a rigorous test of the importance of electoral competition compared to previous research. See Fitzgerald (2005) for a similar research design, but it also uses state fixed effects to control for state conditions.

33. Beck and Katz (1995) argue against using the random effects model for pooled data and instead recommend using ordinary least squares (OLS) regression with panel-corrected standard errors. Through the inclusion of dummy variables for election years, we are also able to control for variation over time.

34. Fitzgerald (2005).

35. Alvarez, Bailey, and Katz (2007).

36. Berinsky (2005).

37. Donovan and Bowler (2004); McDonald and Samples (2006).

38. Tolbert, Smith, and Green (2008); Kousser (2005); Bowler, Brockington, and Donovan (2001).

39. Schattschneider (1975); Hero (1998).

CAROLINE TOLBERT AND DANIEL C. BOWEN

7

Direct Democracy, Engagement, and Voter Turnout

One of the most distinctive aspects of American politics involves direct democracy—the use of state and local ballot propositions or initiatives to resolve controversial policy issues. The constitutions of twenty-four states and hundreds of municipalities permit votes on proposed laws that reach the ballot when advocates submit the signatures of a required number of citizens. This Progressive Era reform was primarily intended to allow citizens to pass public policies that were resisted by state legislatures. However, from the beginning the process was also understood to have educative effects. In addition to promoting the adoption of policies that better reflect citizen preferences, the initiative process can boost voter turnout, increase interest in politics, enhance political sophistication, and promote civic engagement more generally.[1]

Research using the turnout of the voter-eligible population rather than that of the voting-age population shows that each initiative appearing on a state's ballot yields about a 1 percentage point increase in turnout in presidential elections and a 2 percentage point increase in midterm elections.[2] Similarly, using experimental methods, another study finds that citizens voting on referenda in Switzerland show increased levels of participation.[3]

This chapter seeks to address two remaining questions regarding the impact of direct democracy on the individual decision to vote. First, what is the process by which ballot initiatives increase turnout in elections? Second, does this increased turnout reduce the socioeconomic bias of the electorate, or do initiatives reinforce or even exacerbate existing biases within the electorate by stimulating turnout most among those already most likely to vote?

Direct Democracy

In the 2006 midterm election, more than 70 citizen initiatives and 205 legislative referenda appeared on state ballots—the third-highest total since the process was introduced in the 1900s. Both Arizona and Oregon had 10 citizen initiatives on the ballot; Arizona had 19 measures, including 9 legislative referenda. Initiatives targeting gay marriage received the most attention in both 2006 and 2004. But over the last three decades, the initiative has been used for major policy decisions in such areas as elections and governance, affirmative action, the environment, the minimum wage, and tax and spending.

Accordingly, ballot initiatives have attracted an increasing amount of attention from political scientists.[4] Implicit in the literature is a process whereby issue campaigns and the mass media provide information, arguments, and appeals to the electorate. Such campaign and media attention can stimulate interest in politics, which leads to increased participation.

In this account, the supply of information (initiative campaigns) and the demand for participation (citizen interest) work in tandem to increase participation. To date, however, the empirical research has addressed only supply-side factors. Various studies focus on measuring the information available to voters by tallying the number of initiatives appearing on the ballot or the volume of newspaper coverage of those measures.[5] But this research simply assumes that political interest increases in response to these campaigns; it does not estimate that increase. To fill this gap, we utilized two-stage causal models to test the effect of initiatives on political interest and the effect of political interest on turnout. We directly measure the campaign activity generated when initiatives appear on statewide ballots and determine whether political interest and political participation increase with the money spent on initiative elections. We also test whether initiative campaigns have a greater impact on the less educated, potentially reducing the socioeconomic bias of the electorate. If so, initiatives may not only increase turnout but may also modify the composition of state electorates.

The argument builds on Angus Campbell's surge and decline theory of voter turnout in American elections.[6] Campbell argues that a group of "core voters" consistently vote in each election. During high-stimulus elections these core voters are joined by "peripheral" voters with lower political interest. High-stimulus elections bombard individuals with election news and campaign discourse, dramatically lowering the cost of obtaining information and increasing interest in going to the polls. Similarly, by generating controversy and media attention, ballot propositions may stimulate political interest and increase political participation. These effects are likely to be strongest in low-information midterm elections, consistent with previous research on voting.[7]

Ballot Propositions and Political Engagement

Research indicates that, at a minimum, exposure to ballot propositions increases political knowledge. A study drawing on data from the 1992 Senate Election Study merged with a state-level measure of newspaper coverage of ballot initiatives finds that individuals exposed to salient initiatives and referenda show an increased capacity to correctly answer factual questions about politics.[8] Similarly, scholars find that in Switzerland citizens are better informed when they reside in cantons with many opportunities for direct political participation.[9]

Fewer studies link initiatives and referenda to political interest. Research in Canada, though, finds that exposure to referenda leads to increased citizens' interest in and knowledge about politics.[10] Scholars studying direct democracy in the United States report, similarly, that citizens residing in states with frequent ballot initiatives reported higher levels of interest in politics in both the 1996 and 1998 elections (although not in the 2000 presidential elections).[11] Research also suggests that political efficacy or confidence in government responsiveness may be higher when individuals have frequent opportunities to vote on policy issues.[12] But others challenge these findings.[13]

Supply-Side Factors

There has been little focus in the literature on initiative campaigns per se; rather, research has concentrated on the availability of the initiative process or the number of initiatives on statewide ballots. Yet initiative campaigns provide the crucial link between the initiative process and political engagement. Research shows that both political learning and political interest are heavily influenced by the political and information environment.[14] The consumption of political information from media sources, including online news, enhances civic engagement by increasing citizens' knowledge about politics.[15] Campaign advertising has also been shown to increase levels of interest and knowledge among citizens, especially those with low levels of information.[16] Similarly, ballot measure campaigns provide political information, leading to increased opportunities for learning about and being interested in politics. Such campaigns have the potential not only to encourage voting on an individual proposition but also to help set the agenda in candidate elections.[17]

Like the media, political organizations such as parties and interest groups that support or oppose ballot measures may enable citizens to gather information easily.[18] Studies suggest that easily available information shortcuts provide minimally informed voters with the ability to make decisions even on ballot measures that deal with complex policy.[19] Voters use candidates' partisanship to draw meaningful inferences about their policy stances. Similarly, voters can form attitudes on issues without studying them by taking cues from opinion leaders.[20]

Demand-Side Factors

We know from many voting studies that the less educated tend to be the least likely to vote and the least interested in politics.[21] However, salient ballot propositions over controversial policies may spark political interest even among these voters. If that is true, initiatives and referenda may be an important way to engage this portion of the public in politics and to thus alter the socioeconomic composition of state electorates.

Research on media effects finds that campaign ads, even negative ones, can increase civic engagement and political interest, because campaign ads not only convey information about politics but do so in an emotional context.[22] Ballot measure campaigns in which at least one side frames the argument in moral terms—such as same-sex marriage, abortion, affirmative action, immigration, the environment, or stem cell research—rarely present information in dispassionate, emotionally neutral terms.[23] Ballot measure campaigns are skillfully produced, using professional media consultants, pollsters, and campaign ads to persuade voters often using emotional appeals.[24] Emotionally rich issue campaigns frequently provoke responses either directly, through advertising, or indirectly, by way of endorsements from elected officials and interest groups.[25] As a result, initiative campaigns may facilitate the use of the likability heuristic, by which people make informational inferences on the basis of their opinions of other groups in the population.[26] In summary, ballot measure campaigns are rife with both informational and emotional content that may spark public interest in politics, contributing to a more attentive citizenry.

The Evidence

Survey data from the 2004 presidential and 2006 midterm elections suggest that ballot measures do trigger widespread political interest among the public. In the 2004 elections 163 measures appeared on thirty-four statewide ballots. An October 2004 Pew survey found that 86 percent of respondents who were aware of ballot measures in their states were "very interested" or "fairly interested" in the policies on their state's ballot.[27] Comparable numbers of people across the ideological spectrum expressed interest in ballot measures. In 2006, 275 statewide measures were placed before voters in thirty-seven states. A 2006 survey of likely voters aware of initiatives, referenda, or constitutional amendments on their statewide ballot found that 81 percent were interested in the ballot measures (39 percent were very interested and 42 percent fairly interested).[28] Of the policies sparking the most interest among voters in 2004, gambling measures were uppermost in people's minds, followed by proposed constitutional amendments to ban gay marriage. In 2006 gay marriage bans were the most noticed, followed by initiatives to increase the minimum wage and initiatives on education, schools, and school bonds. These surveys, while separate from the data used later in this chapter for empirical analysis, lend support to the notion that when citizens become aware of ballot propositions, most become interested in the ballot campaign.

Research Questions and Data

We can test the link between exposure to initiative campaigns and engagement in politics in both midterm and presidential elections by using survey data and multivariate regression analysis, which allows us to hold constant other factors that may be associated with increased interest in politics. We expect individuals frequently exposed to salient issue campaigns (measured by total spending in initiative elections) to be more interested in politics and more likely to vote than those not so exposed. This hypothesis differs from that of researchers who, although they discuss the educative effects of ballot measures, suggest that these effects are the result of opportunities for direct participation in policymaking (consistent with Progressive reformers' expectations and theories of participatory democracy).[29] We also hypothesize that initiative campaigns have a greater impact on engagement and political interest among the less educated than among those with more education.

To test these hypotheses, we drew on a 2002 postelection Pew survey that included almost 1,000 voters and 1,000 nonvoters, as well as preelection 2004 and 2006 national opinion data also collected by Pew. These surveys measured political interest, or our dependent variable, by asking, "How much thought have you given to the upcoming election?" measured on a four-point scale from "quite a lot" to "none."[30] We found similar results when using the ordinal dependent variable or collapsing the variable into a binary variable where 1 measures political interest ("Quite a lot" and "Some") and zero a lack of political interest ("A little" and "None"). The models reported used the binary dependent variable to simplify interpretation of the findings.[31]

The primary independent variables in our analysis were the number of statewide initiatives appearing on ballots in each respondent's state in the three elections and the total expenditures on ballot initiatives (2002 and 2004) in each respondent's state.[32] (Comparable expenditure data for 2006 were not available at the time of this study.) We believe that the second variable provides a better measure of the information in the political environment and campaign activity, since simple initiative tallies do not take their salience into account.[33]

Spending on initiatives showed great variation from state to state. In 2002 total expenditures on initiative campaigns ranged from $51 million in California to $18,000 in Mississippi.[34] In a number of states, especially when gambling issues were on the ballot, total spending on ballot propositions rivaled or exceeded expenditures for major candidate races, including races for governer and senator.[35] In 2004 expenditures on initiatives ranged from $202 million in California to approximately $10,000 in North Dakota.

In addition to these measures of initiative activity, our models included state and individual contextual variables. To reflect the fact that we expect citizens residing in states with more competitive candidate races to be more interested in the election, we included a variable representing the competitiveness of the Senate and governor's races in 2002, 2004, and 2006 and presidential races in 2004.[36] The model also includes controls for partisanship and a range of demographic factors that affect individuals' interest in the election, including income, educational attainment, age, gender, race, and place of residence.[37] In the 2002 and 2004 surveys, media consumption was measured with binary variables asking whether or not respondents had read the newspaper or watched a national television news program the day before.[38] Previous research reports that the use of online news is important in predicting turnout, and so we controlled for it here as well.[39] Because media consumption variables were not available in the 2006 survey, we instead used a measure of political knowledge, which was not available in the 2002 or 2004 surveys.[40] Our findings are robust whether we control for media consumption or political knowledge.

Findings

Table 7-1 presents logistic regression models predicting political interest in the 2002 and 2006 midterm elections and 2004 presidential election. These data indicate that citizens exposed to more ballot initiatives in the two midterm elections expressed greater general interest in the election, holding constant demographic, attitudinal, media consumption, and the competitiveness of

Table 7-1. *Effects of Ballot Initiatives on Individual Political Interest across Elections, 2002, 2004, 2006* [a]

	2002		2004		2006	
Measure	B	(SE)	B	(SE)	B	(SE)
Number of initiatives on state ballot	0.097***	(0.037)	0.016	(0.023)	0.227***	(0.048)
Newspaper news consumption	0.539***	(0.132)	0.623**	(0.300)	n.a.	
Television news consumption	0.639***	(0.104)	0.300	(0.220)	n.a.	
Online news consumption	1.692***	(0.155)	1.160***	(0.437)	n.a.	
Political knowledge	n.a.		n.a.		0.645***	(0.119)
Republican	0.351**	(0.158)	0.523***	(0.196)	−0.031	(0.150)
Democrat	0.096	(0.164)	0.523***	(0.171)	0.022	(0.144)
Male	−0.232***	(0.086)	0.034	(0.152)	−0.096	(0.142)
Age	0.031***	(0.004)	0.013***	(0.004)	0.016***	(0.004)
Latino	−0.246	(0.204)	−0.605*	(0.333)	−0.369	(0.265)
Black	0.129	(0.154)	0.375	(0.263)	0.061	(0.192)
Asian	−1.131***	(0.272)	−0.449	(0.645)	−0.665	(0.465)
Education	0.174***	(0.039)	0.299***	(0.047)	−0.016	(0.057)
Income	0.081***	0.069**	0.064**			
	(0.026)	(0.032)	(0.031)			
Suburban	−0.229**	(0.112)	n.a.		−0.350**	(0.149)
Urban	−0.118	(0.148)	n.a.		−0.208	(0.202)
Attend church	n.a.		0.053	(0.049)	0.016	(0.038)
Competitive presidential election	...		0.864	(.983)	...	
Competitive gubernatorial election	0.136	(0.205)	0.041	(0.206)	0.202	(0.457)
Competitive senatorial election	0.640***	(0.137)	0.066	(0.206)	0.221	(0.401)
Constant	−3.701***	(0.339)	−2.678***	(1.013)	−3.454***	(0.483)
Wald chi square	1,269.99***		172.28***		223.03***	
Pseudo R^2	.18		.10		.14	
N	1,856		1,284		1,620	

Source: Pew Internet and American Life Daily Tracking Survey, November 2002 (www.pewinternet.org/data.asp); Pew Research Center for the People and the Press, October 24, 2004 (http://people-press.org/dataarchive/); Pew Research Center for the People and the Press, October 26, 2006 (http://people-press.org/dataarchive/).

*$p < .1$ **$p < .05$ ***$p < .01$

n.a. = not available.

a. Unstandardized logistic regression coefficients with robust standard errors (SE, in parentheses) correct for heteroskedasticity. Reported probabilities are based on two-tailed test. Clustering by state used to adjust standard errors for multilevel data.

candidate races in the state. But the number of initiatives on an individual's statewide ballot is not a statistically significant predictor of general political interest in the 2004 presidential election.

Many of the control variables are also statistically significant and in the expected direction. Individuals residing in states with competitive candidate races expressed increased interest in the election in 2002. Consumption of all forms of media (newspapers, television, and online news) was important.[41] Partisans were more engaged in the election than nonpartisans, and those with higher socioeconomic status were also more attentive.

Similarly, as shown in table 7-2, citizens residing in states with higher total expenditures on initiatives expressed more interest in the 2002 midterm election, suggesting that direct democracy may indeed help foster an engaged citizenry.[42] In the 2004 presidential election, increased spending on ballot initiatives did not independently boost interest in the election. Thus ballot measures appear to be particularly important in stimulating engagement in low-information elections, consistent with previous research.[43]

Initiative Campaigns and Voter Engagement

But do initiative campaigns increase political interest among those least likely to be engaged in politics—those with low information? Models 2 (2002) and 4 (2004) in table 7-2 add to the equation an interaction term: respondent's education multiplied by expenditures on ballot initiatives in the respondent's state. These interactive models were used to test whether initiative campaigns have a differential effect on political interest among certain segments of the population. Both interaction terms are statistically significant and negative. The base term for total expenditures on initiative campaigns is positive and statistically significant, indicating that those with less education are more likely to report increased interest in politics when exposed to ballot initiatives' campaigns. Even in high-information presidential elections, initiative campaign spending appears to boost engagement most among the less educated. This is a new finding in the literature and suggests that ballot measures may mobilize the politically disengaged. By extension, initiatives (and their associated campaigns) may alter the composition of state electorates and reduce the socioeconomic bias of the electorate.

Table 7-3 uses probability simulations to summarize the impact of our findings. In 2002 increasing total spending on initiatives by one standard deviation above the mean (from average to high) produced a 7 percentage point increase in the probability that an individual with no more than a high school degree (or its equivalent) had thought "quite a lot" about the election,

Table 7-2. *Impact of Initiative Campaign Spending on Political Interest, 2002 and 2004*[a]

| | 2002 | | | | 2004 | | | |
| | Model 1 | | Model 2 | | Model 3 | | Model 4 | |
Measure	*B*	*(SE)*	*B*	*(SE)*	*B*	*(SE)*	*B*	*(SE)*
Expenditures on ballot initiatives	0.009***	(0.003)	0.018***	(0.005)	0.001	(0.001)	0.008***	(0.002)
Total expenditures	. . .		−0.002*	(0.001)	. . .		−.002***	(0.009e-1)
Newspaper news consumption	0.542***	(0.133)	0.542***	(0.133)	0.624**	(0.300)	0.635**	(0.301)
Television news consumption	0.648***	(0.105)	0.651***	(0.106)	0.302	(0.220)	0.307	(0.222)
Online news consumption	1.688***	(0.156)	1.695***	(0.156)	1.164***	(0.438)	1.199***	(0.439)
Republican	0.336**	(0.158)	0.337**	(0.158)	0.523***	(0.196)	0.516***	(0.195)
Democrat	0.085	(0.164)	0.085	(0.164)	0.524***	(0.171)	0.530***	(0.171)
Male	−0.235***	(0.087)	−0.240***	(0.087)	0.034	(0.152)	0.040	(0.153)
Age	0.031***	(0.004)	0.031***	(0.004)	0.013***	(0.004)	0.014***	(0.005)
Latino	−0.255	(0.195)	−0.256	(0.197)	−0.607*	(0.332)	−0.624*	(0.340)
Black	0.115	(0.155)	0.110	(0.156)	0.374	(0.264)	0.375	(0.264)
Asian	−1.181***	(0.280)	−1.155***	(0.274)	−0.464	(0.643)	−0.415	(0.640)
Suburban	−0.224**	(0.110)	−0.231**	(0.110)	n. a.		n. a.	
Urban	−0.118	(0.144)	−0.122	(0.143)	n. a.		n. a.	
Education	0.176***	(0.039)	0.191***	(0.044)	0.300***	(0.047)	0.335***	(0.046)
Income	0.077***	(0.027)	0.077***	(0.027)	0.069**	(0.032)	0.067**	(0.032)
Attend church	n. a.		n. a.		0.053	(0.049)	0.054	(0.048)
Competitive presidential election	. . .		. . .		0.910	(0.937)	0.862	(0.942)
Competitive gubernatorial election	0.146	(0.213)	0.145	(0.215)	0.057	(0.213)	0.057	(0.212)
Competitive senatorial election	0.668***	(0.152)	0.671***	(0.153)	0.065	(0.198)	0.067	(0.200)
Constant	−3.654***	(0.353)	−3.720***	(0.348)	−2.719***	(0.980)	−2.872***	(0.955)
Wald chi square	1,234.55***		1,306.95***		168.74***		447.53***	
Pseudo R^2	.18		.18		.10		.10	
N	1,856		1,856		1,284		1,284	

Source: Pew Internet and American Life Daily Tracking Survey, November 2002 (www.pewinternet. org/data.asp); Pew Research Center for the People and the Press, October 20, 2004 (http://people-press.org/dataarchive/).

*$p < .1$ **$p < .05$ ***$p < .01$

n.a. = not available.

a. Unstandardized logistic regression coefficients with robust standard errors (in parentheses) correct for heteroskedasticity. Reported probabilities are based on two-tailed test. Clustering by state used to adjust standard errors for multilevel data. Additional models (not presented here) were run with the total expenditures on initiatives variable divided by state population. The substantive results hold for models 1 and 2 but do not hold for models 3 and 4. The education variable in the interaction term is a 7-point ordinal variable of educational attainment; it is identical to the education variable used in the other models.

Table 7-3. *Probability of Being Very Interested in the Election, by Exposure to Initiative Campaign Spending and Education Levels, 2002 and 2004*[a]

	2002		2004	
	Percent	(SD)	Percent	(SD)
Low education (high school graduate)				
Average initiative campaign expenditures in respondent's state	48	(0.04)	68	(0.03)
High expenditures (+1 SD)	55	(0.05)	74	(0.03)
Very high expenditures (+2 SD)	61	(0.06)	79	(0.03)
Change from average to high	+7		+6	
Average education (some college)				
Average initiative campaign expenditures in respondent's state	56	(0.04)	77	(0.02)
High expenditures (+1 SD)	61	(0.05)	77	(0.03)
Very high expenditures (+2 SD)	65	(0.05)	78	(0.03)
Change from average to high percent	+5		0	
High education (bachelor's degree)				
Average initiative campaign expenditures in respondent's state	60	(0.04)	80	(0.02)
High expenditures (+1 SD)	63	(0.04)	79	(0.03)
Very high expenditures (+2 SD)	66	(0.05)	77	(0.04)
Change from average to high	+3		−1	

a. Predicted probabilities estimated with Clarify from models 2 and 4 in table 7-2. Age; income; education; television, newspaper, and online news consumption; and presidential, senatorial, and gubernatorial election exposure set at mean values. Gender set at female and race/ethnicity at white. The respondent is assumed to reside in a suburban region. Simulation estimated for nonpartisans (independents).

holding all other variables at their mean or modal values. In 2004 the same simulation boosted interest among the less educated by 6 percentage points.

The effect of campaign spending on interest decreases as education levels rise, as those with more education are likely to be more interested in politics in general. Increasing issue campaign spending from average to high resulted in only a 5 percentage point increase in the probability of being interested in the 2002 election among those respondents with some college education and only a 3 percentage point increase among those with a bachelor's degree. In 2004 the same increase in campaign spending actually decreased political interest among those with a bachelor's degree and left it unchanged among individuals with some college education.

Table 7-4. *Two-Stage Model of the Impact of Ballot Initiative Campaigns on Political Interest and the Probability of Voting*[a]

Variable	B	(SE)	$p > z$
Political interest (predicted probability from first-stage model)	0.50	(0.21)	.023
Newspaper news consumption	0.08	(0.04)	.063
Television news consumption	0.04	(0.03)	.222
Online news consumption	−0.04	(0.07)	.565
Republican	0.06	(0.03)	.032
Democrat	0.02	(0.03)	.525
Male	−0.01	(0.02)	.555
Age	0.00	(0.00)	.007
Latino	−0.04	(0.03)	.208
Black	0.02	(0.04)	.565
Asian	−0.20	(0.04)	.000
Education	0.03	(0.01)	.060
Income	0.02	(0.01)	.027
Constant	−0.22	(0.09)	.014
F	67.83		.000
R^2	.31		
N	1,414		

a. Second-stage estimates, voting in 2002 election. Instrumental variable regression is used; total expenditures on ballot initiatives in the respondent's state is the instrumental variable. Unstandardized regression coefficients are presented, with robust standard errors in parentheses to correct for heteroskedasticity. Reported probabilities are based on a two-tailed test. Second-stage numbers are estimates. First-stage estimates (similar model) are reported in column 1 of table 7-2.

Initiative Campaigns and Voter Turnout

As a final step in the analysis, we employed a two-stage estimation procedure (instrumental variable regression) to test the hypothesis that exposure to initiative campaigns increases engagement and thereby political participation. Specifically, we modeled the impact of expenditures on ballot initiatives on the probability of being interested in the election. The resulting predicted levels of political interest were then included as an explanatory variable in a second-stage model to predict the probability of voting.[44]

The results in table 7-4 show that the increase in political interest associated with higher initiative campaign expenditures is an important predictor of voting in the 2002 election. We also conducted the analysis using initiative expenditures per capita as the predictor in the first stage of the analysis and obtained similar results (not reported here). In other words, ballot measures appear to increase voter turnout by stimulating interest in elections. Previous researchers have found that states with salient initiatives or referenda on the ballot have higher voter turnout over time; this analysis helps explain the mechanisms behind this increase in turnout.[45]

Implications for Reform

This research suggests the campaigns surrounding ballot initiatives provide alternative sources of information about politics to make democracy possible. Initiative campaigns can convey political information with emotions necessary for civic engagement and participation in a democracy. Proponents and opponents of ballot measures help subsidize the costs of information, and their interest group and political party allies do so as well, distributing voting guides and offering heuristic cues with politically relevant information in an easily digestible form.[46] If ballot initiatives' campaigns create richer political information environments, stimulating interest in politics and voter turnout, direct democracy may serve to, in part, counteract a trend of declining engagement.[47] Further, these effects are exaggerated for those with low political information. Thus initiatives may be able to modify the socioeconomic composition of state electorates by mobilizing the less educated.

A reform implication of this study is that, if increased voter turnout is a goal, expanding the use of the initiative to all fifty states may be beneficial. However, it is one thing to argue that competitive candidate elections increase turnout, for competition is beneficial in terms of stronger political parties. Direct democracy as a turnout mechanism, on the other hand, raises normative concerns. Critics claim that direct democracy can tyrannize minorities and lead to irresponsible fiscal policies, including higher government debt.[48] Empirical research has found, however, that racial and ethnic minorities are no more likely to be targeted via ballot initiatives than they are by state legislatures and that expanding the scope of conflict (statewide versus local initiatives) often limits negative effects on unpopular minorities. Furthermore, the courts will invalidate unconstitutional laws passed by voters.[49] Other studies have found that all racial and ethnic groups "win" most of the time in initiative and referendum contests.[50]

A lingering concern, however, is the indirect effects of initiatives on attitudes about targeted minorities, such as gays and lesbians or immigrants.[51] Most frequently reformers argue on behalf of expanding direct democracy because of policy congruence, or policy outcomes, such as the ability to adopt election reform. The argument made in this chapter is that the initiative may have educative effects, increasing engagement in politics and participation. These goals may be desirable on their own accord and may justify expanding use of the process.

Notes

1. Gerber (1999); Matsusaka (2004); Smith and Tolbert (2004).

2. Tolbert and Smith (2005).

3. Lassen (2005).

4. Gerber (1999); Matsusaka (2004); Boehmke (2005); Nicholson (2005); Bowler and Donovan (1998); Bowler, Donovan, and Tolbert (1998); Magleby (1984).

5. Tolbert, Grummel, and Smith (2001); Smith and Tolbert (2004); Mark Smith (2001); Lacey (2005).

6. Campbell (1966).

7. Nicholson (2003) finds that awareness of ballot propositions is higher in midterm election years, suggesting that ballot measures have a greater engagement effect in midterm rather than presidential elections.

8. Smith (2002).

9. Benz and Stutzer (2004).

10. Mendelsohn and Cutler (2000).

11. Smith and Tolbert (2004). Caution should be used when interpreting these results because the National Election Study (NES) samples randomly within regions but not within states. Thus NES data are not ideal for studying state contextual effects, because all respondents in the NES may reside in one area of a state. Additionally, the NES does not include respondents from some small states, including Western states with the initiative process. In contrast, the Pew Research Center samples randomly within states and includes respondents from forty-eight of the fifty states (Alaska and Hawaii are the missing cases). This makes inferences about state-level effects on individual behavior less biased.

12. Bowler and Donovan (2002); Hero and Tolbert (2004); Mendelsohn and Cutler (2000).

13. Dyck and Baldassare (2006).

14. Nie and Andersen (1974); Nie, Verba, and Petrocik (1979); Luskin (1987, 1990).

15. Delli Carpini and Keeter (1996); Shah, Kwak, and Holbert (2001); Jennings and Zeitner (2003); Uslaner (2004); Mossberger, Tolbert, and McNeal (2007).

16. Freedman, Franz, and Goldstein (2004); West (1997).

17. Nicholson (2005); Smith, DeSantis, and Kassel (2006).

18. Bowler and Donovan (1998).

19. Lupia (1994); Karp (1998); Nicholson (2003).

20. Bowler and Donovan (1998).

21. Campbell and others (1960); Wolfinger and Rosenstone (1980).

22. Freedman, Franz, and Goldstein (2004).

23. Mooney (2001); Haider-Markel (2001); Burden (2005a); Gerber (1999); Chavez (1998); Alvarez and Bedolla (2004); Alvarez and Butterfield (2000); Schrag (1998).

24. McCuan and others (1998); Broder (2000).

25. Bowler and Donovan (1998).

26. Sniderman, Brody, and Tetlock (1991); Wenzel, Donovan, and Bowler (1998).

27. The national random sample telephone survey of registered voters was conducted for Pew by Princeton Research Associates between October 15 and October 19 and included 1,307 registered voters representing all fifty states. Report from the Pew Research Center for the People and the Press, October 20, 2004 (www.people-press.org). Forty-three percent of the respondents said they were aware of ballot measures in 2004.

28. The national random telephone survey was conducted for Pew by Princeton Research Associates among a nationwide sample of 2,006 adults from October 17 to October 22, 2006. Report from the Pew Research Center for the People and the Press, October 26, 2006 (www.people-press.org). Distribution on the awareness question is similar to that in 2004.

29. Nicholson (2005); Smith and Tolbert (2004); Campbell (1966).

30. Respondents in 2002 and 2006 were asked, "How much thought have you given to the upcoming midterm election?" Responses were: "Quite a lot," "Some," "Only a little," and "None," with coding ranging from four to one. Respondents in 2004 were asked, "How much thought have you given to the coming presidential election?" "Quite a lot" was coded four, "Some" was coded three, "A little" was coded two, and "None" was coded one.

31. Ordered logistic regression models are available from the authors.

32. For the first measure, the National Conference of State Legislatures served as the source of these data (www.ncsl.org). We measured ballot initiatives, rather than referenda referred by the legislature, as proposals initiated by citizen petition in general tend to be more salient with the public (Gerber 1999; Bowler and Donovan 1998).

33. The Pearson's r correlation between the number of initiatives on the ballot and total expenditures on ballot initiatives in 2002 was 0.63 ($p < .00$).

34. Data on total expenditures on ballot initiatives in each state in millions of dollars for 2002 and 2004 were downloaded from the website of the Ballot Initiative Strategy Center.

35. Matsusaka (2004).

36. This variable takes the form of 1 minus the vote margin, with the vote margin being the difference in the percentage of the total votes cast for the winning candidate and the percentage of the total votes cast for the runner-up. Higher values indicate more competitive rates.

37. We used dummy variables for ideology (Democratic, Republican, or independent, with independents serving as the reference group), gender, race (African American, Asian, or Latino, with non-Latino whites as the reference group), and region (urban/suburban or rural). Income was measured as an ordinal variable ranging from

1, which indicates that family income ranged from $0 to $10,000, and 8, which signifies a family income of $100,000 or more. Education was measured on a 7-point ordinal scale, ranging from eighth-grade education or less to a doctorate, and age is measured in years.

38. Pew queried respondents about their consumption of online election news by asking, "Have you gone online to get news or information about politics or the campaign" (2004). From responses to this question, we created dummy variables indicating whether respondents had gone online to obtain information about each election (1 = yes; 0 = no).

39. Krueger (2002); Bimber (2003); Tolbert and McNeal (2003). We were not able to control for political discussions or efficacy with the Pew data due to limitations in the survey questionnaire.

40. Media consumption variables are not included in the 2006 survey, but two questions measuring political knowledge are. We would expect those with increased political knowledge (like increased media consumption) to be more interested in the election. We summed positive responses to the following two questions to create a 3-point ordinal score of political knowledge (2 indicates correct answers on both questions, 1 denotes the respondent correctly answered one question, and 0 means no factually correct answer was given). Question 1: "Do you happen to know which political party has a majority in the U.S. House of Representatives?" with 65 percent of the sample correctly answering "Republicans" and 35 percent incorrectly responding. Question 2: "Do you happen to know the name of your current representative in Congress?" with 44 percent correctly responding and 56 percent incorrectly.

41. Delli Carpini and Keeter (1996); Freedman, Franz, and Goldstein (2004).

42. Smith (2002).

43. Nicholson (2003).

44. In the first stage we estimated general interest in the election as a function of a critical set of independent variables employed in the second stage. We began (stage one) by estimating the reduced-form equations for political interest, where the dependent variable was the original four-point ordinal variable, with higher values indicating more interest in the election. From the reduced-form estimates we produced the predicted values for each respondent in the survey. In the second stage, an instrumental variable regression procedure substituted these predicted values for the endogenous variable on the right-hand side of the equation modeling voting.

45. Mark Smith (2001); Lacey (2005); Tolbert, Grummel, and Smith (2001); Smith and Tolbert (2004).

46. Bowler and Donovan (1998).

47. Abramson and Aldrich (1982); Putnam (2000); Verba, Schlozman, and Brady (1995).

48. Cain (1992); Broder (2000); Schrag (1998); Bowler and Donovan (1998).

49. Bowler and Donovan (1998).

50. Hajnal, Gerber, and Louch (2002).

51. Wenzel, Donovan, and Bowler (1998).

PART III

Promoting Responsiveness

THAD KOUSSER

8

Term Limits and State Legislatures

For as long as democracies have existed, legislative term limits have been a topic of debate. These limits are an attempt to ensure that leaders are citizens who take temporary turns in government rather than experts who serve as long as they satisfy voters. Aristotle argued explicitly for term limits, which would set "all over each and each in turn over all," and members of the Athenian *boule* could serve for only a single term.[1] Representatives in the first American Congress set up by the Articles of Confederation were allowed to serve for only three of every six years (Article V), but this measure was eliminated by the Constitution's framers, who sought to create a more muscular Congress.[2]

American states renewed the experimentation with legislative term limits beginning in 1990. Limits have gone into effect in fourteen states and have been in place in some cases for a decade or more. Over this time, a scholarly consensus has emerged on many of their effects (and noneffects). Overall, term limits have fundamentally altered the operation of state legislatures without much changing the type of lawmakers who serve in them or the competitiveness of state elections. That is, the new members voted in because of limits on their predecessors' terms are remarkably similar to their predecessors both in demographics and in an ambition for careers in government. Term limits have not turned political animals into citizen politicians. Term limits have also had little effect on competition in state legislative elections: the average margin of victory in these races has remained constant, and the rate of party turnover in districts is about the same with term limits and without them.[3]

Table 8-1. *Term Limit Laws, by State*[a]

State	Year of impact	Year adopted	Lifetime or consecutive	Limit on years	
				Lower house	Upper house
California	1996	1990	Lifetime	6	8
Maine	1996	1993	Consecutive	8	8
Arkansas	1998	1992	Lifetime	6	8
Colorado	1998	1990	Consecutive	8	8
Michigan	1998	1992	Lifetime	6	8
Arizona	2000	1992	Consecutive	8	8
Florida	2000	1992	Consecutive	8	8
Missouri	2000	1992	Lifetime	8	8
Montana	2000	1992	Consecutive	8	8
Ohio	2000	1992	Consecutive	8	8
South Dakota	2000	1992	Consecutive	8	8
Oklahoma	2004	1990	Lifetime	12 (total)	12 (total)
Nebraska	2006	2000	Consecutive	. . .	8
Louisiana	2007	1995	Consecutive	12	12

Source: National Conference of State Legislatures, "Term Limits," 2007 (www.ncsl.org/programs/legismgt/ABOUT/termlimit.htm [March 2008]).

a. Term limit legislation was passed in another six states but was overturned by courts in four (Massachusetts, Oregon, Washington, and Wyoming) and repealed in two (Idaho and Utah). Only in Oregon, from 1998 through 2001, did limits go into effect by removing veteran members before the limits were overturned. Term limits are due to go into effect in Nevada in 2010.

In this chapter, I review the results of studies analyzing the effects of term limits in the American states. Their findings are organized as answers to three key questions: Who goes to state capitols? What goes on in state capitols? What policies come out of state capitols? Scholars have sought answers to these questions either by comparing behavior in similar sessions held before and after term limits, by comparing states with term limits to states without them, or by combining both methods. Most work is based on observations from many states with slightly different term limit laws. Table 8-1 reports the term limit laws now in effect in the United States.

Who Goes to State Capitols?

In what is perhaps the most surprising finding from the literature on term limits, a host of studies find that the implementation of term limits has not changed either the characteristics of the politicians who inhabit state legislatures or the process that brings them there. Though term limits have opened up more seats, they have not made state elections any more competitive.[4] They have also not removed ambition from politicians.[5] State legislators today appear to be just as careerist as their predecessors before term limits, with the limits simply channeling their electoral ambitions in other directions. Term limits have also failed to open up more opportunities to female or minority candidates, with a few notable exceptions.[6] For better or worse, the politicians who come to state capitols today look much like the term-limited veterans they replaced. As one study reports, "The notion that term limits will sweep out the old politicians is true (almost by definition), but the idea that term limits will sweep in a new breed is not."[7]

Because term limits by definition create more open seats, it is reasonable to have expected that they would lead to more competitive elections. Yet term limits have not increased electoral competition nationally because the increase in the number of open seats has been outweighed by the decrease in the competitiveness of both open seats and races with incumbents.[8] Before term limits, seats often became open in competitive districts; after term limits these openings occurred more randomly. Because one party often dominates these districts, margins of victory in open seats grew significantly. In districts held by an incumbent who is still eligible to run, qualified challengers (at least in one state, California, where their qualifications can be measured) are reluctant to challenge incumbents until they are termed out, making these races less competitive.[9]

Table 8-2 shows that, all told, elections held under term limits have been no closer than elections held in other states or in other years absent this reform. The average margin of victory in legislative contests in term limits states is 26.80 percent, compared to an average margin of 26.84 percent in previous years in these states and in states unaffected by term limits. The rate at which seats change parties is similarly unaffected, registering 7.57 percent under term limits and 7.74 percent in their absence.

The national pattern is also apparent in individual states. One sophisticated analysis of California Assembly elections from 1976 to 2004 finds that "in terms of electoral competitiveness, it appears that incumbents are no more in danger of losing their seats today than they were in the late 1980s."[10] Studies of Michigan elections held before and after term limits also find that term limits did not lead to closer races.[11] An analysis of competition in legislative elections held in Oregon before term limits, after their enactment, and then after their judicial repeal again shows that they failed to bring closer margins

Table 8-2. *Term Limits and Electoral Competition, 1991–2002*

	Number of seats	Contested, Republican vs. Democrat (%)	Number of contested seats	Average margin for contested seats (%)
Legislatures with term limits				
Open seat, due to term limits	698	82.09**	573	24.58**
Open seat, not due to term limits	435	79.54**	346	23.81**
Incumbent	1,399	68.98**	964	29.20
Total	2,532	74.41**	1,883	26.80
Legislatures without term limits				
Open seat	4,754	74.25**	3,528	22.51**
Incumbent	17,131	55.54**	9,485	28.45
Total	21,885	59.60**	13,013	26.84

Source: Cain, Hanley, and Kousser (2006).

**Indicates that the difference between competition levels in the legislatures with and without term limits is statistically significant at the 99 percent confidence level in a two-sample t-test.

of victory or higher levels of party turnover.[12] Finally, an investigation of competition in primary elections shows that term limits appear to bring slight increases in the number of contested primaries and the average number of candidates per primary in Colorado but not in California.[13]

A comprehensive analysis of California elections held from 1976 through 2004 provides evidence that another promise of term limits has gone unfulfilled, at least in that state. Rather than lead to an increase in turnout, the implementation of term limits has been followed by a decline in electoral participation.[14] While this may be due to long-term turnout trends—and deserves further investigation in other states—it provides yet more evidence that term limits have not changed the fundamental parameters of state legislative elections.

Another hope of some term limits' proponents was that this reform would usher a return to the days of citizen legislators. The corresponding fear of its opponents was that legislators stripped of their career ambitions would serve less energetically and faithfully. Neither this hope nor this fear has materialized. Term limits have merely refocused the career ambitions of legislators. A national survey of legislators, conducted under the auspices of the Joint Project on Term Limits (a project organized by the National Conference of State Legislatures, the Council of State Governments, and the State Legislative

Leaders Foundation), shows that very few term-limited legislators plan to retire to private life when their time is up. Only 18 percent of those in lower houses and 28 percent in senates contemplate retirement, while the overwhelming majority plan to run for another elected office, to lobby, or to take an appointive office.[15] Another study shows that 54 percent of the legislators termed out of six state legislatures in 1998 ran for another office and that many others took positions in state agencies or as lobbyists.[16] These itinerant careerists do not always succeed in their political ambitions: term-limited members run for Congress more than state legislators without term limits, but they are also more likely to lose these races.[17]

Many supporters of term limits predicted that they would change the face of state legislatures by creating new opportunities for minority and female representation, but in fact minority representation has increased in only a few cases, and women have not been helped by term limits anywhere. A national study finds "no systematic difference between legislators from term-limited and non-term-limited states" in minority representation.[18] Focusing more closely on individual states, others find that Latinos in California benefited from term limits while African American representation actually declined.[19] The percentage of Latinos in California's population was growing at this time, while the black percentage declined, and the new seats opened up by term limits help to accelerate Latino gains in representation. In states with more stable demographics, term limits led to either minimal (in Michigan) or nonexistent (in Colorado) gains in minority representation.[20]

Although the percentage of seats held by women rose in term-limited states over the prior decade, so did the number of women elected in states without term limits. Reviewing the national data, one study concludes that "there is no evidence that term limits have actually led to an increase in the number of women serving."[21] There are some signs, in fact, that term limits may place some of the gains in female representation that were won in 1992 (Year of the Woman) at risk. One analysis of the 1998 elections reveals that in the 215 open-seat contests held in states with term limits, the number of districts won by women dropped from fifty-eight to fifty-three.[22]

What Goes on in State Capitols?

While the outward characteristics of legislators have changed little, the experience that they bring to state capitols and the incentive structures that they face have transformed legislative operations dramatically. New members have less institutional knowledge and, according to surveys, less expertise in policy and process. With shorter time horizons in office, their views of their role as representatives have changed in important and arguably positive ways. As committee chairs and leaders have become less powerful, the traditional legislative process has begun to break down. Further, it appears that partisan conflict—which was already strong in most states—has sharpened as term limits have erased legislators' common pasts and shared futures.

Increasing the amount of turnover in state legislatures was the primary intended effect of term limit laws, and these increases have indeed occurred, especially immediately following their passage. Limits opened up 58 percent of the seats in the Michigan House and removed 49 percent of the members of the Arkansas House in 1998. Legislative membership typically stabilizes over the next few sessions but then spikes again when members of the initial class brought in by term limits reach the end of their tenure. Overall, term limit laws across the nation have led to an average rise of 14 percent in turnover rates.[23]

What impact has this increase in churn had on the knowledge, behavior, and attitudes of legislators? There are two ways in which it can affect them: by shortening their time horizons and by not allowing them to become experienced legislators. A survey of "knowledgeable observers"—that is, legislative staff, former legislators, executive agency staff, lobbyists, and reporters—conducted by the Joint Project on Term Limits probed the first effect by asking capitol insiders about how much legislators know about statewide issues, the legislative process, and the issues before their committees, compared with legislators ten years earlier. As table 8-3 shows, those in term-limited states are much more likely to note a decline in expertise, an effect that is substantively strong and statistically significant.

Evidence from other surveys indicates that the turnover brought by term limits has eroded the link between legislators and their constituents. A survey of more than 19,000 respondents in all fifty states finds that respondents in states with term limits are less likely to be able to name their state legislators and contact these representatives less often than respondents in states without term limits.[24] The Joint Project on Term Limits survey uncovered a similar pattern by asking members how much time they spend "keeping in touch with constituents" and "helping constituents with problems with government." Legislators in term-limited states report spending less time on both activities.[25] California data show that term-limited legislators spend less money on "constituency outreach" (through mail and by phone) in their last terms.[26] A final piece of evidence on this point comes from the knowledgeable observers' survey. Capitol insiders in term-limited states report that legislators spend

Table 8-3. *Changes in Legislative Expertise, States with and without Term Limits*[a]

Type of expertise	States with term limits[b]	States without term limits[c]
Legislator knowledge about statewide issues	1.94*	2.82
Legislator knowledge about how the legislature operates	1.80*	2.70
Committee member knowledge about issues before the committee	1.96*	2.71

Source: Kousser and Straayer (2007).

*significant at the 0.05 level.

a. Average change in legislators' levels of expertise over ten years, on a five-point scale. An average score of 2 indicates that legislators have "somewhat less" knowledge than legislators ten years before; an average score of 3 indicates that legislators have "about the same" level of knowledge as ten years before.

b. Arizona, Arkansas, California, Colorado, Maine, Ohio.

c. Illinois, Indiana, Kansas.

less time talking to or helping constituents than they did a decade earlier, whereas insiders in the three surveyed states without term limits notice an increase in both activities.[27]

Shortening legislators' time horizons makes them less likely to "support the institution of the legislature."[28] It could also affect whether they view themselves as delegates of their constituents or trustees of the public good, the dichotomy famously set forth by Edmund Burke.[29] To discover whether term limits cause any shift in what representatives view as their proper role, the national survey of legislators posed two questions. The first asked, "When there is a conflict between what you feel is best and what you think the people in your district want, do you think you should follow your own conscience or follow what the people in your district want?" Researchers find that legislators in states with term limits are more likely to say that they follow their consciences, particularly members closest to being termed out.[30]

The second question asked legislators whether they are more concerned with the needs of their district or with those of the state as a whole. Again, those in term-limited states are more likely to answer as trustees, placing a greater emphasis on state concerns, whereas legislators serving in bodies without limits respond as delegates who are more concerned with their districts.[31] Looking at these questions and other measures, another study concludes that term limits brought on a Burkean shift away from the delegate view of district representation and toward a trustee role.[32] Whether this is a positive or negative trend depends upon one's perspective. Early proponents of term limits predicted and celebrated this shift to a more deliberative trustee role, while early opponents argued that the focus on constituency interests created by the electoral connection was a good thing.[33]

Another mathematical certainty that comes with the imposition of term limits is that the tenure of legislative leaders and committee chairs, who sometimes served for decades, declines. This has led to a decentralization of power in legislatures as well as to changes in the process. National studies show that leaders of term-limited houses serve for shorter periods and begin their tenures with less legislative experience, compared with their predecessors before term limits and with the leaders of houses unaffected by limits.[34] A more detailed qualitative study of leaders around the country shows that the nature of leadership has changed as well. Since their peers do not have as much time to evaluate the legislative skills of candidates for leadership posts, there is an "increased emphasis placed on fundraising skills."[35] There is more competition for leadership positions, and the jockeying to be next in line for a leadership post often starts the day after someone else is elected to it.[36] A study of the distribution of contribution patterns in eight states finds that the concentration of money in the hands of legislative leaders (a mark of their power) diminishes after term limits.[37] Finally, a survey of legislative leaders finds that those presiding over term-limited bodies are more likely than those running bodies without limits to say that leaders in their houses lost power over the prior five years, though this difference falls short of statistical significance.[38]

Case studies of states with term limits show that, as the tenure of committee chairs declines, committees become less specialized and know less about policy; in addition, their members are less likely to be collegial and courteous.[39] None of these changes are apparent in states without term limits. Figures from the knowledgeable observers' survey reveal that term limits cause committee members to be less likely (than those in states without limits) to seek public input on legislation, to behave courteously, or to be informed about the issues. Term limits also affect the rate at which committees pass and amend bills, although these effects vary by state.[40]

These changes in leadership and committees have brought about a decline both in levels of knowledge and in adherence to the norms of the legislative process. Insiders in states with term limits see a decline in the number of legislators who "specialize on issues" and who are "knowledgeable about how the legislature operates."[41] Responses to survey questions show that term limits also lead to fewer members who are "concerned about clarity and precision in legislation" and "likely to follow parliamentary procedure on the floor."[42]

Term limits have little systematic impact, however, on the role of staff assistants and the influence of lobbyists. Some opponents of term limits warned that they would shift influence from legislators to unelected, unaccountable staffers.[43] This fear has not been realized, because staff often leave along with longtime legislators. According to the national survey of legislators, there was "no shift toward greater staff influence in term-limited chambers."[44] A fifty-state survey of staff directors asked how staff influence changed over time; the survey finds no differences between states with term limits and those without.[45]

There has also been no broad, consistent change in the role played by interest groups and lobbyists. Analyzing the national survey of legislators, a study finds that term limits have no effect on the perceived power of interest groups, a finding consistent with a prospective survey of term limits conducted in 1995.[46] One analysis finds that states implementing term limits do not experience a sharper rise in the overall impact of interest groups.[47] The survey of knowledgeable observers reveals that term limits do not make legislators significantly more likely to sponsor interest group legislation, although they do lead to a modest rise in the perceived influence of lobbyists relative to the legislature.[48] On this point, one researcher concludes that "there is little evidence of any impact one way or the other of term limits on the broader, macro-level influence of interest groups in state policymaking in general."[49]

By contrast, there is clear evidence that the divisions created by party lines grew more salient after term limits. In state legislatures just as in Congress, party caucuses have grown further apart on the ideological spectrum over the last generation, as liberal voters have become more loyal Democrats and conservatives more reliably Republican.[50] This increase in partisan polarization preceded the term limits movement and cannot be blamed on it. Studies of state legislators in California and Colorado confirm that term limits did not lead to the election of more polarized politicians, a finding consistent with the national evidence.[51]

Yet term limits do change how legislators treat members of the other party. According to one legislator, "The single biggest effect of term limits is increased partisanship. You don't know your colleagues well, and you don't treat them as part of your future."[52] Indeed, an analysis of legislator interactions in Michigan finds that there has been a sharp drop-off in communication and policy consultation across party lines since term limits came into force.[53] Clear evidence that this has changed party dynamics comes from measuring the portion of the bills that each member introduces that becomes law. Without long-term ties across party lines, majority members have been

Figure 8-1. *Gap between Majority and Minority Parties in the Proportion of Legislation Passed, by Term Limit Restrictions, Four States*[a]

Majority party batting average minus minority party batting average

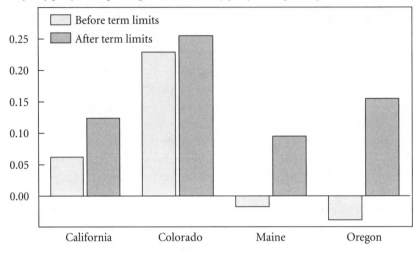

Source: Kousser (2005).

a. Bars represent differences between the mean averages for majority party and minority party legislators in each state. I compiled these means by using legislative records to calculate each legislator's success rate.

free to kill more and more minority-authored bills while passing their own. The legislative climate has grown nastier as terms have become shorter.

Figure 8-1 displays the gap between majority and minority party legislative success before and after term limits. It shows that the gap grew after term limits in all four states that I examined: California, Colorado, Oregon, and Maine. It is of course possible that this trend has occurred in all states, even those without term limits, but the fact that it is so consistent, strong, and present no matter which party is in the majority increases my confidence that this trend reflects a term limits effect.

Further evidence of the growing importance of partisan affiliation comes from an examination of contribution patterns by corporate political action committees (PACs). PAC contributions in California from 1987 to 1998 were tracked to see which legislators possessed enough power to attract them.[54] The study finds that corporate interests increasingly targeted their money on legislative Democrats after the passage of the state's term limit law, indicating that power is increasingly concentrated in majority party hands.

What Policies Come out of State Capitols?

As internal conflict has risen in legislatures since the enactment of term limits, legislators have been less involved with the executive branch and the bureaucracy. Because of this, the policies coming out of state capitols increasingly bear the imprint of governors, and the bureaucracy implements these policies without much oversight. In addition, these policies are less innovative than before term limits.

The clearest objective evidence that term limits shift power away from the legislative branch and toward the executive is the dramatic decrease in the extent to which legislators scrutinize and amend the governor's budget proposal. This effect is sharp and consistent across states. To measure this effect, I compared the outcomes of budget negotiations in pairs of sessions, one held before the passage of a term limit law and the other after its implementation. The sessions were similar in most other important political features.[55] I matched up sessions by party representation in the legislature, by the legislative-gubernatorial party split, and by growth in state spending. I looked at four states with term limits. Two states without them serve as a baseline.

To measure the influence that each branch exerted over the budget in a given session, I conducted a line-by-line comparison of the state spending plan that the governor proposed in January with the final budget passed in the summer. I added up the dollar value of all changes that the legislature made to the budget—counting the absolute magnitude of both reductions and increases—and compared them with the size of the governor's proposals for every budget line to compute the total percentage change that the legislature made to the governor's budget. Figure 8-2 reports these changes in two sets of parallel sessions, held before and after term limits.

In all four states with term limits—California, Colorado, Maine, and Oregon—comparisons reveal a decline in the legislature's use of the power of the purse to check the executive branch. Term limits led to a dramatic drop in the percentage of the governor's budget that was altered by the legislatures in these four states. In contrast, in New Mexico and Illinois, two states without term limits, legislators became more actively engaged in crafting budgets over the period measured. These findings match up with qualitative and survey evidence about the relative powers of the legislative and executive branches. In a national survey, legislators in all fifty states were asked, "What do you think is the relative power of the following actors in determining legislative outcomes in your chamber?" They were then given a list of nine actors, including "Governor" and "Bureaucrats/Civil Servants." On average, legislators in

Figure 8-2. *Changes Made by Legislatures to Governors' Budget Proposal, by Term Limit Restrictions, Six States*

Percent change

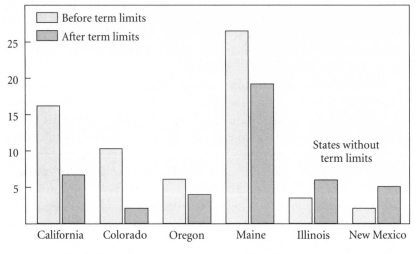

Source: Kousser (2005).

states with term limits rated both the governor and bureaucrats as more powerful than did legislators in states without limits. This difference is statistically significant at the 0.05 level and remains significant even under a multivariate analysis that holds constant the characteristics of legislators and states.[56]

The survey of knowledgeable observers also asked whether power had shifted to governors and agencies over the prior ten years. The power shifts reported in figure 8-3 demonstrate that insiders see the executive branch as being more powerful in five of the six states that implemented term limits over the period. The exception was Ohio, where Speaker Larry Householder was enormously influential after term limits were instituted.[57] But no leader in any other state with term limits has harnessed as much power over state government. The conclusion that term limits are responsible for this power shift is further strengthened by the fact that knowledgeable observers in the three states without term limits—Illinois, Indiana, and Kansas—report that the legislative branch actually grew more powerful over the same period.

Another study finds qualitative evidence of a shift in power to the executive branch.[58] Reviewing case studies containing interviews from term-limited states that attribute the decline in legislative power to the inexperience of new legislators, the short-term futures that they face, and the declining power and

Figure 8-3. *Power Shifts, 1995–2005, in Governorships and State Administrative Agencies, by Term Limit Restrictions, Nine States*

Percent change over ten years

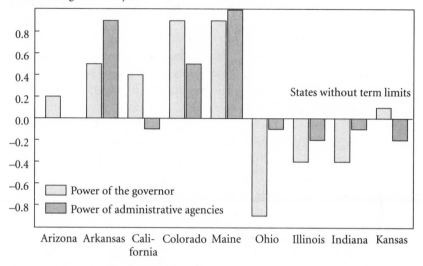

Source: Kousser and Straayer (2007).

expertise of legislative leaders as well as committee chairs, the study finds no reports of such a decline in the states without term limits. Summarizing the survey and case study evidence, the study concludes that "one of the clearest effects of term limits has been to weaken legislatures at the expense of executives. This shift in institutional power represents a significant restructuring of the representative nature of government."[59]

A 2003 study also identifies a strong shift in power toward the executive branch based on a survey of top legislative leaders in both houses in all fifty states.[60] Only 35.2 percent of leaders in houses without term limits say that the governor has grown more powerful in the past five years, compared with 47.6 percent of leaders in states with term limits soon to come and 56.1 percent of leaders in states where limits were going into effect. Similarly, a 1999 survey of lobbyists in California, Colorado, and Maine reveals a strong consensus that term limits shift power to the executive branch.[61]

In addition to strengthening the executive branch's role in the legislative process, term limits appear to weaken legislative oversight of the implementation of laws. Looking only at the California legislature, two researchers find that, after the passage of term limits, legislators make fewer requests to see how state funds are actually spent and order fewer audits of the bureaucracy.[62] A review of case studies shows that this trend is not limited to one state. "Under term limits oversight functions have suffered greatly. As time passes and institutional memory declines, the danger is that legislatures will no longer appreciate what has been lost."[63]

Finally, there is evidence that term limits alter the nature of the laws passed by state governments. Following the passage of term limits, the legislation that emerges from statehouses tends to be less complex and less innovative. In Colorado, Oregon, and Maine the median number of lines per bill—a common measure of the complexity of legislation—declined after the implementation of term limits.[64] As interviews with legislators and veteran staff assistants suggest, bills became shorter and simpler (a potentially positive trend) after term limits, except in California, where experience levels in the legislature initially remained high.[65]

States with term limits are also significantly less innovative in their reactions to federal welfare reform and in setting up new State Children's Health Insurance Programs. Although they are free to diverge from federal guidelines, state legislatures diverged less if term limits had removed their most experienced members. Similarly, states with term limits (compared to states without them) won fewer Council of State Governments' "innovation awards" than their history or their state characteristics would predict.[66]

Implications for Reform

Viewed purely as electoral reforms, term limit laws have not fulfilled their promise. Legislative contests are no more competitive under term limits than they are without them, districts are no more likely to change parties, and there is no evidence that proportionally more voters participate in elections. But term limits have brought major and often unexpected changes to state legislatures. What may have looked like mere tinkering with the qualifications of office at the time has had a profound impact on the operation of government. A recurring theme in the term limits literature is that many of the predictions made both by supporters and by opponents have been flawed, with some of the most consequential changes brought by term limits being the least intended.[67]

The prospects for radical changes in the use of term limits in American politics appear slim. The movement to impose term limits on Congress by passing state laws limiting federal representatives ran into a legal obstacle. In its 1995 *U.S. Term Limits, Inc.,* v. *Thornton* decision, the U.S. Supreme Court invalidated such laws. Likewise, attempts by legislators to remove or ease the term limits that voters placed upon them have run into a political obstacle: voters have so far been unwilling to rescind limits. Ballot measures to extend term limits lost in both Arkansas and Montana in 2004.[68] In February 2008, a California ballot proposition that would have allowed legislators to serve up to twelve years in a single house, rather than six years in the Assembly and eight in the Senate, failed narrowly. It appears that the current wave of experimentation with term limits in the states will last at least a generation, giving scholars more opportunities to study their effects.

Notes

1. See Petracca (1992) for Aristotle's views on term limits and for a history of the debate over limits; and see Thorley (1996, pp. 27–31) for a discussion of term limits in the Athenian boule.

2. Kesler (1990); Erickson (1993).

3. See Moncrief, Powell, and Storey (2007) for evidence on the characteristics of legislators before and after term limits; and Cain, Hanley, and Kousser (2006) for findings on electoral competition.

4. Cain, Hanley, and Kousser (2006); Masket and Lewis (2007); Allebaugh and Pinney (2003); Pinney, Serra, and Sprick (2004); Sarbaugh-Thompson and others (2004).

5. Powell (2003); Lazarus (2006); Steen (2006); Moncrief, Powell, and Storey (2007).

6. Bernstein and Chadha (2003); Caress and others (2003); Cain and Kousser (2004); Carey and others (2006); Moncrief, Powell, and Storey (2007); John A. Straayer, "Colorado's Legislative Term Limits: Final Report for the Joint Project on Term Limits," 2004 (www.ncsl.org/jptl/casestudies/CaseContents.htm).

7. Moncrief, Powell, and Storey (2007; quotation from unpublished manuscript).

8. Cain, Hanley, and Kousser (2006).

9. Cain, Hanley, and Kousser (2006).

10. Masket and Lewis (2007, p. 20). Analyses conducted in the immediate wake of the implementation of California's term limits initiative find that it ushered in closer legislative contests (Clucas 2003; Petracca 1998). However, the apparent term limits effect observed in these studies came from the 1994 through 1998 elections, a time of heightened party competition brought about by the national Republican surge in 1994, coupled with the Democratic resurgence in 1996. The more comprehensive analysis in Masket and Lewis (2007) shows that, since this rise in competition abated, there has been no term limits effect.

11. Allebaugh and Pinney (2003); Pinney, Serra, and Sprick (2004); Sarbaugh-Thompson and others (2004).

12. Cain, Hanley, and Kousser (2006).

13. Cain, Hanley, and Kousser (2006).

14. Nalder (2007).

15. Moncrief, Powell, and Story (2007).

16. Powell (2003).

17. Steen (2006); Lazarus (2006).

18. Carey and others (2006, p. 115).

19. Caress and others (2003); Cain and Kousser (2004).

20. Caress and others (2003); John A. Straayer, "Colorado's Legislative Term Limits: Final Report for the Joint Project on Term Limits," 2004 (www.ncsl.org/jptl/case studies/CaseContents.htm).

21. Moncrief, Powell, and Storey (2007; quotation from unpublished manuscript).

22. Bernstein and Chadha (2003).

23. Moncrief, Powell, and Storey (2007).

24. Niemi and Powell (2003).

25. Powell, Niemi, and Smith (2007).

26. Van Vechten (2003).

27. Powell, Niemi, and Smith (2007).

28. Berman (2007, p. 274).

29. Burke (1774).

30. Powell, Niemi, and Smith (2007).

31. Powell, Niemi, and Smith (2007).

32. Carey and others (2006).

33. Mark P. Petracca, "Pro: It's Time to Return to 'Citizen-Legislators,'" *San Francisco Chronicle,* March 26, 1991, p. A21; also see Will (1992); Glazer and Wattenberg (1996); Polsby (1997).

34. Little and Farmer (2007); Bowser and others (2003).

35. Bowser and others (2003, p. 119).

36. Little and Farmer (2007).

37. Apollonio and LaRaja (2006).

38. Peery and Little (2003).

39. Cain and Wright (2007).

40. Kousser (2005, chap. 4).

41. Berman (2007; quotation from unpublished manuscript).

42. Berman (2007; quotation from unpublished manuscript).

43. Rosenthal (1974).

44. Carey and others (2006, p. 124).

45. Weberg and Kurtz (2007).

46. Carey and others (2006); Carey, Niemi, and Powell (2000).

47. Mooney (2007); this finding is according to a standard measure produced by Thomas and Hrebenar (2003).

48. Berman (2007); Mooney (2007).

49. Mooney (2007; quotation from unpublished manuscript). Although the overall level of power exerted by interest groups has not changed, their behavior and the distribution of influence across lobbyists do seem to have shifted. Mooney (2007) shows that interest groups hired lobbyists at a faster rate after term limits came into effect in their states. Quotations from legislative insiders reported in Kousser (2005, chap. 2) and Mooney (2007) indicate that lobbyists who relied on their connections to individual legislators became less powerful as term limits removed these legislators; groups that could afford to hire new lobbyists grew in influence. Finally, both Mooney (2007) and Thompson and Moncrief (2003) report that lobbyists say that they have had to work much harder at their jobs after term limits were instituted.

50. McCarty, Poole, and Rosenthal (2006); Jacobson (2007).

51. Cain and Kousser (2004); Straayer (2004); Carey, Niemi, and Powell (2000).

52. Cain and Kousser (2004, p. 61).

53. Sarbaugh-Thompson and others (2006).

54. Gordon and Unmack (2003).

55. Kousser (2005, chap. 6).

56. Carey and others (2006).

57. Kousser and Straayer (2007).

58. Powell (2007).

59. Powell (2007; quotation from unpublished manuscript).

60. Peery and Little (2003).

61. Thompson and Moncrief (2003).

62. Cain and Kousser (2004).

63. Powell (2007; quotation from unpublished manuscript).

64. Kousser (2006).

65. Kousser (2006).

66. Kousser (2005).

67. Kurtz, Niemi, and Cain (2007); Kousser (2005, chap. 8); Sarbaugh-Thompson and others (2004, chap. 11); Cain and Kousser (2004, chap. 6).

68. Bowser and Moncrief (2007).

CHRISTOPHER A. COOPER

9

Multimember Districts and State Legislatures

Although many Americans may think of government structures as static, a close examination of the history of the American electoral system reveals frequent changes. For instance, since the time of the Constitution's ratification the country has moved from indirect election of senators to direct election, believing that direct election of senators would lead to better representation. The country has also capped the number of U.S. House members at 435 and passed a series of laws to increase ballot access.

One change that has received comparatively less attention is the move from multimember districts to single-member districts in many state legislatures. Until the 1960s most states elected at least some state legislators in multimember districts (MMDs) rather than the single-member districts (SMDs) that are more familiar today.[1] Under an MMD system, in each election voters choose more than one legislator to serve their district. A single citizen in an MMD system would therefore be represented by several legislators in the same legislative body. By contrast, candidates who run in SMD elections are running for a lone seat, which will represent the entire district. Although many states continue to use MMDs, there has been a clear decline in their use.

Theoretically, MMDs should affect both constituents and legislators. Because of the increased number of legislators in each district, constituents should be less likely to identify with and know their legislators in MMDs, making it less likely that they will contact them with problems or recognize their names on a ballot. Similarly, legislators in MMDs face different electoral circumstances. Whereas SMD incumbents likely face competition from political amateurs, who do not have the resources or experience to provide a competitive challenge, MMD legislators must compete with other incumbents—legislators who have experience and resources. MMD legislators also do not need a plurality of votes to be elected, providing very different incentives for running an election and relating to constituents once in office. These markedly different electoral circumstances for both voters and legislators produce markedly different political outcomes.

In this chapter I discuss the current state of MMDs in the American states and then review the literature on multimember districts, concentrating on the effects for descriptive representation, constituency relations, reelection, party strength, and ideological extremity. At times I present new data to illustrate the effects of MMDs, but most of the analysis in this chapter reflects work conducted elsewhere.

An Overview of Multimember Districts

Multimember districts were once a common way to elect legislators in the United States. Until the Apportionment Act of 1842, 345 members of Congress were elected in MMDs.[2] In addition, many citizens, particularly in the South, once elected part or all of their state legislators under this systems. As late as 1979, "twenty-nine states elected all members of the lower house from single-member districts, eight states elected all from multimember districts, and thirteen states used a combination of the two."[3] In the past few decades, however, the prevalence of MMDs has declined significantly. Much of this decline stems from legal battles waged in the 1960s in which the legality of MMDs was called into question. In one of the earliest and most prominent cases, the court ruled in *Reynolds* v. *Sims* that apportionment should be made by population and that MMDs might violate the one man, one vote principle. The current prevailing opinion can be found in *Thornburg* v. *Gingles*, in which the court ruled that MMDs were not necessarily unconstitutional. As long as they were not instituted to dilute minority representation, they could stand as a legal, and acceptable, means of apportionment.

As of 2001 eleven states still elected legislators using MMD systems:[4]
—Arizona: 100 percent of lower chamber
—Arkansas: 2 percent of lower chamber
—Maryland: 71 percent of lower chamber
—Nevada: 31 percent of upper chamber
—New Hampshire: 56 percent of lower chamber
—New Jersey: 100 percent of lower chamber

—North Carolina: 19 percent of upper chamber; 17 percent of lower chamber

—North Dakota: 100 percent of lower chamber

—South Dakota: 100 percent of lower chamber

—Vermont: 77 percent of upper chamber; 29 percent of lower chamber

—West Virginia: 100 percent of upper chamber; 42 percent of lower chamber

Many local governments also use MMDs to elect school boards and other local offices. The MMD structure is not limited to the United States. Globally, more legislators are elected using MMDs than SMDs.[5]

In this chapter I consider only the "pure" form of the MMD, that in which more than one candidate is elected to the legislature simultaneously in a single, free-for-all election. Some states employ variants of the MMD system, such as the seat-designate system (Washington State), where legislators run for a designated seat. This system more closely mirrors a series of single-member elections than a true MMD. Similarly, some states use a staggered-term system, in which different legislators run in different years—representing the same area but never appearing on the same ballot. The most prominent example of this system is found in the U.S. Senate.[6]

Descriptive Representation

One of the oldest and potentially most important questions in political science addresses descriptive representation—the extent to which a legislative body looks like the people it represents.[7] For instance, if a legislative body were made up entirely of men while the constituency was 50 percent female, the legislative body would be low in descriptive representation.

Theoretically, descriptive representation should lead to more equitable government policies and processes that are fair to the minority as well as the majority of citizens. Considerable evidence suggests this is true. For instance, African American legislators have been found to propose and pass policies directly benefiting those in poverty and those who live in urban areas.[8] Perhaps as a result, the representative bureaucracy literature finds that African Americans are more satisfied with government in areas with higher proportions of African American political representation.[9] Further, states with district structures that suppress black representation have less generous welfare policies than states with district structures that aid in minority elections.[10] Another study comes to similar conclusions but cautions that minority influence may be conditioned by political context and party control.[11]

Table 9-1. *Professionalism of Legislatures, by District System and Term Limit Descriptors, Eight States*

State, district system	Professionalism	Term limits (year enacted, year effective)
Arizona, MMD	.185	Yes (1992, 2000)
Oklahoma, SMD	.188	Yes (1990, 2004)
South Dakota, MMD	.065	Yes (1992, 2000)
Maine, SMD	.098	Yes (1993, 1996)
North Dakota, MMD	.058	No
Kentucky, SMD	.053	No
New Jersey, MMD	.320	No
Pennsylvania, SMD	.283	No

Latino representation has been found to lead to less political alienation among Latino citizens.[12] Similarly, women tend to have higher political efficacy in states with a greater proportion of female state legislators.[13] Female legislators are more likely than their male counterparts to act on bills on health, family, and women's issues.[14] There is also evidence that female representation affects constituents' opinions of government.

Female Representation

District structure has a substantial influence on female representation. States that elect legislators from MMDs have about 5 percent more women in office than SMD states.[15] A study of states that shifted from SMDs to MMDs provides similar evidence.[16] A study of legislators in ten states supports this outcome, as do studies of local and international representation.[17]

To provide a simple demonstration of the consequences of MMDs for female representation, I collected data on female representation in 2007 for the four states (Arizona, North Dakota, New Jersey, and South Dakota) that have a lower chamber completely elected from MMDs. I also collected data from four states (Oklahoma, Maine, Kentucky, and Pennsylvania) using SMDs but that are each similar to one of the first four regarding term limits and legislative professionalism (table 9-1).[18]

Of course simply comparing the upper houses across states would provide a poor demonstration of this hypothesis, as some states are more likely to elect women due to other features of the state (such as public opinion or female labor force participation). Figure 9-1 graphs the difference between the percentages of women in the upper and lower chambers (House representation

Figure 9-1. *Female Representation, Upper and Lower Chambers, Eight States, 2007*

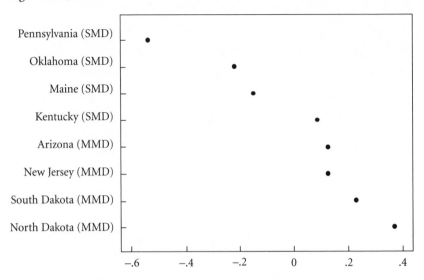

Source: Center for American Women and Politics (2007). See www.cawp.rutgers.edu.
SMD = single-member districts; MMD = multimember districts.

minus Senate representation). MMD states show a greater difference between the two chambers, as the theory suggests. While not a rigorous test, this exercise provides a simple graphic demonstration of the influence of district structure on female representation and shows that MMDs tend to produce greater numbers of women in office than SSDs.[19]

The empirical demonstration of the relationship is fairly straightforward, but the literature on the theoretical reasons behind this relationship is more unsatisfying. One theory suggests that party leaders are more likely to support and recruit female candidates in MMD environments.[20] A second theory argues that it is the voters, rather than the party elites, who act differently in MMD elections. This hypothesis holds that "voters may practice a form of sexual affirmative action in MMDs. Those with reservations about women's qualifications for political office may cast one of their ballots for a woman in an MMD and reserve their other votes for male candidates."[21] A third theory suggests that because of lower name recognition in MMD elections, other distinctive characteristics, such as gender, become more important and provide an easy heuristic for voters to make decisions.[22]

In sum, although political scientists have demonstrated convincingly that district structure is related to the probability of electing a woman, they have spent much less time and energy discovering why. Judging from the extant literature, it is almost impossible to distinguish among these potential causes.

Minority Representation

Conventional wisdom holds that the probability of electing a minority legislator is highest when a minority group is geographically concentrated and district lines are drawn proximate to these minority concentrations. Given that MMDs are often larger than SMDs, many argue that these districts suppress the election of minority legislators. "Lower houses having a substantial minority of black legislators are ones that use single-member districts exclusively: Alabama, Georgia, Louisiana, South Carolina, Tennessee, and Texas. The states with very few black representatives are all ones using large multi-member districts in metropolitan areas: Arkansas, Florida, Mississippi, Virginia and North Carolina."[23]

Although minority candidates sometimes win in MMD elections, they are more likely to gain election in cumulative voting systems than in more traditional voting systems.[24] Similar findings can be found in studies of city councils.[25] There is some reason to question these findings, however. First, MMDs frequently occur in urban areas; therefore, it could be the urban nature of the district, rather than the district's structure, that retards minority representation.[26] Second, we know that MMDs were frequently used explicitly to discriminate against minorities. Indeed, many southern states instituted MMDs expressly to dilute minority representation.[27] Certainly the nature of race relations in America has changed over the past two decades, suggesting that the effects of MMDs may have changed as well. Third, many studies include staggered and seat-designated MMD systems and categorize them alongside pure MMD systems, conflating theoretically and practically distinct concepts.[28] Finally, it is possible that the effects of minority representation are difficult to discern given the lack of ethnic diversity in many of the MMD states (such as Vermont, North Dakota, South Dakota, New Hampshire, and West Virginia, where the percentage of the voting-age population that is black never rises above 3 percent).

For many of these reasons, a reduction in minority representation is not an automatic result of switching from MMDs to SMDs.[29] Further, MMDs may actually increase the number of minority officeholders.[30] Or they may hurt black male representation but increase black female representation.[31] A study analyzing the effects of district structure on minority (black and Hispanic) representation across three decades finds no relationship.[32] Consequently, it appears that MMDs may no longer have the effect on racial representation that they once had. At a minimum, given the mixed findings, we can no longer assume that MMDs are bad for the representation of minorities.

Constituency Relations

In addition to the demographic differences cited above, considerable evidence suggests that representational styles are different in MMDs and SMDs. Because constituents in SMDs are represented by only one legislator, the probability of a constituent being aware of her legislator is fairly high. Contrast this with an MMD system, in which each constituent is represented by two or more legislators, giving the constituent more legislators to follow and be aware of. Consequently, if a constituent in an MMD has a problem, it is less likely that she will approach her state legislator for help, simply because of a lack of name recognition. Similarly, because legislators do not need a majority (or even a plurality) of votes to be reelected, legislators in MMDs tend to spend less time on—and place less emphasis on—constituency service and casework than their counterparts in SMDs. Interviews with legislators in the 1970s show evidence to support this conclusion, noting that "single-member districting makes the legislator more directly responsible to constituents."[33]

Many legislative scholars have used the terms *delegate* and *trustee* to refer to a legislator's focus. Delegates refer to legislators who believe the constituents' interests should be the primary determinant of a legislator's actions. Trustees, however, believe that the legislator is elected to make the best judgment she can, regardless of constituent opinion. Interview data suggest that legislators from SMDs are more likely to be delegates. Using survey data from eight states, another study comes to a similar conclusion, finding that legislators who represent multimember districts are significantly more likely to consider themselves trustees—even when controlling for a host of other individual and institutional factors.[34]

To provide a further test of the hypothesis that legislators in MMDs are less focused on their constituency, I used data from a survey of more than 3,000 legislators across all fifty states.[35] Researchers asked these legislators to rate on a scale of 1–5 how much time they spend on casework. The responses to this question make up the dependent variable in an ordered logit model to explain time spent on casework (table 9-2). I control for a number of factors, including sex, education, age, whether the legislator intends to have a career in politics, party identification, chamber, and legislative professionalism.

Table 9-2. *Predicting Legislators' Time Spent on Casework*
(Ordered Logit Model)

Factor	B	(robust SE)
MMD member	−0.679**	(.126)
Male	−0.331**	(.086)
Education	−0.254**	(.045)
Year born	−0.004	(.003)
Career in politics	−0.039	(.064)
Republican	−0.428**	(.074)
Chamber	0.123*	(.052)
Professionalism	1.500**	(.165)
Chi square	206.41**	
N	3,341	

Source: Carey, Niemi, and Powell (2000).
*$p < .001$ **$p < .05$

The results suggest that all of the predicted variables are statistically significant except for age and whether the legislator plans to spend a career in politics. Notably, district structure has a statistically significant and substantially important influence on the time legislators spend on casework. When all other variables are held at their sample means, a legislator from an SMD has an 81 percent probability of putting a great deal of time into casework (4 or 5 on the scale), while a legislator from an MMD has a 71 percent probability—a difference of 10 percentage points. SMD legislators are also less likely (5 percent) than their MMD counterparts (8 percent) to report that they spend hardly any time on casework.

Reelection and Turnover

Legislators are motivated by many factors, but most scholars argue that reelection is the most important. After all, if a legislator is not reelected, he cannot pass policy or achieve power within the institution. As one legislator commented, "The thought of reelection may not occur to a first-term legislator within the first five minutes after winning the election, but I would not count on that."[36] Fortunately for legislators, reelection rates in the state legislature are often quite high, although there are important differences across states.

Along with term limits and professionalism, multimember districts are one of the most frequently cited predictors of turnover, with most studies

Figure 9-2. *Institutional Changes and Turnout in State Legislatures with Two-Year Terms*[a]

Effect on turnover

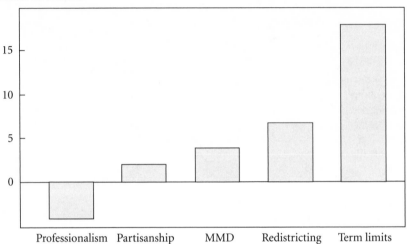

Source: Moncrief, Niemi, and Powell (2004).
a. This figure summarizes the first model in table 6 of Moncrief, Niemi, and Powell (2004). The bars represent the size of the coefficients. Professionalism was rescaled to be representative of likely changes rather than of the effect of moving across the entire system.

finding that MMDs have a small, positive influence on turnover.[37] To illustrate this relationship and how it compares to other potential predictors of turnout, figure 9-2 summarizes the results from one model.[38] The bars represent the effect of each of the potential independent variables on turnover in states with two-year terms. For instance, we can see that moving from a relatively unprofessional to a professional legislature reduces turnover by almost 5 percentage points. Of course, term limits have the largest effect, translating into an increase in turnover of about 17 percentage points. Multimember districts have a significant but not massive effect. Turnover in MMDs is about 3.9 percentage points greater than turnover in SMDs.

The causal mechanism behind this finding is most likely name recognition, which has been found to be one of the most important factors aiding in incumbent reelection.[39] When a constituent is represented by only one legislator, the likelihood of knowing his name is relatively high. As the number of legislators expands, the probability of any constituent knowing a legislator decreases substantially. At the same time, the value of being a legislator may decrease: "Serving in a multimember delegation is less satisfying than being the sole representative of a constituency, thus leading more legislators *not* to run for reelection."[40]

Influence of Party

Legislators depend on political parties to be elected, but the dynamics of party importance vary across time and space. District structure is often presumed to affect the power and influence of political parties. MMD elections, for instance, were found to promote an electoral environment in which it is easier for one party to sweep elections and dominate the legislature.[41] Further, legislators believe that parties play a larger role in MMDs.[42] Given the relative weakness of their name recognition and constituency relations, legislators from MMDs tend to rely on other agents to help them get elected and pass policy once in office. For example, MMD legislators are likely to rely on endorsements and on party organization. MMD voters rely on party cues in deciding how to vote. "There is a feeling that the shift from at-large to single-member districts in the urban counties, which took effect in 1966, reduced the influence of party organizations over incumbents."[43]

District Structure and Ideological Extremity

In SSDs in which candidates must win a plurality of the vote to win an election, candidates and legislators maximize their likelihood of winning elections by appealing to the median voter. This dynamic drives candidates toward the political middle. In MMDs, the incentive structure is different, because candidates can win with a much smaller portion of the vote. Accordingly, they may benefit by receiving active support from a smaller group, rather than receiving passive support from a larger group, as they would in an SMD. This may drive them to ideological extremes. The evidence in the American states and internationally provides evidence for the polarizing effects of MMDs.[44]

Figure 9-3, which presents results from a study of the Arizona State legislature, supports this contention. Recall that the Arizona legislature includes an MMD lower house and an SMD upper house, each with identical district lines. The figure shows on the extreme left and on the extreme right the proportion of each chamber that is ideologically moderate, demonstrating that, at least in this case, the MMD system in the lower house produces more ideologically extreme legislators than the SMD system in the upper house.

Figure 9-3. *Ideological Extremism in the Arizona State Legislature with Multimember Districts*

Percent

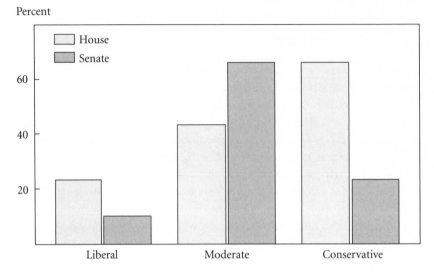

Source: Richardson and Cooper (2004).

Implications for Reform

MMDs are an important feature of legislative organization in the American states, in local governments, and across the globe. Despite their prominence, they are not given the attention they deserve, particularly in the legislative literature. Although the number of MMD states is limited, this chapter suggests that they have effects distinct from their SMDs. MMDs increase female representation (if not necessarily minority representation), increase ideological extremity, decrease constituency service marginally, promote an attitude of trusteeship among legislators, and increase the importance of party.

What this literature lacks, however, is a clear understanding of why these changes occur. In particular, our understanding of the causal mechanism behind why MMDs affect descriptive representation can be charitably described as mixed, and perhaps more accurately described as unsatisfying. Future work in this area needs to work harder to explain why we find the differences we find. Given the vast variation in the American states, across cities, and across counties, it should not be difficult to parse out different tests for each of the competing theories. The result will be a more satisfying understanding of electoral choice and legislative behavior.

In the meantime, while the evidence does not make it possible to recommend multimember districts for all states, depending on the characteristics of the state, MMDs may be an effective reform. In areas with little chance for minority representation, but where the legislative institutions have struggled to increase their female membership, MMDs may be worth considering. Similarly, in areas where constituents want less centrist and more distinct candidates, MMDs may be one good option. Legally, and practically, MMDs are not difficult to implement. Many states still employ them; created responsibly and carefully, they could well withstand legal scrutiny.

Notes

1. Klain (1955).
2. Calabrese (2000).
3. Jewell (1982a, p. 24).
4. Larimer (2005).
5. Crisp and Desposato (2004).
6. Schiller (2000).
7. Pitkin (1967).
8. Bratton (2002); Bratton and Haynie (1999); Grose (2005).
9. Marschall and Ruhil (2007).
10. Larimer (2005).
11. Preuhs (2006).
12. Pantoja and Segura (2003).
13. Atkeson (2003).
14. Thomas (1994).
15. Arceneaux (2001).
16. King (2002).
17. Moncrief and Thompson (1992); Bullock and MacManus (1991); Welch and Studlar (1990).
18. MMD states also have identical district boundaries for the two chambers. In other words, two House seats have identical district lines to one Senate seat. Legislative professionalism refers to the institutional capacity of the state legislature. Professional legislatures have more staff members, longer sessions, and higher salaries than their counterparts. The professionalism scores can be interpreted as the proportion of resources of the U.S. Congress (the paragon of professionalism). For instance, a score of 1 would indicate that a legislature has an equal number of staff, equal session length, and equal salary to those of the U.S. Congress. A score of 0.5 would indicate 50 percent of the resources of Congress, and so on (King 2000).
19. Although the majority of the literature supports this conclusion, see Bullock and Gaddie (1993) and Darcy, Welch, and Clark (1985) for an opposing view.
20. Carroll (1994).

21. King (2002, p. 163).

22. Darcy, Welch, and Clark (1985).

23. Jewell (1982b, p. 130).

24. Gerber, Morton, and Rietz (1998).

25. Engstrom and McDonald (1981, 1986); Karnig and Welch (1982).

26. MacManus (1978).

27. McCrary (1990).

28. In a seat-designate MMD election, candidates indicate which seat they are running for. This system mimics an SMD election. In a staggered MMD election, legislators run in different years. Thus they represent the same area but never appear on the same ballot.

29. Bullock and Gaddie (1993).

30. Welch and Karnig (1978).

31. Darcy, Hadley, and Kirksey (1993).

32. Richardson and Cooper (2006).

33. Jewell (1982a, p. 120).

34. Cooper and Richardson (2006).

35. Carey, Niemi, and Powell (2000).

36. Rosenthal (2004, p. 50).

37. Niemi and Winsky (1987).

38. Moncrief, Niemi, and Powell (2004).

39. Herrnson (2004).

40. Moncrief, Niemi, and Powell (2004, p. 372).

41. Calabrese (2000).

42. Jewell (1982a).

43. Jewell (1982a, p. 31). Some argue that this shift may instead be a result of the decline in party organization.

44. Adams (1996); Dow (1998); Magar, Rosenblum, and Samuels (1998).

MICHAEL P. MCDONALD

10

Legislative Redistricting

*It requires no special genius to recognize the political consequences of
drawing a district down one street rather than another.*
—Justice White, *Gaffney* v. *Cummings*

As a new census nears, state governments prepare for the decennial
political ritual of legislative redistricting. This task is typically entrusted to
state legislators, who have a self-interest in using redistricting to secure their
reelection or maintain their party's control of the legislature. Consequently,
many good government groups have rallied to the cause of redistricting
reform. Leading up to the 2000 census, the League of Women Voters and
Common Cause advocated successfully for redistricting reform through ballot initiatives in Washington, Idaho, and Arizona. Since then, prominent
politicians have joined the reform movement and are pressing their state legislatures to adopt alternative redistricting methods.

Such efforts face significant obstacles. One is the complexity of the redistricting task. Most reform proposals can be designed to secure specified outcomes. For example, while scholars and policymakers may debate the wisdom
of enacting term limits, laws or constitutional amendments limiting the number of terms a state representative can serve are unquestionably effective in
achieving their stated goal. By contrast, redistricting has multiple, often conflicting goals, such as competitiveness and minority representation, and the
best method for achieving any of those goals—let alone all of them—is often
unclear.

The design of the redistricting process also poses challenges. Even if a reasonably "fair" set of criteria for drawing districts can be identified for a given
point in time, these criteria are rendered obsolete when the political landscape
changes as populations move and political allegiances realign. A solution is to
give the redistricting authority considerable discretion when it comes to bal-
ancing between conflicting redistricting criteria. But reformers must then

147

ensure that this discretion is not abused, often by adopting procedures designed to select a redistricting authority composed of "independent" actors.

If the challenge of designing redistricting reform were not daunting enough, proponents must then have that reform enacted, either by the legislature, which has an inherent conflict of interest, or through a ballot measure. Recent experience suggests this is a difficult proposition. In the mid-2000s reform bills cleared one legislative chamber or were reported out of committee for a floor vote in California, Ohio, Texas, and Virginia, but they all failed to become law. In California and Ohio voters rejected ballot reform measures in 2005. Still, reformers were successful in Alaska, Arizona, and Idaho in the 1990s, so reform is possible.[1]

This chapter's goal is to provide better information for such reform efforts by summarizing what political science and legal scholars know about redistricting institutions and criteria. In addition, it discusses the political circumstances that support successful reform.

Redistricting Reform

An insightful typology of redistricting reforms, distinguishing among outcome-based regulations, process-based regulations, and institution-selecting regulations, was published in 2004.[2] Process-based regulations require a redistricting authority to implement (hopefully) neutral criteria, such as the requirements that districts have relatively equal population. Outcome-based regulations are a subset of process-based regulations that require a redistricting authority to achieve a political goal, such as the creation of minority-majority districts, as required by the Voting Rights Act. By contrast, institution-selecting regulations fundamentally change who draws the lines. For example, this type of reform may place redistricting in the hands of a commission that is divorced, as much as possible, from politics. The three types of reform are not mutually exclusive; indeed, they are often packaged together within a reform proposal.

Process-Based Regulations

Federal criteria constrain redistricting in all fifty states. A series of U.S. Supreme Court decisions, starting with *Baker* v. *Carr,* have stipulated that districts must be of relatively equal population.[3] Practically, this means that redistricting must occur at the start of each decade following the census.[4] In imposing this standard, the Court generally permits a 1 percent population deviation between the largest and smallest congressional districts in a state and a 10 percent deviation among state legislative districts.[5] Federal law further requires single-member congressional districts and adherence to the Voting Rights Act, which I discuss below as an outcome-based regulation.

When the Supreme Court first mandated equal population districts in the 1960s, scholars expected to see a significant reduction in partisan gerrymandering.[6] Yet some argue that "population equality guarantees almost no form of fairness beyond numerical equality of population."[7] And another argues that "there is general pessimism about the ability of process-based regulations . . . to thwart partisan gerrymandering efforts."[8] General criteria, such as equal population or compactness standards, are typically too permissive to meaningfully constrain a redistricting authority. Moreover, practice may make perfect: when required repeatedly to draw districts, redistricting authorities may learn to gerrymander despite legal constraints.[9]

In addition to complying with federal criteria, redistricting authorities must often comply also with state regulations. In many states, reform movements and efforts to adapt to evolving federal race standards have resulted in the adoption of more and sometimes complex redistricting criteria. Litigants seeking to overturn a district map have increasingly turned to state courts, leading some analysts to herald the current period of redistricting litigation as the "non-federal criteria period."[10]

There are many state criteria. Some states codify equal population standards that are more constraining than the 10 percent deviation permitted for state legislative districts under federal law. Some states also prohibit middecade congressional redistricting, although a recent Supreme Court decision authorizes this practice.[11] State law often includes relatively noncontroversial contiguity and compactness criteria, and some states require districts to follow existing political boundaries, such as those of counties, cities, townships, precincts, and wards. They may also require districts to respect "communities of interest" and may even codify specific political goals.

Ohio's 2007 House Joint Resolution 1, which was sponsored by Ohio Republican House Speaker Kevin DeWine, is instructive regarding the political machinery required to redistrict. The joint resolution requires that political subdivisions be kept together to the extent possible but recognizes that some may need to be split in order to create districts of equal population. The resolution prioritizes which political subdivisions below the county level will be kept together, stating that "preference shall be given to a township, a city ward, a contiguous municipality, and a village in the order named." Noncontiguous townships are scattered throughout Columbus and other Ohio municipalities. The preference for keeping together townships over dividing the municipality of Columbus has a real political effect, since it forces Franklin County to be divided like a pie, with wedges extending from the Democratic city core to Republican suburbs, which in this case is an effective Republican gerrymander. Ohio Democrats may thus prefer to keep municipalities intact while dividing townships.

One of the weaknesses of process-based regulation is the fact that redistricting criteria are often poorly defined. For example, a number of states are silent on the definition of *compactness*.[12] The absence of a concrete standard was a factor behind the Supreme Court decision, in the *Shaw* cases, to strike down racially motivated districts that were simply "bizarre" in shape.[13] In response to the *Shaw* line of court cases, which rejected maps based predominantly on racial intent, state legislators came up with the concept of "communities of interest" (essentially a euphemism for racial communities). They reasoned that districts drawn on this basis would survive court scrutiny, since federal law allows oddly shaped districts to be drawn in the pursuit of nonracial goals.[14] However, there is no objective definition of communities of interest, making this a particularly nebulous standard that logically applies to any community with a shared interest. Line drawers may thus appeal to protecting communities of interest to justify any district borders.

A further complication in enacting process-based regulation is that criteria may conflict with one another. In Arizona, for example, Proposition 106 both established the Arizona Independent Redistricting Commission and presented it with a list of criteria that included respecting federal law, creating contiguous and compact districts, respecting political subdivisions, protecting communities of interest, and creating competitive districts where doing so did not conflict with the other goals.[15] In practice, drawing competitive districts was difficult. Arizona is a Republican-leaning state, and it is required under section 5 of the Voting Rights Act to draw minority-majority districts. After the heavily Democratic Native American and Hispanic districts were drawn to comply with the Voting Rights Act, there were few Democrats left in the remainder of the state, limiting opportunities to draw competitive districts. The commission made this task even harder by deciding not to place politically dissimilar communities of interest together in order to promote the goal of "protecting communities of interest." For example, the commission rejected a proposal that would have created a competitive district by placing a Democratic area surrounding the University of Arizona in the same district as a retirement community to the southeast of Tucson. The resulting maps were little more competitive than those drawn by the legislature in the previous decade (that had no competition requirement).

This discussion suggests four lessons. First, criteria vary in their ability to constrain the choices of redistricting authorities. Second, seemingly neutral criteria may have significant, predictable political effects, as the Franklin County example illustrates. Third, ambiguously defined or conflicting criteria may be manipulated to achieve political goals, particularly since courts are deferential to the political process for all but the most egregious violations.[16] Fourth, the impact of any criterion is likely to vary significantly from jurisdiction to jurisdiction. For example, Ohio's 2007 House Joint Resolution 1 might have quite a different effect outside Franklin County. For these reasons, perhaps the most promising avenue for studying criteria effects is to analyze maps drawn by simulation under alternative criteria.[17]

Outcome-Based Regulations

Outcome-based regulations are a special case of process-based regulations that require redistricting to achieve explicit political goals. For example, the federal courts, which have taken the lead in enforcing outcome-based regulations, have frequently sought to prevent the dilution of minority representation by ruling against racial gerrymandering.[18] There is wide consensus among academics that, when racially polarized voting is present, the way in which minority communities are divided among districts affects the ability of minorities to elect, in legal parlance, their "candidates of choice."[19] The debate over race-based redistricting has since shifted to how to distribute minority voters into districts to maximize their substantive representation and the policy implications of drawing such districts.[20]

The courts have shown little enthusiasm for formulating or enforcing outcome-based regulations on nonracial grounds.[21] Even though the Supreme Court entertained partisan gerrymandering claims in *Davis* v. *Bandemer,* the recent *LULAC* v. *Perry* decision reveals that Justice Anthony Kennedy, who is the swing vote on partisan gerrymandering claims, believes the issue is justiciable but has yet to find a standard to his liking.[22] In the meantime, a number of states have stepped into the breach by codifying outcome-based regulations related to political goals. In Hawaii, the constitution stipulates, "No district shall be so drawn as to unduly favor a person or faction," and Idaho, Iowa, and Washington have similar regulations in place.[23] Arizona, Washington, and Wisconsin require competitive districts, and Arizona and Iowa operationalize this mandate by forbidding their redistricting authorities access to election data and knowledge of where incumbents live.[24] Thus enforcement of outcome-based regulation by state courts is possible. But current litigation in Arizona over the state's competitiveness criterion suggests that such enforcement, if indeed warranted, may be elusive.[25]

The potential effectiveness of partisan and competitive regulation is a matter of scholarly debate. There is universal consensus among politicians, practitioners, and scholars that political parties and incumbents are motivated to manipulate district boundaries to secure legislative majorities and bolster their reelection chances. However, there is less agreement on their effectiveness in achieving these goals, which raises questions concerning the effectiveness of outcome-based regulation. Some scholars find political parties secure electoral advantage when they control redistricting, whereas others find political parties realize little or no advantage.[26] Some scholars find districts are less competitive following redistricting while others find no link between redistricting and district competitiveness.[27] In addition, some scholars find that redistricting does little to protect incumbents.[28] Changing district boundary lines often upsets incumbents' reelection constituencies and encourages challengers to emerge.[29]

A related debate is whether or not redistricting reform should be a tool to achieve such goals as partisan fairness or increased district competitiveness. Some scholars argue that the legislative arena is the proper place to resolve inherently political redistricting questions.[30] Others advocate active regulation to counter potential abuses by self-interested legislators and propose partisan gerrymandering standards based on minimizing partisan bias or on maximizing partisan symmetry.[31]

Value trade-offs among proposed criteria are cast in stark relief when the topic of political outcomes is broached. Political scientists have long recognized that the rules used to aggregate votes into election outcomes cannot simultaneously achieve all possible representational goals.[32] For example, if one values effective representation for partisan voters above all else, then uncompetitive districts stacked with partisans would be desirable since they reduce the number of voters who cast a ballot for a losing candidate.[33] However, always being on the winning side within a district is just one value, as is being on the winning side in the majority of the legislature, a topic the voting rights community is particular sensitive to, as creating uncompetitive minority-majority districts may perversely move a legislature ideologically to the right.[34] Moreover, a legislature composed of nothing but extremely safe districts would be nearly impervious to changes in public mood. While it is difficult to juggle these competing goals, a mix of competitive and noncompetitive districts ensures that legislatures are responsive to the public will but not to such an extent that all districts change hands when the public mood shifts, thereby minimizing the political minority voice in legislative deliberations.[35]

Institution-Selecting Regulations

There are two basic types of redistricting processes, those that follow the legislative process and those that use a commission at some stage. Twenty states empower commissions as the sole congressional or state legislative redistricting authority, a source of proposals to the legislature, or a backup if the legislative process fails.[36] However, such commissions often produce gerrymanders similar to those that would emerge from the legislative process. Redistricting commissions are typically designed to protect, not diminish, the power of party leaders, as commissioners are often either elected officials or their handpicked lieutenants.

There are two general types of redistricting commissions, partisan and bipartisan. A partisan commission typically grants majority representation to one of the parties, allowing it to engineer a partisan gerrymander. A bipartisan commission typically has an equal number of members from each party and uses a supermajority rule to adopt an electoral map, resulting in a bipartisan gerrymander that protects the interests of both parties. Commissions that adopt maps by a majority vote may break deadlocks by the appointment of a tie-breaking member, selected either by a commission majority vote or by an outside authority. When a commission internally selects a tiebreaker, the agreement between the parties on the tiebreaker often leads to a bipartisan gerrymander. When a tiebreaker is imposed from the outside, a partisan is often appointed, resolving the dispute in favor of that party.

A "neutral" tiebreaking member is needed to thwart a gerrymander. Two examples are illustrative. In 2000 the New Jersey Supreme Court appointed the Princeton political science professor Larry Bartels as the tiebreaking member of the state's legislative commission. Bartels had partisan members bid for his vote by stating he would support the map scoring best on his proposed "neutral" criteria. In a less direct way, the Arizona commission seeks a similar outcome by forbidding the tiebreaking member from being registered with a major political party.

Another method to increase a commission's independence from political pressures is to apply qualifications to all members, not just the tiebreaking member.[37] The 1960 Alaska Constitution innovated this approach by prohibiting public employees and officials from serving on the redistricting commission.[38] In addition, in Hawaii, Missouri, Idaho, and Alaska commissioners are forbidden from running for office in the districts they draw.[39] Prospective Arizona commission members must abide by these combined qualifications and are further vetted by the state's Commission on Appellate Court Appointments.[40]

A Model Reform Proposal

The history of redistricting reform suggests that process-based regulation may be most successful when implemented with institution-selecting regulation; that is, a redistricting commission that operates under strict criteria. Recent court decisions suggest that state courts will hold commissions to a higher standard than a legislature. For example, court cases in Alaska and Idaho required the states' redistricting commissions to address violations of their states' constitutions.[41]

Four components of proposed model redistricting reforms are

—Independence: the commissioners must be selected through a nonpartisan process.

—Criteria: the commission must draw districts conforming to an objective set of criteria.

—Transparency: all commission meetings must be open to the public.

—Public submissions: the commission must solicit public input and comments on proposed maps.

Good government groups have successfully promoted the creation of redistricting commissions by way of ballot initiatives in Washington (1983), Idaho (1994), and Arizona (2000).[42] The archetype is Arizona's Independent Redistricting Commission, which is distinguished from other states' commissions in that it is designed to promote the independence of commissioners, adhere to a defined set of criteria, be transparent, and provide mechanisms for public input.[43]

The reform model summarized above seeks to put commissioners removed from politics (insomuch as that is possible) in charge of redistricting and to broadly constrain the commission through objective criteria, but the model also provides the commission with enough discretion to correct course if it sails into dangerous waters. To make sure that the commission is functioning properly, public oversight is provided for in open meetings, where the commission can hear public feedback on its actions. Those opposing redistricting reform note that Arizona failed in its promise to create a substantial number of competitive districts and conclude that redistricting reform is generally unlikely to affect political outcomes.[44] Reformers are more sanguine and have learned from Arizona's experience that institutional details matter. Reformers in California, Florida, Minnesota, Ohio, New York, Wisconsin, and Virginia (among others) are tinkering with the Arizona model to devise the reform that will work best for their state.

Adopting Reform

Once the difficult task of crafting reform is accomplished, reformers face the even more daunting task of making it law. There are two pathways to redistricting reform. One path goes through the voters by way of a constitutional amendment adopted by ballot initiative. The second path goes through the legislature and either ends in sufficient legislative action or continues in a constitutional amendment by ballot referendum. Neither pathway is an easy route to reform, given legislators' interests in controlling redistricting.

Politicians believe deeply that the fates of their parties, their careers, and racial representation are at stake during redistricting. If one party currently controls the redistricting process or has high confidence that it will control the process in the future, then it has little incentive to trade control of the process for reform that increases the uncertainty of redistricting outcomes. When political actors are uncertain as to who will control the process or are stalemated in a divided control situation, then they have a greater incentive to seek reform.

Ohio's experience in 2006—following the failure of a 2005 ballot initiative (Issue 4), which would have required a proposed commission to automatically adopt the map that scored best on constitutionally codified criteria—illustrates the legislative politics underpinning redistricting reform. Ohio's seven-member state legislative Apportionment Board comprises four members appointed by the majority and minority leaders of the two legislative chambers and includes three statewide officers: the governor, the auditor of the state, and the secretary of state.[45] Partisan control of the commission is therefore determined by which party controls at least two of the three statewide offices. In 2005 the failed ballot initiative was supported by Democrats and opposed by Republicans. In 2006 it was the Republicans' turn to press for reform and the Democrats' turn to oppose it. When the Republicans failed to win the three-fifths vote they needed in the statehouse to send their reform proposal to the voters as a referendum, they repackaged the Democrats' 2005 ballot initiative and held a vote. Republicans voted for the new plan, and Democrats voted against it.[46] The reason for the shifting mantle of reform was simple: in 2005 Republicans were considered likely to control the Apportionment Board; in 2006 Democrats were the odds-on favorites to win two of the three statewide offices, which they did.

Assuming redistricting reform survives these legislative hurdles, how are voters likely to react? To answer this question, just before the 2006 midterm election, the Pew Research Center in association with the Brookings Institution and the Cato Institute conducted a national survey on attitudes toward electoral competition and redistricting reform. The survey reveals that the low amount of information voters have about redistricting and the low salience of the issue pose significant hurdles for reformers to overcome. Only 9 percent of respondents reported that they had heard or read "a lot" about the redistricting debate, 38 percent "a little," and 51 percent "nothing at all." When asked who drew district lines, 47 percent did not know or refused to answer the question. When asked about their satisfaction with the redistricting process in their state, 13 percent were satisfied, 14 percent were dissatisfied, and 70 percent had no opinion. (The margin of error is 2.5 percentage points.)

These findings are consistent with studies that find the public has generally low levels of political information, especially on issues that involve arcane matters of process.[47] However, there is evidence that people learn when exposed to the issue. Three states figure prominently in the recent redistricting debate. In 2005 reform was on the ballot in California and Ohio; in 2003 Texas adopted a controversial mid-decade congressional map favoring the Republicans (the map had been engineered by the former House majority leader Tom Delay). Respondents in these states were 8 percentage points less likely to respond that they had not heard anything about redistricting. They were also 7 percentage points more likely to respond (correctly) that legislators drew the congressional districts in their state.[48]

Interestingly, levels of dissatisfaction in California, Ohio, and Texas were nearly identical to those in other states, perhaps as a consequence of the perceived partisan character of the debate. In 2006 redistricting was widely seen as favoring the Republicans nationally. Being on the losing side seemed to increase awareness among self-identified Democrats, who were 8 percentage points more likely than Republicans to say that they had heard at least a little about the debate. They were also 7 percentage points more likely to express dissatisfaction.

While redistricting may have favored Republicans nationally, partisan beneficiaries varied among the states. The last round of redistricting helped Republicans in Ohio and Texas but hurt them in California. When California Republican respondents are grouped with their Democratic counterparts in Ohio and Texas, 22 percent of respondents on the losing side of redistricting expressed dissatisfaction, compared to 9 percent on the winning side. Still, while the levels of awareness were higher in these states and among Democrats nationally, 71 percent of respondents in the three states expressed no opinion on satisfaction, underscoring that even in high-information circumstances the public is quite ambivalent about an issue they know little about.

The same legislative politics concerning redistricting reform emerge in electoral politics. For reform to be successful it must be appear to be nonpartisan or bipartisan and it must not mobilize opposition from the majority party in a state. Arizona's success in adopting Proposition 106 can be partially traced both to the bipartisan appearance of reform and to the Republican Party's delay in mobilizing against it.[49] Strong opposition and fragmented support coalitions characterized reform defeats in California and Ohio in 2005. In California, Democrats mobilized against Governor Schwartzenegger's Proposition 77, which was further crippled by conservative dissenters within the Republican Party skeptical of the benefits of drawing competitive districts.[50] In Ohio, Republicans opposed Issue 4 and organized early behind a well-funded group called Ohio First; reform was further crippled by Democratic African American legislators skeptical that the plan would protect minority representation.[51] With so little knowledge about redistricting among voters, ballot initiatives are easily defeated by strong opposition, especially if they are able to frame the debate as a partisan power grab. Framing the debate in these terms was made easier in California and Ohio by a mid-decade redistricting requirement packaged into the reforms, invoking analogies to the partisan re-redistricting in Texas that had made national headlines in 2003.

Implications for Reform

Scholars and activists hold little hope for meaningful outcome-based redistricting regulation from the courts, which have proven reluctant to enter the political thicket on issues other than race. In the few states where outcome-based regulation is codified into state constitutions, state courts may play an important role in adjudicating violations. However, even here the hope may be fleeting since the exemplary case of outcome-based litigation in Arizona was still in the state courts in 2007, years after the map had been adopted. Reform, if it is to come, must happen through legislative or initiative action— and will likely continue to be addressed state by state.

The favored reform among good government groups melds institutional reforms with process- and outcome-based regulations in the form of a redistricting commission that operates under strict criteria. Formulating reform is perhaps easier than adopting it. Since redistricting is a zero-sum game when one party controls the process, it is almost ensured that, under a modest degree of certainty about who will control a state's redistricting authority, one party will expect to benefit from the status quo and the other will expect to benefit from reform. This split is likely to be reproduced if redistricting reform appears on the ballot, since voters have little knowledge about the issue and are likely to follow the cues provided by party leaders. Only under the greatest uncertainty over the future balance of power will the two parties come together to adopt redistricting reform. This situation may arise when elections are competitive or when control of the process is divided and stalemate may hand redistricting to judges who do not value political goals to the same degree as legislators. The circumstances favorable for reform do not arise often, but this is not to say that reform is impossible—only that the obstacles are daunting.

Notes

1. McDonald (2004).

2. Cox (2004).

3. *Baker v. Carr* 369 U.S. 186 (1962).

4. See *Reynolds v. Sims* 377 U.S. 533 (1964) (finding redistricting that did not follow a regular timetable was constitutionally suspect).

5. *Karcher v. Daggett* 462 U.S. 725 (1983); but see also *Cox v. Larios* 124 S. Ct. 1503 (2004) (striking down Georgia State legislative districts that purposefully underpopulated Democratic districts within a 10 percent deviation). In practice, states may need to justify any deviation, particularly for congressional redistricting, which is why redistricting authorities often strive for absolute equality; see *Vieth v. Pennsylvania* 195 F. Supp. 2d 672 (MD Pa. 2002) (striking down a Pennsylvania congressional map with a nineteen-person population deviation).

6. See Cox and Katz (2002); Musgrove (1977); White and Thomas (1964).

7. Gelman and King (1994, p. 553).

8. Cox (2004, p. 756).

9. Niemi and Winsky (1992).

10. Cain, MacDonald, and McDonald (2005, p. 16).

11. Levitt and McDonald (2007). See *League of United Latin American Citizens (LULAC) v. Perry* 126 S. Ct. 2594 (2006) (upholding a mid-decade Texas congressional redistricting but overturning parts of the plan on voting rights concerns).

12. Conventional wisdom holds that compactness standards favor Republicans (for example, Cox 2004), though some argue otherwise (Polsby and Popper 1993), and one of the few articles on the political effects of compactness standards finds compactness standards reduce minority representation (Barabas and Jerit 2004).

13. McDonald (1998); *Shaw v. Reno* 509 U.S. 630 (1993).

14. Cain, MacDonald, and McDonald (2005).

15. This discussion is based on my experience as a consultant to the Arizona Independent Redistricting Commission, as described in McDonald (2006a).

16. For example, a Michigan court declared that the redistricting criteria adopted in a previous legislative session were nonbinding on the legislature that drew the maps. See *O'Lear* v. *Miller,* No. 01-72584-DT (E.D. Mich. May 24, 2002).

17. The Columbus, Ohio, example is derived from a mapping project funded by the Joyce Foundation. For similar analyses of California Proposition 77, see Cain, MacDonald, and Hui (2006); and Johnson and others (2005).

18. A suit challenging the constitutionality of the Voting Rights Act, which was renewed in 2006, is currently being litigated in district court, *Northwest Austin Municipal Utility District Number One* v. *Gonzales* (1:06-cv-1384).

19. Brace and others (1988).

20. On the first issue, see, for example, Cameron, Epstein, and O'Halloran (1996); Lublin (1999). On the second, see, for example, Thernstrom (1987); Swain (1995).

21. See for example Issacharoff and Karlan (2004).

22. *Davis* v. *Bandemer* 478 U.S. 109 (1986); *League of Latin American Citizens* v. *Perry* 548 U.S. (2006).

23. See Hawaii Constitution, Article IV §6; Idaho Code, 72-1506; Iowa Code, Title II §42.4; and Revised Code of Washington, §44.05.090.

24. McDonald (2006b). See Code of Washington §44.05.090; Arizona Constitution, Article IV, Part 2 §1; and Wisconsin Code, 4.001(3). (Wisconsin imposes this requirement only for state legislative districts.) See Iowa Code, Title II §42.4. These criteria conflict with the Voting Rights Act, which demands knowledge of incumbent homes and analysis of election data.

25. See *Minority Coalition for Fair Redistricting et al.* v. *Arizona Independent Redistricting Commission* CV2002-004380 (2003).

26. For the first position, see, for example, Abramowitz (1983); Cain (1984); Gelman and King (1994); King (1989); Niemi and Winsky (1992). For the second, see, for example, Glazer, Grofman, and Robbins (1987); Squire (1985); Campagna and Grofman (1990).

27. For the first position, see, for example, McDonald (2006a); Swain, Borrelli, and Reed (1998). For the second, see Abramowitz, Alexander, and Gunning (2006a).

28. Campagna and Grofman (1990); Gelman and King (1994).

29. Ansolabehere, Snyder, and Stewart (2000); Hetherington, Larson, and Globetti (2003).

30. Lowenstein and Steinberg (1985).

31. See, for example, Berman (2005); Cox (2006); Issacharoff and Karlan (2004); King and Grofman (2007).

32. Arrow (1951).

33. Brunell (2006); Buchler (2007).

34. Cameron, Epstein, and O'Halloran (1996); Lublin (1999).

35. McDonald (2006b).

36. McDonald (2004).

37. McDonald (2006b).

38. Alaska Constitution, Article VI §6.

39. Hawaii Constitution, Article IV §2; Missouri Constitution Article III §7 ; Idaho Code 72-1502; Alaska Constitution, Article VI §8.

40. Arizona Constitution, Article IV, Part 2, Section 1(3).

41. See *In re 2001 Redistricting Cases,* 47 P.3d 1089 (Alaska 2002); and *Smith* v. *Idaho Commission on Redistricting,* 38 P.3d 121 (Idaho 2001).

42. Alaska's commission was established in 1960 and amended in 1998 by a ballot referendum forwarded to voters by the Republican legislature. I do not consider the 1998 referendum a reform effort since a motivation was to reduce the influence of the Democratic governor, who appointed all commissioners.

43. Common Cause, "California Common Cause Redistricting Guidelines" (www. commoncause.org/site/pp.asp?c=dkLNK1MQIwG&b=366007); League of Women Voters, "Redistricting Reform" (www.lwv.org/AM/Template.cfm?Section=Redistricting); and Reform Institute, "Principles for Redistricting Reform," August 1, 2005 (www. reforminstitute.org/DetailPublications.aspx?pid=56&cid=2&tid=5&sid=5). All websites accessed January 27, 2006.

44. Abramowitz, Alexander, and Gunning (2006b); Hill and Hertzberg (2006).

45. Ohio Constitution, Article XI §11.01.

46. "House Democrats Need to Back Plan to Improve Ohio's System of Creating Legislative Districts," *Ohio Dispatch,* May 28, 2008, p. 4D.

47. Delli Carpini and Keeter (1993).

48. All differences among subgroups discussed here are statistically significant at a p value of .10 or less.

49. Amy Silverman, "What's My Line?" *Phoenix New Times,* October 5, 2000.

50. Gary Delsohn, "Poll: Support for Key Ballot Measures Failing: Governor's Backing May Be Hurting Their Chances on November 8," *Sacramento Bee,* November 1, 2005, p. A3; and Jim Sanders, "Parties Doubtful about Prop. 77, Redistricting Plan May Not Create Competition and May Make Other Problems," *Sacramento Bee,* October 17, 2005, p. A1.

51. John McCarthy, "Outside Groups Funding Bid for Election Changes," Associated Press State and Local Wire, October 4, 2005; and William Hershey, "Redistricting Plan Draws; Lawmakers Ask Whether State Would Send Fewer Blacks to Columbus, Washington," *Dayton Daily News,* July 25, 2005, p. B1.

BARRY C. BURDEN

11

Multiple Parties and Ballot Regulations

For more than a century American politics has been dominated by two major political parties. The duopoly enjoyed by Democrats and Republicans is largely the result of Duverger's law: the tendency of a system of single-member districts to produce two-party competition.[1] Minor parties fail in a single-member district system for two reasons. First, the winner-take-all approach does not reward candidates who finish third. Second, citizens vote strategically to avoid "wasting" their votes on hopeless candidates and spoiling the election.[2]

Perhaps owing to the apparent strength of Duverger's law, most scholarly research on minor parties has focused on the electoral system rather than on other forms of party regulation.[3] Yet the United States is unusual in that the Constitution gives states the authority to regulate ballot access as they see fit. The result is a nationwide crazy quilt of ballot access laws. In this chapter I examine the effects of these laws on minor party and independent candidates.[4] I find that raising the proportion of the state's electorate that must sign petitions for ballot access sharply reduces the number of candidates on the ballot. But the number of votes cast for minor party and independent candidates is largely determined not by ballot access regulations but by the closeness of the race between the major party candidates. In concluding, I argue that ballot access restrictions do little harm to the two-party system. I also provide some considerations for lawmakers.

The Australian Ballot

The regulation of ballot access became a state matter about a century ago. For much of U.S. history, ballots were provided by parties rather than by state governments. There was no unified ballot that listed all of the candidates seeking office. Rather, voters sought ballots from parties and deposited these tickets into ballot boxes. Since parties could print their own tickets, such minor parties as the Know Nothings, Progressives, Free Soilers, Socialists, and others were a regular part of American electoral politics.

Things changed in the late nineteenth century as the so-called Australian, or secret, ballot was introduced. As part of a larger progressive agenda to eliminate corruption, the Australian ballot was implemented as a way to reduce voter intimidation. Because the government then became the official distributor of ballots, decisions had to be made about which parties qualified for space on the ballot. Ballot access immediately became both an administrative and a political question for states to resolve. By 1900 nearly every state had adopted the Australian ballot and along with it varying definitions of what qualified as a ballot-worthy political party.[5] Under the new rules, big, established political parties qualified for ballot access almost automatically and used primaries to choose their nominees. In contrast, new or minor parties, if they were permitted on the ballot at all, were required to submit petitions signed by hundreds or thousands of supporters. Insurgent candidates were thus encouraged to channel their energies within major parties rather than circumvent them.

Ballot Access Laws

Early ballot restrictions were often used solely to facilitate efficient and honest election administration. Petitions typically required just 1–2 percent of the vote in signatures, and filing deadlines were often just a few weeks before election day. That legacy remains in place today. In nearly every state, minor party and independent party candidates must collect signatures on nominating petitions and submit them to state officials by a prescribed deadline to appear on the ballot. Although write-in candidacies are also possible, being granted a line on the ballot alongside Democrats and Republicans provides a visibility, credibility, and ease of selection that is hard to match.

But ballot lines can be difficult to achieve. In order to appear on the ballot in every state and Washington, D.C., in the 2008 general election, a minor party or independent presidential candidate would need at least 690,000 petition signatures.[6] No minor party presidential candidate even won this many *votes* in 2004. A minor party hoping to run candidates in all 435 congressional districts would need close to 2 million signatures. Moreover, since inevitably some signatures are invalidated due to illegibility, false names, lack of qualification as a citizen or registered voter, and other flaws, candidates must submit more than the required minimum to provide some insurance. In response to this practice, some states have instituted signature maxima. For example, an independent candidate running for president or statewide office in Wisconsin needs to submit at least 2,000 but no more than 4,000 signatures. This requirement can easily block access to the ballot. In 2004 Nader delivered twice the required numbers of signatures in Ohio and Pennsylvania yet was not given ballot access in either state because some signatures were forged and some circulators did not demonstrate their residency status.[7]

Reflecting the nation's decentralized electoral administration, there are fifty-one different sets of laws regulating ballot access. In 2004 a presidential candidate needed only 677 signatures to qualify as a minor party nominee in Hawaii and about 3,000 to run as an independent. In contrast, North Carolina required new parties to submit 58,842 signatures by May to earn a place on the November ballot. In New York a statewide candidate must collect either 15,000 signatures or 5 percent of the total number of registered voters, whichever is less. There is also a geographical distribution requirement: at least half of the state's congressional districts must provide 100 signatures each. In Texas independent presidential candidates must submit more than 64,000 signatures in early May, but they are not permitted to begin collection until early March. Further, each signatory must affirm that she is a registered voter but has not voted in a party primary that year, will not do so, and will not sign the petition of another independent candidate running for the same office.

Most states allow a party to qualify itself for the ballot and then select nominees. But eleven states do not provide explicitly for minor party ballot access; instead the new party must select nominees and then qualify them individually. The signature requirements, qualifications for petition circulators, filing fees, and deadlines are often different for new parties and independent candidates and across offices. These inconsistencies can be frustrating for a party or candidate seeking national office or attempting to field a coordinated team of candidates in multiple states. They also frequently provide the kindling for legal battles.

Existing Research

The scholarly literature provides little evidence that ballot access signature requirements matter. One otherwise comprehensive analysis never directly tests whether ballot access laws influence third-party showings.[8] It nonetheless concludes that "potential third party candidates do not seem to be deterred by legal barriers to candidacy."[9] In fact, it suggests that being on fewer state ballots actually may help a presidential campaign with limited resources by encouraging it to focus on only these states.

A history of notable third-party presidential candidates scarcely mentions ballot access hurdles, noting that Henry Wallace in 1948 and George Wallace in 1968 found their way onto state ballots with minimal effort.[10] Others find no evidence that the introduction of the state ballot harmed third parties, although they note that their methodological approach did not allow them precisely to rule out delayed effects of ballot access.[11] Another researcher shows that the number of minor parties was actually lower from 1892 to 1930 than from 1964 to 1996 despite the existence of less restrictive ballot access laws in the earlier period.[12] This surprising result conflicts with an earlier finding by the same researcher that more lenient ballot access laws are associated with minor party victories.[13] A different study of state legislative elections finds no evidence that signature requirements affect the number of minor party candidates on ballots.[14] And a study of the 1996 presidential election produces the "surprising finding . . . that ballot access laws explain very little of the variance in either the number of minor party candidacies or the vote for them. These results suggest that activists—as well as scholars—are overstating the importance of ballot access."[15]

Only a few studies dissent from this conventional wisdom. Casually inspecting data from the most and least restrictive states, one study reports a "very direct correlation between the severity of the [raw] signature requirements in the different states and the number of third-party candidates who appeared on the ballot in the states."[16] Another shows that raw signature requirements affect the likelihood that a moderately strong minor party (in this case the Natural Law Party in 1992) appears on ballots.[17] Yet the Natural Law Party was also more likely to get on the ballot in states with more electoral votes, in apparent contradiction of the fact that these states have higher signature standards. Moreover, the statistical model includes no control variables beyond these two measures. A study of congressional elections finds only limited evidence that ballot access requirements affect the number of candidates running for office.[18] One study reports that incumbents are more likely to be opposed when signature requirements are lower, which might mean that more minor party candidates run in low signature states.[19] But this evidence is only circumstantial. So while a few studies purport to show that signature thresholds deter minor party and independent candidates, the results are tenuous. In addition, all these authors only consider the raw number of required signatures without regard for state population.[20]

Two recent and comprehensive studies employ better methodological approaches than earlier work, although their conclusions are completely opposite to each other. One finds that signature requirements do indeed deter minor party gubernatorial candidates.[21] But the other—a broad analysis of historic U.S. House races—concludes that "third-parties were often more successful in states where the signature requirements were higher."[22]

The overwhelming conclusion among political scientists is thus that signature requirements are not a real deterrent to minor party ballot access. Yet precisely why this should be true is unclear. From a candidate's perspective, ballot access would seem to be extremely difficult and expensive. Paid circulators are often used because they deliver valid signatures more reliably than do volunteers, and even campaigns that rely on volunteers face substantial legal and administrative costs. Independent presidential candidate John Anderson spent roughly half of his $15 million campaign war chest on ballot access, most of it for legal fees. In 1992 Ross Perot spent a quarter of his $73 million to get on the ballot.[23] In fact, the $18 million Perot spent on ballot access is more than Ralph Nader raised in his 2000 and 2004 campaigns combined.

Perhaps the power of Duverger's law swamps any small effects due to ballot restrictions. Or maybe none of the restrictions on the books happens to be severe enough to represent a serious deterrent. Alternatively, it is possible that minor party and independent candidates are simply too irrational to respond strategically to institutional incentives and constraints.[24] Regardless of the reason, it would seem that ballot restrictions are inconsequential. But most of the existing studies only test their effects indirectly or use inappropriate methodologies. I now turn to a fairer test of how petition requirements affect minor party and independent candidates.

Data and Research Questions

I begin with two dependent variables that gauge the success of minor party candidates. The first is a simple count of the number of minor party and independent candidates listed on the ballot. The second is the percentage of the vote earned by these candidates. I analyze the 2000 and 2004 presidential elections and the 2006 gubernatorial and senatorial elections. The two elections display different dynamics, with far fewer minor party candidates on the ballot in 2004. Yet reducing the number of candidates on the ballot does not necessarily decrease the number of votes going to independent and minor party candidates. The correlation between the number of candidates and the vote share of non-major parties is weak, ranging between 0.29 and 0.33. Thus

I hypothesize that clear impediments to the ballot should affect the number of candidates listed but not necessarily their vote shares.

Two important aspects of ballot access are the number of petition signatures required and when those petitions must be delivered to elections officials. The deadline measure is simply the number of days before the general election when the nominating petitions are due, under the assumption that earlier deadlines are more difficult to meet. The average state required petition delivery about three months before the election, although some set significantly earlier deadlines. The signature measure is scaled to the size of the electorate in a state by dividing the raw number of required signatures by the voting-eligible population.[25] The rationale is that signatures are easier to collect in more populous states. Many states require that candidates collect a percentage of total registered voters or a percentage of the vote cast in a recent election. I collected this information for all states and the District of Columbia, determining the actual number of signatures required in each case, regardless of whether the formulas depend on the last presidential election, the last gubernatorial election, overall state population, or some other standard. I measure the number of signatures required using either the number required for an independent candidate or the number required for a minor party candidate, whichever is less. For consistency's sake I then compute the simple percentage of the eligible electorate that must sign a petition in order for this candidate to achieve ballot access.[26] In 2000 the typical state required about 10,000 signatures for presidential candidates, or about 0.3 percent of the eligible electorate. As this threshold rises, the number of candidates on the ballot should decrease.

By contrast, I do not expect ballot access regulations to affect the share of the vote won by minor party candidates. In the vote share models I add variables that are thought to affect how many votes are cast for such candidates. The variable of greatest interest to minor party advocates is fusion. With the advent of the Australian ballot, minor parties began formally cross-endorsing major party candidates. The practice, known as fusion, allows a minor party to have a spot on the ballot without forcing citizens to "waste" their votes on a candidate who is not viable. Also referred to as cross-endorsement, fusion allows multiple parties to nominate the same candidate. A candidate may thus be listed on the ballot multiple times, one for each party that endorses him.

Because it prevents the possibility of spoiling an election, fusion has been identified as a remedy to the handicaps inherent in a system of single-member districts. Some believe that passage of antifusion laws are responsible for the dampening of third-party activity in the twentieth century compared to the nineteenth century.[27] One history of the antifusion movement concludes that fusion has led directly to the "non-viability of third parties."[28] Based on experience in Minnesota, another researcher makes an extensive plea for fusion as the best way to solve the dilemma of Duverger's law.[29] Other analyses of elections in New York also argue that fusion has buoyed minor parties such as the Conservatives there.[30] Also studying New York, another researcher argues that fusion laws are important enough that Duverger's law should be amended to specify that it holds only where fusion is outlawed.[31] A strong advocate of multiparty politics believes that antifusion laws are critical barriers to third parties, second only to the single-member district system itself.[32] So while scholars have doubted the ability of signature requirements to deter candidates, they seem confident that the lack of fusion hurts minor parties. To determine if fusion buoys minor parties as suggested, I include a dummy variable for the states where fusion is legal at the presidential level.[33] Depending which election is being considered in the models below, eight to nine states permit fusion.

If minor party supporters are concerned about spoiling and wasting votes, then the psychological mechanism behind Duverger's law should be more salient when the race between the Democratic candidate and the Republican candidate is close. In contrast, when the major party race is lopsided, minor party supporters are free to support their nominees. Two studies show that strategic voting hurts minor parties more as the contest between the two major parties tightens.[34] This is also the logic behind an analysis of the ratio between the first- and second-place finishers.[35] To test this hypothesis, I include a measure of closeness that is calculated as 100 minus the absolute value of the difference between the Democratic vote percentage and the Republican vote percentage. Minor party vote shares should decline as this indicator increases, since high values represent close races.

I also consider two other possible factors. One indicator is whether the ballot format permits a voter to cast a straight-party ticket by pulling a single lever, checking a single box, or some other simple action. Since this option is most beneficial to major parties that field more complete slates of candidates, straight-party voting should decrease the vote for minor party and independent candidates. One study does find that a straight-party ballot mechanism hurts minor party candidates for Congress.[36]

In addition, because minor party voters often become interested in the election closer to the end of the campaign, it is possible that an early closing date for voter registration depresses minor party voting. It has been argued that Reform Party candidate Jesse Ventura's successful gubernatorial campaign in Minnesota was due to the availability of same-day voter registration.[37] Yet

Table 11-1. *Ballot Regulation Effects in the 2000 and 2004 Presidential Elections*[a]

	Number of candidates (Poisson count model)		Minor/ independent vote % (Linear regression)	
Explanatory variable	2000	2004	2000	2004
Petition signatures required as %	−0.79**	−1.06**	−2.29**	0.01
of electorate	(0.25)	(0.31)	(0.81)	(0.21)
Days before general election when	−0.002	−0.002	−0.003	−0.0005
petitions must be submitted	(0.003)	(0.003)	(0.010)	(0.003)
Fusion candidacies permitted			−1.10	0.16
			(0.64)	(0.15)
Straight-party voting mechanism on ballot	. . .	. . .	−0.86*	−0.09
			(0.50)	(0.12)
Closeness of major party election	. . .	. . .	−0.07**	−0.009*
			(0.02)	(0.004)
Voter registration closing date	. . .	. . .	0.03	−0.007
			(0.03)	(0.006)
Minor party/independent vote share	0.03	0.06*	0.63**	0.19**
in last presidential election	(0.02)	(0.03)	(0.09)	(0.02)
Constant	1.68**	1.50**	3.87*	1.33**
	(0.39)	(0.31)	(2.01)	(0.45)
Adjusted R^2			.58	.64
Log likelihood	−91.67	−94.59		
N	51	51	51	51

a. Cell entries are coefficients; standard errors are in parentheses.
*$p < .05$ **$p < .01$ (one-tailed test)

Nader's vote in 2000 was unrelated to the lateness of either the candidate filing deadline or the voter registration closing date.[38] Further, minor party support tends to wane as election day approaches.[39] I allow for both possibilities by including a variable measuring the number of days before the general election by which a voter must register.

In all models I control for previous minor party and independent candidate strength in the state. This measure (total percentage of the popular vote earned by minor parties) should roughly reflect support for third parties in a state, which could be due to political culture, organization, population demographics, or other endogenous factors. To the degree that support the last time around is also a product of ballot access laws, this is a strong control variable.

Table 11-2. *Ballot Regulation Effects in the 2006 Gubernatorial and Senatorial Elections*[a]

Explanatory variable	Number of candidates (Poisson count model)		Minor/ independent vote % (Linear regression)	
	Governor	Senator	Governor	Senator
Number of signatures required as %	−1.10**	−2.06**	−0.60	−6.95
of electorate	(0.43)	(0.66)	(4.18)	(7.60)
Days before general election when	0.003	0.0001	0.07	−0.04
petitions must be submitted	(0.003)	(0.0025)	(0.04)	(0.05)
Fusion candidacies permitted			−2.22	9.89
			(3.68)	(6.54)
Straight-party voting mechanism on ballot	...	...	−0.79	−0.68
			(3.12)	(4.50)
Closeness of major party election	...	...	0.11	−0.29**
			(0.10)	(0.10)
Voter registration closing date	...	...	−0.01	0.15
			(0.13)	(0.22)
Minor party/independent vote share	0.66**	0.28	3.67	6.06
in last presidential election	(0.24)	(0.22)	(2.87)	(3.80)
Constant	−0.15	0.72	−15.85	20.93*
	(0.59)	(0.49)	(9.88)	(11.02)
Adjusted R^2			.003	.46
Log likelihood	−58.36	−55.59		
N	35	33	35	33

a. Cell entries are coefficients; standard errors are in parentheses.
*$p < .05$ **$p < .01$ (one-tailed test)

Results

Tables 11-1 and 11-2 summarize the main results. Petition signature requirements have statistically significant effects on the number of candidates on the ballot. In the 2000 presidential election, shifting the threshold upward from the lowest signature state to the highest reduces the number of candidates by 4.2. Put another way, states with no signature requirements list about 6 minor party and independent candidates on the ballots, while those with the most severe requirements have about 2 such candidates. In 2004 the effect is similar at −3.8.

The effects in the 2006 gubernatorial and senatorial elections are a bit more modest. Varying the signature requirement from the minimum state to the maximum state decreases the number of gubernatorial candidates by 2.1 and the number of senatorial candidates by 2.6. While these effects are smaller, the number of gubernatorial candidates was smaller overall. The typical state ballot lists only about four non-major-party presidential candidates and two non-major-party gubernatorial and senatorial candidates. Increasing the signature threshold to that of the highest state—roughly 1.4 percent of the eligible electorate—effectively eliminates alternatives to the Democratic and Republican nominees. In none of the models does the deadline for petitions matter, so all of the action is in the number of signatures required.

Although lower signature requirements increase the number of minor party and independent candidates on the ballot, the major parties' vote shares are not harmed. In the four models of vote share, the signature requirement is statistically significant in only one. It would seem that lower signature requirements provide more ballot choices without jeopardizing the two-party system.

The models show that the main variable determining the votes for minor party and independent candidates is the closeness of the major party campaign. Just as Duverger's law would suggest, when the race between the Democratic and Republican candidates is close, supporters of other candidates tend to abstain or vote strategically to avoid spoiling the election. In three of the four models the closeness variable is statistically significant, with effects ranging between –0.7 and –28.0 percentage points. Stated positively, minor party and independent candidates earn more votes when the major party contest is a runaway. It is the lack of competitiveness, not ballot regulations, that determines how much of the vote goes to major and minor party candidates.

None of the other variables show much effect on minor party and independent vote shares. Despite the claims made by proponents of ballot fusion, in none of the models is the availability of fusion related to votes for minor parties. Perhaps cross-endorsement has the potential for sustaining minor parties, but these parties are not taking advantage of the opportunity in states where fusion is allowed. The effect of fusion might also depend on larger forces related to major party competition.[40] Likewise, the voter registration closing date has no effect on minor party and independent candidate votes. Although Ventura might have been helped by a swell of last-minute registrants, the relationship between registration deadlines and minor party success is generally nonexistent. Finally, in only one of the four models does the presence of a straight-party voting mechanism hurt minor parties. In 2000 minor party candidates running for president earned about 1 percentage point less in states with this device than in states without it. It is possible that straight-ticket voting, fusion, and other factors affect races further down the ballot more significantly since voters have less information about those candidates.

Implications for Reform

Ballot access regulations have a clear impact on the number of candidates who run for office. The greater the share of the electorate required to sign nominating petitions, the fewer minor party and independent candidates appear on the ballot. Increasing the percentage by even a trivial amount nonetheless reduces the number of candidates. Extrapolating a bit from the data, it would seem that a requirement as high as 2 percent of the electorate would effectively eliminate all competition to the Democrats and Republicans. On the other side, even the most lenient signature requirements result in about six presidential candidates and four senatorial and gubernatorial candidates from outside the major parties.

Some proponents of strict ballot access requirements believe that an excessive number of candidates on the ballot will cause "clutter" and voter confusion. This seems unlikely. We have seen that even states with no signature requirements seldom have more than half a dozen minor party and independent candidates on the ballot. Compared to the other choices that voters are required to make, even ten candidates on the ballot would not seem unmanageable. For example, ballot initiatives require voters to make much more complex decisions, read lengthy ballot text, and have considerable outside knowledge of the issues at hand. Voters in other democracies have managed for years to choose among multiple parties without much difficulty. There is no reason to believe that American voters are any less capable.

Signature requirements have much less impact on the number of votes that minor parties and independents actually receive. (In only one of the four models was it significant.) Although minor parties have at times played the role of spoiler, this is the result of voter choices, not ballot access laws. Even low petition thresholds do not cut into the votes earned by Democrats and Republicans. Vote shares are affected by the larger winner-take-all electoral system, which harms minor parties via the "wasted vote" phenomenon. As the closeness of the major party race grows, votes for non-major-party candidates decline in number. The availability of fusion appears not to dampen this fundamental relationship, at least in recent elections. In light of the evidence, minor party activists' emphasis on fusion as a means for overcoming strategic voting seems misplaced.

These findings suggest that state lawmakers should not be hesitant to liberalize signature requirements since this measure requires only a minor statutory change and does not threaten the two-party system. The findings also highlight the importance of signature requirements, as opposed to deadlines for submission or voter registration closing dates, as targets of electoral reform. Both advocates of choice and defenders of the traditional two-party system should agree that lower thresholds provide voters with more options without threatening the dominance of the two major parties. Only abandonment of the underlying electoral system can do that.

Notes

1. See Duverger (1963). Single-member district systems are as also known as "first past the post," or simply plurality rule, elections. More generally, an "nth past the post" system will produce $n + 1$ parties (Cox 1997; Reed 1990). A district magnitude of one seat thus results in two-party competition. The Electoral College is a special case of first past the post, since electoral votes are usually allocated on a winner-take-all plurality rule within each state.

2. Cox (1997); Riker (1982). It does not take many votes to "spoil" a close election. In the 2000 presidential election, George W. Bush famously beat Al Gore by just 537 votes in Florida. Ralph Nader's nearly 100,000 votes in Florida were easily enough to flip the outcome. But so were the votes of seven other minor party candidates who earned votes in Florida. Nader also collected enough votes in New Hampshire that year to cost Gore the victory (Burden 2003). More recently, the Democrats' new majority in the U.S. Senate is due in part to minor party candidates who drew Republican votes in two key states in the 2006 midterms. In Montana a Libertarian won more than 10,000 votes, and Jon Tester defeated Republican Conrad Burns by just 3,500 votes. In Virginia Jim Webb defeated George Allen by just over 9,000 votes, while a conservative independent candidate won 26,000. Republicans, however, managed to win governorships in Minnesota and Texas with a little help from progressive minor party candidates.

3. Since the 2000 presidential election, research on ballot formats and technology has also blossomed.

4. Although cumbersome, I use the terms *minor party candidate* and *independent candidate* to describe non-major-party candidates. While commonly referred to as *third-party candidates,* the terms I apply better reflect the legal definitions of non-major parties in the states.

5. Rosenstone, Behr, and Lazarus (1996); Rusk (1970).

6. This estimate was provided by Richard Winger. Interestingly, the total number of signatures needed reached its high point in 1964 at nearly 1 million, despite the fact that the voting-age population has nearly doubled since then.

7. Winger (2006).

8. Rosenstone, Behr, and Lazarus (1996).

9. Rosenstone, Behr, and Lazarus (1996, p. 213).

10. Penniman (1980).

11. Hirano and Snyder (2007).

12. Winger (2006).

13. Winger (1997).

14. Strattman (2005).

15. Collett and Wattenberg (1999, p. 230).

16. Smallwood (1983, p. 255).

17. Lewis-Beck and Squire (1995).

18. Robeck and Dyer (1982).

19. Brown (1997).

20. Strattman (2005) also inappropriately uses linear regression to model a count process.

21. Lem and Dowling (2007).

22. Tamas and Hindman (2007, p. 13).

23. Rosenstone, Behr, and Lazarus (1996).

24. Herrnson (2006).

25. Similar to the measure used in Lem and Dowling (2007).

26. I used the "voting eligible population" as provided by Michael McDonald at http://elections.gmu.edu/voter_turnout.htm. A related aspect of signature requirements that I do not measure is the geographic distribution requirements noted earlier. It is possible that requiring signatures to be dispersed across the state is especially difficult for a minor party that is strongest in a particular region.

27. Morse and Gass (2006).

28. Argersinger (1980, p. 304).

29. Disch (2002).

30. Mazmanian (1974); Spitzer (2002).

31. Scarrow (1986).

32. Lowi (1999).

33. Morse and Gass (2006). Fusion is directly banned in general elections in about half of the states. In many others it is indirectly banned by preventing nominees selected in primaries from accepting the endorsement of other parties in the general election (www.nmef.org/statebystate.htm).

34. Burden (2005b); Strattman (2005).

35. Cox (1997).

36. Collett and Wattenberg (1999); also Winger (1997).

37. Lentz (2002).

38. Allen and Brox (2005).

39. Rosenstone, Behr, and Lazarus (1996).

40. Tamas and Hindman (2007).

DANIEL A. SMITH

12

Direct Democracy and
Election and Ethics Laws

State legislators are likely to alter institutions so as to keep power and win elections. As such, we should not expect lawmakers to adopt either election or ethics reforms that may diminish their chances of winning and holding office. In nearly half of the American states, though, citizens may circumvent their state legislatures and adopt statutes and constitutional amendments that alter the institutional design of state government, including election and ethics policy.[1] This chapter offers a comparative and historical examination of the popular adoption and policy impact of a variety of election and ethics ballot initiatives in the American states. It also examines recent efforts by state legislatures to regulate and restrict the use of the initiative. It concludes by assessing the successes and failures of initiated ethics and election reforms in the states.

History of Ethics and Election-Initiated Reforms

Beginning with the passage of the first governance initiative in Oregon in 1904 (requiring the direct primary for the nomination of candidates) and continuing through 2006 with the defeat of the Voter Reward Act in Arizona

I would like to thank the Ballot Initiative Strategy Center, the Initiative and Referendum Institute, and especially Jennie Drage Bowser at the National Conference of State Legislatures for making data on the historical usage of the initiative available to me. For valuable feedback on the draft of this chapter, I thank Bruce Cain, Caroline Tolbert, and the anonymous reviewers. I also thank Aaron Retteen for helping me collect and code current ethics and election laws in the American states.

(which would have awarded a $1 million lottery prize to one lucky voter), citizens have approved 154 of 258 initiated ethics and election reforms appearing on the ballot.[2] Ethics and election reform initiatives have a much higher success rate (60 percent) than initiatives in general (40 percent).

This aggregate adoption rate, however, masks an important difference between the two types of reform. Over the past century, initiatives proposing ethics reform have been far more successful than initiatives proposing election reform. Voters have rejected just two of twenty-four ethics-related statewide initiatives on the ballot—a 1934 measure in Arizona that would have changed nepotism rules and a 1976 measure in Utah that would have given voters the right to recall their state officials. Every other ethics reform initiative has received a majority vote. Voters have passed initiatives requiring the disclosure of financial interests of legislators, limiting their outside business interests, and curtailing the gifts bestowed upon them, as well as initiatives clamping down on legislative salaries, creating independent ethics commissions, and regulating the activities of lobbyists, giving ethics reform initiatives a success rate of 92 percent.

In contrast, over the same period, voters have approved 132 of the 234 election reform initiatives on the ballot, a 56 percent approval rate. Within this category, only legislative term limits (76 percent), proxy term limit initiatives calling for self-limit pledges, informed-voter notations, none-of-the-above ballot options (69 percent), and campaign finance initiatives (60 percent) come remotely close to the success rate of initiated ethics reforms. The overall passage rate for election reforms is greatly inflated by the 59 legislative term limits initiatives (of which 45 passed) and the 46 campaign finance initiatives (of which 28 passed). The balance of initiated election reforms have been met in large part by voter skepticism.

When term limit initiatives are removed from consideration, slightly less than half (87) of the remaining 175 election reform initiatives have been approved by voters. Some of the big losers among election reforms have been initiatives promoting woman suffrage (7 of 9 initiatives were defeated in the early 1900s), calling for a unicameral legislature (Nebraska's 1934 initiative was successful, but 2 others were defeated), redistricting and reapportionment efforts (21 of 31 initiatives were defeated), approving independent redistricting commissions (6 of 10 initiatives have failed), changing the way candidates are nominated by their parties (only 4 of 10 initiatives calling for nonpartisan elections have passed: fusion, open primaries, blanket primaries, and the end of caucuses), and altering the method of voting (only 7 of 16 initiatives have been approved that call for voting by mail, election day registration, and no-excuse absentee voting). In 2005 voters struck down 4 election reform initiatives in Ohio and a redistricting measure in California.[3] The following year voters rejected election reform initiatives allowing voting by mail and giving a $1 million reward to a lucky voter in Arizona, providing public financing to candidates in California, limiting the terms of judges in Colorado, allowing candidates in Massachusetts to cross-list with multiple parties, and term limiting state legislators and imposing campaign finance restrictions in Oregon. In 2006, 4 initiatives were successful at the polls: in Alaska a measure limiting campaign contributions and requiring greater lobbying disclosure passed, as did 1 limiting the state legislature to a ninety-day session, and voters approved ethics reform measures in both Colorado and Montana. Between 2001and 2006 voters passed all 7 statewide ethics reform initiatives on the ballot, but they struck down 26 of 30 election reforms.

Support for Reform Initiatives

A closer examination of the history of ethics and election ballot initiatives suggests that they are shaped by two separate dynamics that may increase or undermine popular support at the polls. Mechanistically, of course, the initiative provides a majoritarian system of governance. As such, it is prone to both populist and factional tugs and pulls. Both dynamics in the plebiscitary process are powerful and at times can be synergistic. The populist dynamic taps an oppositional sentiment among the electorate, counterpoising citizens against their elected officials. As one observer notes, "Populism divides the political world into Us, the People, and Them, the professional politicians and bureaucrats who actually rule."[4] This rhetorical trope exploits the sentiment that ordinary citizens can use the process "to challenge, if not outright repudiate, their elected officials and the institution of representative government."[5]

Governance policies like tax and expenditure limits and other antitax measures, election reforms such as term limits and campaign finance limits, and many ethics reforms are classic examples of this populist dynamic at play. Whether the goal of reformers is to crack down on corruption of public officials or malfeasance within government by creating an independent ethics commission, to rein in legislative salaries or restrict the outside financial interests of state legislators, to restrict lobbying or make it more transparent, or to limit the gubernatorial appointment power of U.S. senators, we can rest assured that supporters will rely on the populist cry of Us versus Them when rallying the masses. If it is not possible to throw the bums out, reformers can at least place on the ballot laws regulating the public actions of elected officials and those seeking to influence them.

In contrast, other election and ethics reforms are driven predominantly by a factional dynamic. These factional reforms do not alter the relationship between citizens and their elected officials or attempt to regulate the conduct of elected officials. Rather, factional governance policies might be best characterized as a struggle of Us versus Us, since the aim of the reforms is to disrupt the status quo of who is permitted to participate in the electoral process, the manner in which citizens nominate and elect candidates, and the way in which elections are conducted. Initiatives advanced by good government groups such as Common Cause and the League of Women Voters typically aim to enhance electoral participation (especially among apathetic or marginalized segments of the electorate), alter the nomination process of political parties, grant electoral rights to the disenfranchised, or expand the voting rights of members of minority groups. From giving women the right to vote to establishing the direct primary and eliminating the appointment of U.S. senators to rectifying malapportioned state legislative or congressional districts to allowing election day voting to permitting fusion candidates to crosslist their parties' affiliation to allowing crossover voting in blanket primaries, the explicit normative goal of these good government policies is to enlarge or enhance the electoral opportunities of certain citizens.

The initiative, then, is conducive to the adoption of some, but not all, election reforms. Not every citizen wants to change the electoral system; many may prefer, and may even benefit from, maintaining the status quo. As a result, there is the potential for the electorate to become factionalized over these governance initiatives, and it is reasonable to expect that many of these reforms will be rejected at the polls. "As a majoritarian institution, direct democracy requires majorities of voters to support a particular policy and, by definition, minority groups are disadvantaged."[6] Good governance election reforms intended to level the playing field and expand political access and opportunities for minorities or marginalized groups have at times provoked a factional rift that stems from an electoral majority sensing it is being pushed aside by those gaining political power at their expense.[7] Election-related initiatives motivated by a factional divide within the electorate, while not as extensive, include efforts in the 1960s across many states to overturn reapportionment plans by state legislatures and, more recently, to require stricter identification requirements in Arizona for citizens to register and vote.

Direct Democracy and Election Reforms

In theory, even if many election reform initiatives go down to defeat, the initiative process can still promote the adoption of election reforms by stimulating action in state legislatures. In the words of Woodrow Wilson, the option of an initiative may serve as a "gun behind the door," compelling legislators to act in accordance to the will of the people.[8] However, when it comes to election reforms, the evidence on the efficacy of this instrument is mixed. Looking over time at ten election reforms, one study finds that states with and without the initiative do not seem to have very different election laws,[9] and another, which controls for some demographic and ideological factors, finds (with the exception of term limits) that the presence of the initiative historically does not have much impact on the adoption of fifteen election-related laws.[10] In contrast, an earlier study finds that "citizen usage of the initiative is a powerful explanation for the adoption of legislative term limits and constraints on governmental taxation and spending."[11] In a follow-up study that controls for a number of socioeconomic variables, legislative professionalization, and state political ideology, the same scholar concludes that states with frequent use of the initiative were "more likely to adopt the nine contemporary political reforms" by 1996 than lower-frequency initiative users and those without the process.[12] Between 1984 and 1998, states with a higher historical average use of the initiative were similarly found to be more likely than other states to adopt stricter restrictions on individual contributors and on contributions from parties and political action committees.[13]

There may be good reason to be somewhat circumspect about the effect of the initiative on the adoption of election reforms.[14] When trying to extrapolate the historical impact of the initiative on governance reforms more broadly, it is possible that the adoption of some reforms may be historically bounded. In particular, the overwhelming success of legislative term limits across initiative states during the 1990s has come and gone.[15] It is also possible that when governance reforms are combined into a single index, a few policies (specifically, term limits and tax and expenditure limits) may be driving the results.[16] Finally, it may be the case that governance reforms were initially stronger in noninitiative states and that initiative states were simply trying to catch up during the period studied.[17] As such, it may be an overreach to conclude that "a state history of active citizen participation using the process is necessary to explain the adoption of governance policies."[18]

Table 12-1 provides bivariate correlations of two measures of the initiative (the presence or absence of the initiative and the average number of statewide

Table 12-1. *Statewide Initiative and Election Reform Correlations*

Reform[a]	Initiative permitted	Average number of initiatives on the ballot, 1980–2004
State legislative term limits	.594**	.605**
Multimember Senate districts	.127	.094
Multimember House districts	.027	.048
Felon voter restoration in prison	−.008	−.004
Felon voter restoration on parole	−.157	−.134
Felon voter restoration during probation	−.196	−.241
Index of campaign finance regulations	.046	.071
Campaign finance disclosure	.330*	.340*
Public financing of campaigns	−.147	−.166
Campaign finance contribution limits	−.088	−.010
Redistricting commission for state legislative seats	.402**	.382**
Redistricting commission for congressional seats[b]	.043	.076
Index of principles governing congressional redistricting[c]	−.061	.018
Index of state election administration reforms	.007	.032
No straight-party voting	.402**	.428**
Election day voter registration	−.053	−.100
No-excuse absentee voting	.412**	.448**

Source: National Conference of State Legislatures (2007).

a. *N* = 50, unless otherwise noted.

b. *N* = 44. Seven states (Alaska, Delaware, Montana, North Dakota, South Dakota, Vermont, and Wyoming) have a single, at-large congressional district, but Montana has a redistricting commission for congressional districts (Barabas and Jerit 2004; McDonald 2004).

c. *N* = 43. Seven states have a single, at-large congressional district.

*significant at 0.05 level (two-tailed); **significant at 0.01 level (two-tailed)

initiatives on the ballot between 1980 and 2004) with seventeen measures of election reform in the American states.

The ordinal measures of recent election reforms include

—Legislative term limits and multimember Senate or House districts.[19]

—Allowing felons to vote (while in prison, on parole, or on probation).[20]

—A composite stringency index of twenty-two state campaign finance regulations as well as disaggregated measures of state campaign finance disclosure, public financing of campaigns, and contribution limits.[21]

—A redistricting commission for either state legislative or congressional redistricting.[22]

—A seven-point index of the principles governing congressional redistricting decisions.[23]

—A composite index of twelve election administration reforms (new voting equipment, voting equipment standards and procedures, a ban on punch cards, a new or improved central registration database, improved registration list maintenance and purging procedures, voter intent, recount procedures, absentee voting procedures, provisional ballots, poll workers, polling place and voting machine accessibility for elderly and disabled voters, and improved voter education).[24]

—Straight-party voting, election day voter registration, or no-excuse absentee voting by mail.[25]

We should take the results presented in table 12-1 as suggestive, rather than definitive, as they do not use multivariate statistical controls for state economic, demographic, and political factors. Though other possible factors are not held constant, the adoption of five of the seventeen election reforms—term limits on state legislators, stringency of campaign finance disclosure, the use of a commission for state legislative redistricting, no straight-party voting, and no-excuse absentee voting by mail—are statistically related to the presence or use of the initiative. It comes as little surprise that the adoption of legislative term limits is positively related to both the presence of the initiative and actual initiative use.[26] States with the initiative (and those using the process more frequently) are also less likely to allow party-line voting, which again should be expected, as one of the major Progressive Era reforms was to weaken party machines. The adoption of campaign finance disclosure, redistricting commissions, and no-excuse absentee voting are all positively related to having (and using) the initiative.[27] However, the fact that more than two-thirds of the election reforms are not tied to either the presence or the use of the initiative is somewhat eye-opening. Initiative states are not more likely to overturn felon disenfranchisement laws or use multimember legislative districts. There is also no statistically significant relationship between the presence (or use) of the initiative and a wide spectrum of campaign finance reforms (except for disclosure) or the index of state election administration reforms.

Direct Democracy and Ethics Reforms

Little scholarly work has been done on the impact of the initiative on the adoption of ethics reforms in the American states. A few studies use a dichotomous dummy variable indicating the presence or absence of the initiative to examine comparative levels of corruption in the states, but results are mixed.[28]

Table 12-2. *Statewide Initiative and Ethics Reform Correlations*

Reform	Initiative permitted	Average number of initiatives on the ballot, 1980–2004
Statehouse reporters' ranking of public corruption ($N = 47$)	−.198	−.298*
Ethics laws, jurisdiction to investigate index ($N = 47$)	−.061	−.033
Ethics laws, authority to investigate index ($N = 44$)	−.193	−.181
State legislative lobbying regulation, 1990–91 ($N = 50$)	−.088	.039
State legislative lobbying regulation, 2003 ($N = 50$)	.001	.093
State legislative lobbying regulation, 2003 (plus penalties) ($N = 47$)	−.073	.016

Source: National Conference of State Legislatures (2007); Council of State Governments (2006).
*significant at 0.05 level (two-tailed)

In a more rigorous treatment of the adoption of ethics laws in the states, one scholar also uses a dummy variable to capture the impact of the initiative on the adoption of various state ethics laws in the states over three time periods.[29] In 1954–72 and 1989–96, the study finds that the presence of the initiative does not have an impact on the likelihood of a state adopting legislative ethics codes or on explaining a state's overall change in its legislative ethics laws. During the post-Watergate period (1977–88), however, the presence of the initiative contributed to the overall strengthening of state legislative ethics laws. Citizens in four states used the initiative to authorize the adoption of independent legislative ethics commissions between 1970 and 1996 (California, 1974; Maine, 1975; Michigan, 1975; Arkansas, 1990), and the initiative process played an indirect role in the adoption of a commission in Massachusetts (1978) after Common Cause threatened to place a measure on the ballot. However, the study also finds that the initiative did not affect whether a state adopted an independent legislative ethics commission between 1973 and 1996.

Table 12-2 provides bivariate correlations among the alternative measures of the initiative and five measures of ethics reform in the American states, as well as a normalized ranking of perceived public corruption from a survey of statehouse reporters.[30] The ethics reforms include separate indexes measuring the jurisdiction and authority of state ethics committees to investigate on their own authority, and three measures of state legislative lobbying regulations.[31] Correlations between the presence and average use of the initiative over time and the five ethics reform measures suggest that states with or that frequently use the initiative are no more likely to adopt reforms giving ethics commissions more authority to investigate misconduct or to adopt stricter lobbying regulations. The increased use of initiative, however, appears to be weakly related to lower levels of perceived public corruption by the capitol beat press corps. As with the relationship between the initiative and various election reforms, the findings here are suggestive, not conclusive.

Legislative Backlash? Regulating the Initiative

It comes as no surprise that initiated efforts to regulate ethics and elections have not been well received by many state legislatures. Faced with a threat to their own livelihood, lawmakers have tried continually to rein in the process of direct democracy. Though legislative hostility toward the initiative is often driven by concerns over substantive outcomes resulting from ballot measures, legislators undoubtedly are also frustrated by the ethics and elections sanctions imposed by initiatives.

Legislative efforts to regulate and restrict the initiative process are not new. Before the ink had even dried on the constitutional amendments granting citizens newfound plebiscitary powers during the Progressive Era, state lawmakers tried to make it more difficult for groups to place measures on the ballot.[32] In Oregon, the first state to have a statewide initiative on the ballot, the state legislature passed a law in 1907 requiring circulators to sign an affidavit when collecting signatures. In California, following the 1914 general election, which had forty-eight statewide measures on the ballot, the state legislature passed a law making it a criminal offense for signature gatherers to misstate the contents of a measure. Lawmakers in Washington passed a statute in 1915 that required registered voters to sign their names on petitions in the office of a county clerk from 6 p.m. to 9 p.m. over a ninety-day period. Perhaps appropriately, the law never went into effect, as it was immediately overturned by a popular referendum.[33] During the 1920s and 1930s state legislatures passed a series of laws pertaining to the financing of ballot measures. In 1933 Oregon lawmakers passed a statute requiring proponents and opponents of ballot measures to report their contributions and expenditures and, in the following legislative session, prohibited "any person to give, pay, or receive any money or other valuable consideration for securing the signatures of electors on direct legislation petitions."[34] By the 1970s more than half of the initiative states passed laws restricting campaign contributions and expenditures in ballot campaigns.[35] Over the years, state legislatures also have passed laws placing geographic distribution requirements on the signature-gathering phase in qualifying ballot measures. Roughly a dozen states still require signatures to be collected from a minimum number of geographic units (usually congressional districts).[36] As a result of these regulations, there is considerable variation across states with regard to the ease and availability of the initiative process.[37]

State lawmakers continue to place restrictions on the initiative process, with the unmistakable intention of making it more difficult for proponents to qualify their measures. Many legislative efforts to regulate the process focus on fraudulent gathering of signatures for petition drives. Some of these regulations include requiring signature gatherers to be residents of the state, requiring petitioners to sign affidavits or have the petitions they are circulating notarized, and shortening the time in which valid signatures may be gathered. Today, every state permitting the initiative has criminal penalties for both circulators and signatories if they falsify information on petitions, including fines upward of $5,000 and up to two years of jail time.[38]

Many of these restrictions on the initiative subsequently faced court challenges. In 1978 campaign finance restrictions that states had placed on ballot measure campaigns were overturned by the U.S. Supreme Court in its 1978 decision in *First National Bank of Boston* v. *Bellotti.* In reviewing a Massachusetts statute that prohibited contributions and expenditures by corporations in ballot campaigns unless the issue materially affected the corporation's business, the court found that expenditure limits in ballot campaigns were unconstitutional. Three years later, in *Citizens against Rent Control* v. *City of Berkeley,* the justices ruled that any limits on contributions to ballot issue committees were unconstitutional infringements on free speech.[39] In 1988 the U.S. Supreme Court invalidated a Colorado law banning paid signature gatherers in its decision *Meyer* v. *Grant.* Several other states, including Maine, Mississippi, North Dakota, Washington, and Wyoming, were required to take bans off the books.[40] In its 1999 decision *Buckley* v. *American Constitutional Law,* the high court struck down another Colorado law that required petition gatherers to be registered voters, to wear identification badges, and to report how much they were being paid, ruling that the restrictions were "undue hindrances to political conversations and the exchange of ideas." Recently, the high court has been quite dubious of state legislative efforts to restrict the initiative process.[41]

Despite judicial rulings striking down legislative efforts to regulate the process of direct democracy, the legislative effort to restrict the initiative process seems to have picked up steam. According to data compiled by the

National Conference of State Legislatures, between 2001 and 2006 more than 400 bills dealing with the process of direct democracy were filed in the twenty-four states that permit the initiative, with more than 1 of 8 of these bills becoming law.[42] In 2007 alone, legislators in the two dozen initiative states filed more than 200 bills aimed at regulating the process. Some of the more popular legislature-sponsored regulations include requiring a financial impact statement for measures that qualify for the ballot, changing the format of petitions, tightening single-subject standards, placing additional restrictions on paid petition gatherers, and providing more disclosure of campaign finance activities. Certainly, the efforts of state lawmakers to rein in the process is not solely a reaction to ethics and election initiatives, but these initiatives likely contribute at the margins to the hostility shown by state legislatures toward the process of direct democracy.

Implications for Reform

The use of the initiative might not be the best institutional antidote for reformers interested in reforming the electoral process, although it may play an indirect role in setting the reform agenda across the states. Reformers who sponsor ethics and election initiatives that tap into a deep populist sentiment will likely continue to be rewarded at the polls.[43] But absent a populist dynamic, election reform efforts using the initiative will face the same uphill battle as other factionalized ballot initiatives. Furthermore, regardless of the success or failure of ethics and election reforms placed on the ballot via the initiative, it is certain that state lawmakers will continue to cast a skeptical eye on the process. The legislative backlash against the initiative arose during the origins of direct democracy, and regulations placed on the process are likely to persist. At its heart, though, the initiative remains a majoritarian system of governance; the voice of the people (or at least that of the electorate) will have the final say on whether altering the status quo is perceived to be beneficial.

Notes

1. Smith and Tolbert (2007).

2. Data are from the Ballot Initiative Strategy Center, National Conference of State Legislatures, and the Initiative and Referendum Institute and were coded by the author. Several initiatives contain both ethics and election reforms and are counted twice for the purposes of this analysis.

3. Tolbert, Smith, and Green (2008).

4. Citrin (1996, p. 268).

5. Smith (1998, p. 28).

6. Donovan, Wenzel, and Bowler (2001, p. 173).

7. Cain (1992).

8. Quoted in Smith and Tolbert (2004, p. 2).

9. Persily and Anderson (2005).

10. Matsusaka (2006).

11. Tolbert (1998, p. 184).

12. Tolbert (2003, p. 487).

13. Pippen, Bowler, and Donovan (2002).

14. See Persily and Anderson (2005); Matsusaka (2006).

15. Smith (2003); Tolbert (1998).

16. Tolbert (2003).

17. Pippen, Bowler, and Donovan (2002).

18. Tolbert (1998, p. 187).

19. Council of State Governments (2006).

20. Sentencing Project (2006).

21. Witko (2005).

22. McDonald (2004).

23. Barabas and Jerit (2004).

24. Palazzolo and Moscardelli (2006).

25. Kimball (2003); Council of State Governments (2006).

26. See Tolbert (1998); Persily and Anderson (2005); Matsusaka (2006).

27. Pippen, Bowler, and Donovan (2002).

28. Alt and Lassen (2003); Meier and Holbrook (1992).

29. Rosenson (2005).

30. Boylan and Long (2003).

31. Council of State Governments (2006); Newmark (2005).

32. Donovan and Smith (2008).

33. Lapalombara and Hagan (1951).

34. Lapalombara and Hagan (1951, p. 415).

35. Daniel Smith (2001).

36. Waters (2003).

37. Collins and Oesterle (2005); Bowler and Donovan (2004).

38. Donovan and Smith (2008); Council of State Governments (2006).

39. Smith (2001).

40. In 2002 voters in Oregon approved Measure 26, an initiated measure that requires signature gatherers to be paid by the hour and be classified as paid employees rather than independent contractors.

41. Daniel Smith (2001).

42. National Conference of State Legislatures (2007).

43. Citrin (1996); Smith (1998).

TODD DONOVAN

13

A Goal for Reform

There is consensus among reform proponents that "something" must be done to restore "faith" in American elections. This consensus has given rise to a broad range of reform proposals. Some address problems in the administration of elections. Others aim to increase participation by making the act of voting more convenient. A third category targets the structure of the election system, such as the way in which electoral maps are drawn. Each of these reforms may have beneficial effects. Few people, for example, would quarrel with the statement that election rules should ensure that only eligible voters vote and that their votes are counted accurately. Most would also agree on the desirability of flawless voter registration and record keeping, perfectly trained poll workers, and optimally designed polling places with ample resources.

But to what extent would such reforms increase engagement with representative democracy? Would participation in elections rise? Would elections become more meaningful? Would more people believe that elections make government pay attention to the public or that voting gives them a say in what government does? In this chapter, I argue that, to answer these questions, we need to identify the root causes of what currently ails American democracy. I suggest that the failure to count votes accurately, the fact that eligible voters find they are unable to vote, the inability of minor parties to access ballots, the power of wealthy donors, and the lack of civility in political discourse all contribute to public cynicism about elections. But the fundamental causes of this syndrome include the polarized party system and the prevalence of uncompetitive elections, which fail to mobilize or engage many citizens. If contemporary reform proposals are truly to succeed, they must address these basic problems.

Reforms of Old: The Responsible Party Model

Ironically, the roots of some of today's problems may be traced to an earlier push for political reform. In 1950 the American Political Science Association produced a report titled "Toward a More Responsible Two-Party System," which called for wholesale changes in how American political parties operated. In 1950 "weak" parties were the target of reformers, who believed that such parties did not provide an adequate opportunity for the electorate to hold government accountable. Parties in power were unable to control their members in office, coordinate the branches of government, or implement goals. The lack of intraparty cohesion left voters unable to assign responsibility to a party and unable to select between parties on the basis of governing and programs.

The 1950 report proposed several reforms to make the two major parties more hierarchical, cohesive, programmatic, and distinct. These included strengthening national party offices by increasing funding and staff resources, changing rules to give parties a meaningful role in financing congressional campaigns, increasing party discipline in Congress, closing participation in nomination contests to registered partisans, giving rank-and-file party members direct control over delegate selection to national conventions, and placing greater emphasis on national policy in congressional elections and party platforms. For decades after 1950 the fragmentation of the party system at the elite level, the shift to candidate-centered presidential nominations, the decline of attachments to parties among the electorate, and the lack of collective responsibility in the political system remained problems of concern for political science.[1]

Today, at least some of the changes recommended in the 1950 report have taken place. By the late 1990s party identification played a considerably stronger role in structuring voter behavior.[2] Party leadership in Congress, although by no means parliamentary, is more cohesive and hierarchical than in decades past.[3] Even with "soft" money excluded, parties now play a much larger role in recruiting congressional candidates and financing races. And evidence that parties are more internally cohesive and ideologically distinct can be seen in floor voting in Congress and in public attitudes and behavior.[4] The proportion of floor votes in the House that fell largely along party lines increased through the 1970s, 1980s, and 1990s.[5] At the same time, realignment in the South and New England has made the constituency base of the national parties more internally cohesive. Conservative southern voters have migrated from the Democratic to the Republican Party, while liberal Republicans have been migrating to the Democrats.[6] By accident or by design, the American political system is now characterized by polarized party elites and by polarized partisans.

The sources of this polarization lie both in demographic trends and in the structure of the election system.[7] Nomination processes in homogeneous districts, "extremist" party activists, and ideologically motivated patrons who control campaign funds have shaped the pool of successful candidates and increased the distance between the parties.[8] Equally important, the vast majority of members of the U.S. House of Representatives are now from safe seats. In 2002 there were fewer two-party competitive U.S. House districts than at any point since 1900.[9]

The growing prevalence of safe seats is important because these districts elect members who are more extreme ideologically than the national median voter (or the median district nationally).[10] Figure 13-1 plots the scores for members of the 109th Congress, categorized by the incumbent candidates' 2004 vote share. These scores represent how liberal or conservative a representative's voting record was. Higher scores reflect more conservative voting, lower scores more liberal voting. The figure shows that the safest Democrats had the most liberal floor votes while Democrats in marginal districts had more centrist records.[11] Similarly, the most centrist Republicans were those in the most marginal districts.

Figure 13-2 shows the impact of these dynamics on the distribution of representation in Congress. It displays the number of representatives in the 109th Congress across the ideological range. This bimodal distribution demonstrates the absence of a center in the American political system. It is a distribution at odds with the distribution of ideological self-placement across the American electorate, which has the qualities of a normal, bell-shaped distribution.[12]

Figure 13-3 plots the frequency of responses to the American National Elections Study ideological self-placement question for Democrats, Republicans, and independents. It demonstrates that a plurality of Americans call themselves moderates (including almost half of all independents and a plurality of all Democrats). Yet the party system produces few moderate representatives. In the House the median Democratic representatives in the 109th Congress were liberal members such as Patrick Kennedy (R.I.) and Howard Berman (Calif.) and the median Republicans were conservatives Dennis

Figure 13-1. *Floor Votes of Members of 109th Congress, by Their Vote Share in Previous Elections*[a]

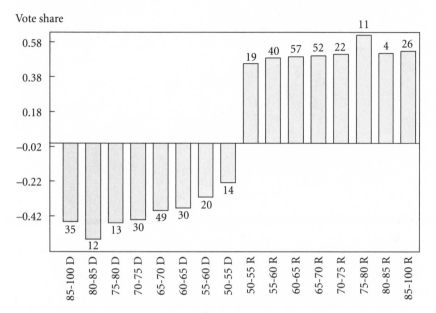

Source: Author's calculations.
a. Each bar represents the average DW-NOMINATE score for representatives in each type of district. −1 = most liberal, 1.0 = most conservative. Representatives are grouped on the horizontal axis based on how competitive their district was (based on their 2004 vote share). Those in the center of the figure come from the most competitive districts. The vertical axis represents the average DW-NOMINATE score for representatives for each category of district competitiveness.

Hastert (Ill.) and Virgil Goode (Va.), a vocal opponent of Muslim immigration. In 2004 the presidential candidates were also linked to the ideological poles of their parties. John Kerry's floor votes placed him to the left of most of the senators from his party, while George W. Bush's (inferred) issue positions placed him to the right of nearly all Republican senators.[13]

In addition to promoting ideological polarization, the growing prevalence of safe seats makes the election system less responsive to changes in the mood of the electorate. As a result of the decline in competition, it may now take a larger swing in public sentiment to move fewer seats.[14] A 5.5 percent vote swing against the majority party in 2006 yielded a thirty-seat midterm loss, which was below average for comparable elections since World War II. In 1994 the 6.3 percent Republican swing against Democrats produced a fifty-five-seat loss. The post-Watergate swing of 5.8 percent against Republicans in

Figure 13-2. *Distribution of Representation in the U.S. House,*
109th Congress[a]

Number

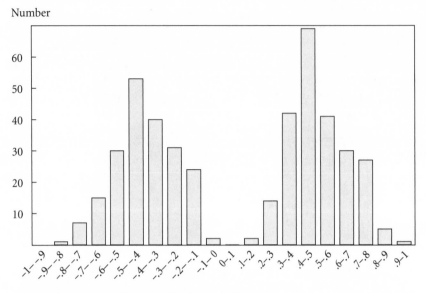

Source: Author's calculations using data from voteview.com.

a. Bars reflect the number of representatives with DW-NOMINATE scores in the ranges listed on the x-axis. Values to the left are more liberal, values to the right more conservative. $N = 434$, mean $= -0.02$.

1974 produced a forty-eight-seat loss. A 5 percent swing yielded a forty-seven-seat loss in 1958.

Be Careful What You Wish For

Since the APSA's call in 1950 for a stronger party system, the two major parties have indeed become more ideologically distinct. But the reformers' goals have only partially been achieved. Despite the increase in polarization among party elites and party identifiers, there has been little progress toward a *responsible* two-party system. The system described in the 1950 report was modeled on the assumption of legislative supremacy or at least legislative parity with the executive. This is a form of government that has been on the wane. Furthermore, one forgotten aspect of the report is its emphasis on the need to "give all sections of the country a real voice" in elections, notably presidential elections, rather than continue with the "blight of one-party monopoly" that results in the concentration of campaign resources in a few pivotal areas.

Figure 13-3. *Ideological Self-Identification of Democrats, Republicans, and Independents, 2004*[a]

Percent of respondents

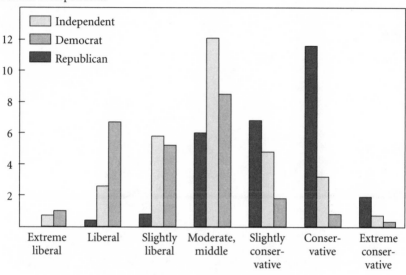

Source: American National Election Studies (www.electionstudies.org).
a. Partisan categorization based on the three-point party identification question.

Today the United States has polarized parties without competitive elections. Even with the one-party South transformed, fewer U.S. House contests are two-party competitive now than they were in 1950. Presidential and House elections are now structured such that many people live in places where they have no influence on elections. Most voters are not exposed to national election campaigns unless they live in a handful of competitive presidential states, such as Ohio, or in a rare, competitive U.S. House district. Many people face irrelevant elections in which they are offered choices between candidates from parties that may be too extreme for them and in which only one candidate has a chance of winning.

The trend toward greater polarization and less competitiveness has been associated with a significant decrease in faith in representative democracy. As of 2004 cynicism about elections was near (or at) the highest levels recorded in the era of modern American survey research. Attachments to major parties reached a record low in 2000. Although partisanship may now play a stronger role in structuring the votes of people who identify with a party and who

Figure 13-4. *Opinion, by Political Party, of Whether Government Follows Voters' Desire a Good Deal of the Time, 1964–2004*

Percent

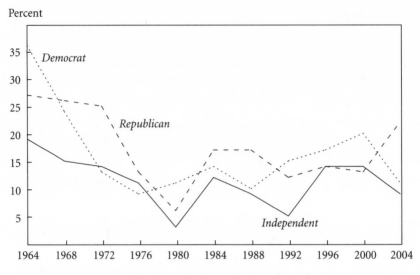

Source: American National Election Studies (www.electionstudies.org).

continue to vote, fewer people identify with parties today. The 2000 American National Election Study measure of partisan affiliation found 40 percent of Americans identifying themselves as independent, the highest level since the survey began in 1952. It is true that most of these independents report "leaning" toward a major party when prompted, and when their vote choices are limited to candidates from the major parties they are, behaviorally, quite similar to partisan identifiers.[15] But when it comes to their attitudes about the two-party system, independent leaners appear more like pure independents than partisans. Leaners have little regard for maintaining the two-party system, they are more likely to support third-party candidates, and they prefer divided government.[16] Thus a substantial proportion of Americans fail to identify with a party system that presents increasingly polarized choices. And while barriers to voting have been reduced, turnout declined (outside the South) or at best remained stagnant from 1972 to 2000.[17]

The rise of ideologically cohesive parties has not engaged more citizens nor led them to think that elections provide a mechanism to hold government accountable. Figure 13-4 illustrates that people are less likely to believe government listens to what people think, compared with previous decades. Using the standard NES measure of "having a say in government," figure 13-5

Figure 13-5. *Opinion, by Political Party, of People Who Think They Have a Say in Government, 1956–2004*

Percent

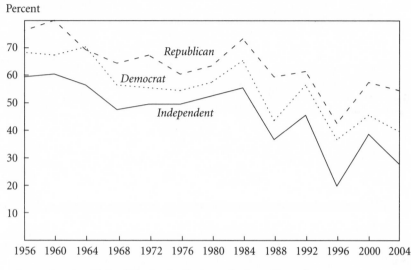

Source: American National Election Studies (www.electionstudies.org).

illustrates that in 2004 the nation was approaching a record low of political efficacy for Americans. Data such as these suggest a malaise about the efficacy of elections and representative democracy that has persisted since the 1980s.

What are the sources of such attitudes? Clearly, experiences such as Vietnam, Watergate, revelations about soft money, Iraq, and assorted political scandals explain much about these trends. But cynicism about representative democracy may also reflect public frustration with elections and the party system.[18] Safe, politically homogeneous legislative seats not only produce representatives further from a national median voter, but also these uncompetitive districts have less campaign activity, which translates into less engagement, especially for the young and for people with less interest in politics than partisans.[19]

Table 13-1 displays the results of a simple model of factors that affects beliefs regarding government responsiveness and political efficacy, based on survey data gathered immediately after the 2004 presidential election. People were asked, "How much attention does government pay to what people think when it decides what to do?" and whether they agreed that "people like me" have no say in government. Responses are estimated as a function of education, income, gender, and identification with the party that just won the election (in

Table 13-1. *Association between Electoral Competition, Individual Efficacy, and Governmental Responsiveness*[a]

Variable	People like me have a say in government	Government doesn't pay attention to what people think
Electoral competitiveness	−.71*	−.88+
(higher value = more competition)	(.40)	(.69)
White	.003	−.13
	(.09)	(.16)
Age	−.002	.001
	(.002)	(.004)
Education	.12**	−.12**
	(.03)	(.05)
Union household	.10	.07
	(.10)	(.18)
Household income	.014**	.001
	(.007)	(.01)
Female	−.05	.24*
	(.08)	(.13)
Strong Democrat	.02	.32*
	(.12)	(.19)
Strong Republican	.50**	−.91**
	(.12)	(.20)
Weak Republican	.27**	−.39*
	(.12)	(.21)
Weak Democrat	−.03	.22
	(.12)	(.20)
Constant 1	2.33**	−3.00
	(.22)	(.21)
Constant 2	.17	
	(.67)	
Number of cases	963	957
R^2	.07	.06

Source: American National Election Studies (www.electionstudies.org).

*$p < .05$ **$p < .01$ +$p = .10$ (one-tailed)

a. OLS coefficients in first column, ordered logit estimates in second column. Standard errors in parentheses. Competitiveness is measured as the 1 minus the margin between Bush and Kerry in the respondent's state of residence. Higher values for electoral competition reflect a closer election.

this case, Republicans)—all factors that are likely to increase efficacy. In addition, the model includes the competitiveness of the presidential election in a respondent's state, which is measured as 1 minus the vote margin between Bush and Kerry in a respondent's state in 2004. (Higher values represent greater competitiveness.) A state's vote margin in 2004 was highly correlated with television advertising and campaign visits and thus provides a solid measure of exposure to presidential campaigns.

The first column in table 13-1 presents estimates for a model that uses the propensity to think government listens "to people like me" as the dependent variable. The second model (results shown in column 2) treats opinions about whether government listens to people as the dependent variable. In both cases, the results support initial expectations. In 2004 people with higher education, Republicans, and the wealthy were more likely to think that "people like me" had a say. Likewise, those with more education and Republicans were less likely to think government did not pay attention to people, while women and strong-identifying Democrats were more likely to hold this belief.

The effects of electoral competition are less consistent but interesting nonetheless. People in states with the most competitive presidential races were less likely to agree that "people like me" had a say, but they were also somewhat less likely to agree with the idea that "government does not pay attention to what people think." In other words, constant bombardment with campaign ads may have an adverse effect on personal efficacy but a positive effect on a person's sense that government actually listens to people. It should be stressed that these data provide only a snapshot of political attitudes and that the sampling method used in the survey is not the best suited for assessing state-level effects. But the results suggest exposure to electoral competition (or a lack of exposure) may affect the attitudes plotted in figures 13-4 and 13-5.

Electoral Polarization, Competition, and Reform

Partisan polarization, then, by combining with uncompetitive elections, has gone from being part of the preferred solution to what ails the American system to quite possibly being a large force driving discontent with representative government. Consequently, it should also be of central interest to those interested in election reform. If either the failure to represent the large center of the American electorate or the dearth of meaningful elections (or both) are sources of discontent with representative democracy, then we must consider how various contemporary reform impulses affect party polarization and electoral competition.

For example, many efforts to reform election administration have been driven by perceptions of inaccuracy in voter registration, lack of fairness in vote counts, problems with butterfly ballots and hanging chads, and the latest revelations about improper behavior by legislators and lobbyists. However, the most accurate registration records and vote-counting systems would likely do little to affect electoral competition nor affect how the major parties and the electoral system represent (or fail to represent) the preferences of marginally interested Americans who think of themselves as centrists or moderates. Administrative reforms, such as those promoted by the Help America Vote Act, may make it more difficult to steal elections, but they fail to address the fact that most elections in most places remain so uncompetitive that they are not worth stealing.

Similarly, reducing barriers to voter participation is often promoted as a means to get more citizens engaged with elections, and there is evidence that election day registration increases turnout over time.[20] However, the effects of other efforts to make voting easier and more convenient, such as early voting, are typically modest.[21] Without increasing mobilization efforts and interest in elections, convenience voting will have limited effects on turnout and the composition of the electorate.

Reforms that target the rules that structure electoral competition may seem to have greater promise. For example, measures that reduce barriers to candidate entry might provide voters with more choices. In practice, however, while ballot access rules have clear effects on whether minor party candidates appear on ballots, the addition of these candidates has little effect on election outcomes.[22] Indeed, their vote share is inversely related to the competitiveness of races they enter. In a single-member simple plurality system where such candidates have little chance of representation, they remain a protest vehicle.

Changes in districting practices offer another potential avenue for increasing electoral competition. But few states have adopted outcomes-based redistricting practices that emphasize competition, and it is unclear whether state courts will enforce competition-related redistricting criteria.[23] Moreover, if uncompetitive elections are mainly the product of a natural pattern of like-minded partisans locating in similar places (rather than gerrymanders), even the most nonpartisan, independent redistricting plans may be unable to affect electoral competition.[24] Our awkwardly representative party system may be built on an electoral system that is simply incapable of responding to the new geography of American politics: a shrinking pool of Democrats live near Democrats and a shrinking pool of Republicans near Republicans. There may be no way to produce responsive, representative elections in this context under the old single-member district system.

Implications for Reform

The primary goal of election reform should be to increase competition. Electoral competition is the mechanism that makes elections more responsive to the distribution of mass preferences, the mechanism that provides accountability, and the mechanism by which citizens are mobilized and engaged by representative democracy. A significant body of literature suggests that people respond to meaningful electoral choices and electoral competition. Competition in U.S. House races increases turnout.[25] Multiparty systems have higher voter turnout and greater citizen satisfaction with how democracy works.[26] Referenda and initiatives bring people to the polls, and choices associated with these may stimulate political efficacy.[27] Local semiproportional representation systems, which are rarely used in the United States, can expand the range of candidates competing for office and thus increase campaign activity and voter turnout.[28]

Efforts to improve poll workers' training and improve the accuracy of vote tabulation and voter registration rolls are necessary and laudable, but errors associated with voting machines and duplicity in election administration are most likely to have consequences where election outcomes are relatively uncertain. Thus an electoral context where more contests are marginal may increase incentives for fraud. This is an unavoidable by-product of making elections worth stealing.

The argument here about many of the electoral reforms discussed in this book may be understood in terms of a baseball analogy. Administrative reforms that improve the integrity of elections are analogous to perfecting how balls, strikes, and base running are called in a baseball game. Accurate calls are critical, but they are not likely to fill the stands with fans. Reforms that lower the costs of voting are analogous to giving away free tickets to the game. In the end, people watch a game because they support one of the teams, because they are excited about the game, or because they know it is an important game. Perfect scoring and free tickets are not going to fill the stands if only one team takes the field, and attendance will suffer if two teams are playing that no one can cheer for.

Notes

1. See, for example, Polsby (1983); Wattenberg (1991, 1998); Fiorina (1980).
2. Bartels (2002).
3. Sinclair (2006).
4. Groseclose, Levitt, and Snyder (1999); Poole and Rosenthal (1997).
5. Donovan and Bowler (2004).

6. Rhode (1991); Black and Black (2003).

7. McCarty, Poole, and Rosenthal (2006); Cox and Katz (2002); Jacobson (2005).

8. Burden (2004); King (1997).

9. Donovan and Bowler (2004).

10. Homogeneous one-party districts may elect ideologically extreme members. Ansolabehere, Snyder, and Stewart (2001) find competitive races are more likely to produce moderate candidates. Also see Fiorina (1973); Sullivan and Uslaner (1978).

11. Marginal, centrist Democrats (according to DW-NOMINATE scores) include Salazar (Colorado, 3), Higgins (New York, 27), Bean (Illinois, 80), Costa (California, 20), and Barrow (Georgia, 12).

12. Fiorina, Adams, and Pope (2005).

13. Clinton, Jackman, and Rivers (2004).

14. Issacharoff and Nagler (2007).

15. Keith and others (1992).

16. Donovan, Parry, and Bowler (2005); Bowler and others (2004).

17. The Supreme Court has reduced advance registration to a maximum of thirty days. Motor voter registration, early voting, and no-excuse absentee voting have also expanded. Yet turnout has been stagnant. Turnout by voting-age population oscillated below a high point of 55 percent from 1972 to 2004, after being higher in the 1960s.

18. See, for example, Amy (2002).

19. Donovan and Tolbert (2007).

20. See chapter 6, this volume.

21. See chapter 5, this volume.

22. See chapter 11, this volume.

23. See chapter 10, this volume.

24. Abramowitz, Alexander, and Gunning (2006c).

25. Cox and Munger (1989).

26. Blais and Carty (1990).

27. Tolbert and Smith (2004); chapter 7, this volume.

28. Bowler, Donovan, and Brockington (2003).

BRUCE E. CAIN

14

From the Last Generation
of Reform to the Next

Since the 1960s there has been a continuous flurry of electoral reform activity in such diverse areas as campaign finance, term limits, redistricting, election administration, conflict of interest regulation, and direct democracy. Some of these changes have been court instigated: the move to equal population as the almost universal basis for legislative representation and the removal of racially discriminatory electoral and franchise arrangements. Others have come through conventional legislative or direct democracy channels. But what has all this activity brought us? What can we learn from it? What does it imply for the next generation of reforms?

Hits and Misses

The short answer is that the last generation of reforms yielded successes and failures, anticipated results, and unintended consequences. Although the overall record is generally mixed, some areas of electoral reforms fared better on average than others. Drawing on the distinctions made in the first chapter, participation reforms (notably those promoting racial equality in voting but also those making voting and registration easier and more convenient) made more headway than electoral responsiveness reforms (that is, measures making elections more competitive or outcomes more representative) and integrity reforms (efforts to prevent corruption and promote impartial, efficient, and accurate electoral administration). In part, this is because the courts were much more sympathetic to, and willing to act on, the pursuit of voter equality than they were to responsiveness or integrity issues. Relying on the

Fourteenth Amendment and the 1982 amended version of the 1965 Voting Rights Act, the courts struck down laws and electoral institutions that disfranchised and diluted underrepresented minorities. The consequence was a dramatic expansion of minority voting rights and of the number of minority elected officials over the last three decades.

While this book does not focus on voting rights issues, it does consider some reforms that had the effect of increasing minority participation and representation. For instance, by opening up more seats in state legislatures and providing more opportunities for challengers to face other challengers rather than entrenched incumbents, term limits led to significant gains in Latino representation in the states where Latino population growth was most dramatic (chapter 8). Reforms to the redistricting process, particularly after *Thornburg* v. *Gingles* gave blacks and Latinos greater opportunities to elect representatives of their own choice by keeping reasonably compact protected minority neighborhoods wholly contained within a single district rather than being splintered across several seats.[1] While some of these redistricting opportunities were brought about by the threat of Voting Rights Act litigation, Latino and black activists also played important advocacy and informational roles. And as more minority representatives were elected to office, they came to play a greater role in shaping the representation of their communities (chapter 10). Some local jurisdictions switched to semiproportional, multimember district systems (such as cumulative and limited vote) to enhance the electoral prospects of minority groups without the self-conscious actions of an affirmative action gerrymander, but where multimember, at-large systems worked against racial and ethnic minorities, they have usually been abandoned for single-member districts (chapter 9).

On the face of it, attempts to make voting more convenient (such as same-day registration) should also help disadvantaged racial and ethnic voters, who tend to participate at lower rates than well-educated, home-owning, and wealthier individuals. However, chapters 4, 5, and 6 remind us that merely making voting more convenient does not necessarily expand the universe of voters or increase diversity. Convenience voting is less important to participation than having competitive elections in which the outcome is in doubt and in which all voters, including racial and ethnic minorities, feel they have something at stake.

Compared to the achievement of greater racial and ethnic fairness, there has been less success in defining and achieving partisan fairness in redistricting (chapter 10). The Supreme Court failed yet again to find a manageable standard for determining partisan unfairness in the *Vieth* v. *Jubelirer* and

League of Latino American Citizens v. *Perry* cases, leaving political parties to fend for themselves in the political rough and tumble that comes with dividing up seat shares.[2] Attempts to move away from America's historical reliance on a single-member, simple plurality, two-party political system have encountered resistance from voters, elected officials, and the courts. Signature requirements and antifusion laws passed by state legislatures and condoned by the courts have made it harder for minor parties to stay on the ballot (chapter 11), further cementing what some call the party duopoly problem (chapter 13).[3] Critics of the current system say that the two major parties do not represent all the ideological dimensions and continuum extremes very well. But this structural unfairness is not widely seen by the public as a problem, and arguments for more European-style systems have made no headway so far. Indeed, the strong negative reaction to Lani Guinier's mild recommendation to consider alternative vote systems has put a damper on making such suggestions in many reform circles, especially in the civil rights community.[4]

In the areas of responsiveness and integrity, the courts have been far less helpful, and reform successes, such as they are, have more often come through direct democracy measures or even traditional legislative action (such as the passage of the Help America Vote Act by Congress in 2000). Where the equal protection clause has often facilitated the expansion of voting reforms, the First Amendment has more often struck down or seriously restricted proposed new reforms. To take the most obvious example, the First Amendment rights of association and speech have circumscribed legislative attempts to control the amount of money contributed to and spent on political campaigns, essentially gutting the comprehensive federal reforms of the 1970s, leaving only disclosure, contribution limits, and voluntary public financing in place. When the contribution limits became too restrictive, the parties creatively switched to a soft money strategy (that is, unlimited donations to the parties that came to be used for negative candidate advertising), leading ultimately to yet another congressional fix, the 2002 McCain-Feingold bill. But with no ability to cap total funding, independent spending, or personal expenditures (because equalizing speech is not a compelling state purpose), the Supreme Court essentially created huge loopholes for campaign money to pour through that no constitutionally valid reform can plug. Public financing schemes can only be voluntary, and the consequence is that those who opt in are often not involved in serious competitive races. The situation is particularly bad in the case of presidential funding. Most serious candidates in the 2008 primary races chose not to handicap themselves by accepting the restrictions that come with accepting public money.

Even when the courts have not gutted the proposals, there have been some difficult problems associated with integrity or corruption reforms. In part the highly decentralized structure of the U.S. government is the culprit. For instance, since the 2000 presidential elections it has been apparent that voting machines and ballot administration sometimes have failed to produce accurate results in very important contests. When elections are not competitive, which is the normal state of affairs, this democratic sloppiness goes unnoticed. But with a closely divided Congress and party identification levels near parity, even minor error margins are important. Congress passed HAVA in the wake of the 2000 presidential election controversy, encouraging numerous states to discard their punch-card machines and to improve their administrative procedures. But preparing volunteer poll workers to do a politically sensitive task under much pressure and scrutiny (see chapter 3) and preserving a sense of public confidence in the electoral process (see chapter 2) have proved to be much more difficult than people anticipated. Because the skills of voters, the quality of poll workers, and the resources available to local election officials vary socioeconomically, the transition to new machines has not been successful everywhere. Suspicions about the veracity of the outcomes remain high in certain quarters. The Supreme Court's reluctance to apply the equal protection doctrine beyond *Bush* v. *Gore* has removed any sense of legal compulsion to provide a uniform national system, and the inertial forces in state and local governments, barring a major scandal, are too strong to expect rapid change without external compulsion.[5] Even if the perceptions of vote administration problems are greater than the reality, they diminish confidence in the system nonetheless and, hence, need to be addressed in some way in the future.

Another aspect of system integrity growing in importance is conflict of interest law. There has been a great proliferation of conflict of interest regulations at all level and branches of U.S. government, aspiring to limit situations in which people might be tempted to exploit public positions for private gain. While not denying their obvious value in restoring confidence in government, these requirements are not cost free: increased reporting burdens and potential criminal liabilities for failure to comply have raised the potential downside cost of public service and on the margin may have decreased the pool of those willing to serve. Moreover, the more disclosure we have, the more we make constituents aware of violations. Thus even though most experts would agree that the total amount of corrupt activity and self-serving behavior in public office has diminished, the overall perception of corruption has not. With the rising sophistication of political consultants and their use of opposition research, almost every questionable activity can be found out and used in a political campaign or fed to the press. So the efforts of reformers to reduce corrupt activity have been offset to some degree by rising public expectations, fed by the political opposition and the press.

Perhaps the area of most concern recently, and the one that has experienced the least progress to date, is responsiveness. Chapters 13 and 10 best express this sentiment. The concern about having enough competitive seats and elections has grown in the United States during the post–World War II period. Beginning in the 1970s, political commentators and political scientists began to note with alarm the growing resources that incumbents had at their disposal (like the franking privilege, pork spending, name recognition, campaign finance advantages) and the high rates of incumbent reelection. The goal of many reforms was to lessen the incumbency advantage through term limits, campaign finance regulation, or restrictions on staff and resources. While term limits at the state level did increase the rate of officeholder turnover, it did not prevent incumbents from one office from carrying their advantages to running for other offices. Thus officeholders from lower houses had a big advantage running for offices in the upper houses. Campaign finance reform also tried to address the incumbency entrenchment problem through public funding schemes and has had some modest success: challengers are more likely to take the public money, and the pool of candidates has expanded in some states as the result of adopting public financing programs.

Competition has emerged as a serious redistricting concern only recently. Commissions have not had a good record on this score, partly because other criteria take legal precedence but also because social sorting and communities of interest have made it hard to create competitive seats where they do not naturally exist. Perhaps more than the areas of integrity and participation, there is considerable normative dispute as to the benefits of more electoral competition. Minorities fear that their hard-earned voting rights districts might be undermined, and partisans worry that competitiveness will come at the sacrifice of fair representation. Still, at the extreme, a noncompetitive system would be undesirable, and so this discussion is far from finished.

Lessons for the Next Generation of Electoral Reforms

Looking into the future is a hazardous activity for social scientists, fraught with the dangers of relying too much on the past and not anticipating shifts or departures from the normal. But without trying to predict exactly what the future challenges might be, it is possible to summarize some rules of thumb for would-be reformers that follow from what we have discussed in this volume.

The Role of the Courts

The courts played an important role in the last wave of reform, especially in expanding the participation and representation of historically underrepresented groups. However, First Amendment doctrine will likely continue to strike down reforms that impinge on speech and association rights for good government purposes that the courts do not find to be "compelling state purposes." Moreover, while racial and ethnic discrimination continues, conditions on the ground have improved, and there are far fewer instances of overt discrimination. To date, direct democracy has not been the best avenue for measures that improve minority representation. Most likely any future progress in this area will have to come from laws passed by elected officials.

As for integrity and responsiveness reforms, their prospects in the political arenas are good. In most cases, some kind of scandal or coalescing event is needed to spur political efforts at reform. This is especially true of legislative action, but initiatives are not guaranteed to succeed either (see chapter 12). This cycle of scandal and response means that reforms lurch forward unevenly, often lying latent until events make their enactment more pressing. Whereas the courts can proceed in a manner less detached from public opinion, political responses need the nest to be visibly fouled before proposed changes can overcome the strong inertial forces of U.S. state and federal governments.

The Role of Strategy

Reforms have to anticipate strategic behavior. The law of unanticipated consequences is not quite right. Sometimes there are consequences that no one can imagine, but more often than not efforts to circumvent or undo reforms are the predictable, rational calculations of actors responding to the incentives they face. This means that reform proposals should try to anticipate what people will do to get around the constraints that a new reform places on their behavior. There was quite a bit of this kind of thinking in the McCain-Feingold bill that eliminated soft money and attempted to distinguish more clearly between pure issue ads and candidate ads that were disguised as issue ads. The bill sponsors anticipated that the national parties might try to avoid regulation by shipping money to and funding political ads through the state parties. Another example of rational anticipation being built into reforms is the provision in some public financing schemes that releases candidates from fund-raising restrictions if they face wealthy self-financed candidates or opposing candidates that opt out of regulation.

One problem with this kind of rationally anticipated design is that it can lead to very elaborate and sometimes convoluted laws that are complex and possibly interfere with many parts of the system simultaneously. This then invites judicial scrutiny into whether the measure is sufficiently narrowly tailored to the regulatory purpose, a test that often leads to the demise of the law. Still, there is no real alternative to this kind of strategic anticipation if reformers want their laws to be effective.

It is also important to realize that elected officials, consultants, interest groups, and the like are not the only strategic actors in the system. Voters are increasingly strategic both in the choices they make and their participatory behavior. The presidential nomination systems have revealed that voters often dispense with unrealistic choices early and focus on the feasible candidates (those that have a chance to win). This is strategic voting in the classic sense. But voters are also strategic in the sense that they are more likely to invest time and effort when elections matter (see chapter 13). In the classic version of political participation, people vote as a matter of civic duty, irrespective of whether the election is meaningful. In the modern era and a culture of higher cynicism and complacency, citizens are more strategic in their citizenship decisions, responding to cues about relative costs and benefits. Reform measures have to incorporate more modern notions of citizenship if they are going to have any chance of success.

The Role of Venue

Reformers will have to venue shop. Several of the chapters in this book explore the biases of different avenues of reforms. The courts are responsive to reforms that seek to reduce corruption but have less sympathy for reforms that try to increase equity or competition. Initiatives are majoritarian venues that tend to favor populist reforms, striking down the abuses of higher office and the excessive power that some groups have. Elected officials are often resistant to change unless they need reforms in order to stay in power.

Reformers have to be sensitive to the timing of their proposals and shop in the appropriate venues. Minority rights measures (participation) are more likely to succeed in the courts or the legislature. Integrity measures will have more success through direct democracy, or the legislature under duress. Competition and responsiveness may be orphans, but if there is any chance of future adoption it will likely come from direct democracy (see chapters 12 and 7).

The Role of Consensus

Reforms will often have to settle for second best. Given First Amendment constraints and the lack of consensus about reform goals, reforms often come through the political process looking very different from what they were when they started. The hardest place to achieve reform is in the area of regulating direct democracy. The courts regard initiatives as essential First Amendment political exercises and therefore are loathe to accept even modest proposals for limiting campaign contributions or requiring volunteer signature gatherers. And reforming the initiative process often means going through the process itself to get change. Just as elected officials are resistant to reform that makes their lives harder, those who benefit from direct democracy will view changes skeptically. A decade of discussions about improving direct democracy has scaled back expectations about what is feasible.

The key question in evaluating second-best solutions is to ask whether the reform as scaled back will improve things marginally or not. Sometimes when you get half a loaf you really have not advanced your cause at all. Arguably, this has been true of contribution-only campaign finance reforms, causing elected officials to spend more time, not less, on raising political funds. Had the contribution limits been accompanied by mandatory spending limits and bans on personal and independent expenditures, the purposes of contribution limits might have been achieved.

The Role of Political Scientists

Too often reforms are placed before the public without any empirical or scholarly vetting. And too often political scientists prefer to focus their research on literature-based questions rather than the practical questions of the day. Fortunately, as this book shows, this trend is changing, and political scientists are developing a greater interest in—and a body of findings about—the effects of reform measures. Of course, evaluating whether a measure has had a given effect is only part of the reform process. There are also important questions about the goals and purposes of reforms that have to be addressed. But choices informed by facts are more likely to be successful, and that is a cause we hope we have advanced in this volume.

Notes

1. *Thornburg* v. *Gingles* 478 U.S. 30 (1982).
2. *Vieth* v. *Jubelirer* 541 U.S. 267 (2004); *League of Latino American Citizens* v. *Perry* 548 U.S. (2006).
3. Issacharoff and Pildes (1998).
4. Guinier (1994).
5. *Bush* v. *Gore* 531 U.S. 98 (2000).

References

Abramowitz, Alan I. 1983. "Partisan Redistricting and the 1982 Congressional Elections." *Journal of Politics* 45: 767–70.

Abramowitz, Alan, Brad Alexander, and Matthew Gunning. 2006a. "Don't Blame Redistricting for Uncompetitive Elections." *PS: Political Science and Politics* 39: 87–90.

———. 2006b. "Drawing the Line on District Competition: A Rejoinder." *PS: Political Science and Politics* 39: 95–98.

———. 2006c. "Incumbency, Redistricting, and the Decline of Competition in U.S. House Elections." *Journal of Politics* 68: 75–88.

Abramson, Paul R. 1983. *Political Attitudes in America*. San Francisco: Freeman.

Abramson, Paul, and John Aldrich. 1982. "The Decline of Electoral Participation in America." *American Political Science Review* 76: 502–21.

Adams, Greg D. 1996. "Legislative Effects of Single-Member vs. Multimember Districts." *American Journal of Political Science* 40: 129–44.

Aldrich, John H. 1993. "Rational Choice and Turnout." *American Journal of Political Science* 37: 246–78.

Allebaugh, Dalene, and Neil Pinney. 2003. "The Real Costs of Term Limits: Comparative Study of Competition and Electoral Costs." In *The Test of Time: Coping with Legislative Term Limits,* edited by Rick Farmer, John David Rausch Jr., and John C. Green. Lanham, Md.: Lexington Books.

Allen, Neal, and Brian J. Brox. 2005. "The Roots of Third Party Voting: The 2000 Nader Campaign in Historical Perspective." *Party Politics* 5: 623–37.

Alt, James, and David Lassen. 2003. "The Political Economy of Institutions and Corruption in American States." *Journal of Theoretical Politics* 15: 341–65.

Alvarez, Michael, Delia Bailey, and Jonathan Katz. 2007. "The Effect of Voter Identification Laws on Turnout." Paper prepared for the annual meeting of the Society of Political Methodology, Penn State University, July.

Alvarez, R. Michael, and L. Bedolla. 2004. "The Revolution against Affirmative Action in California: Racism, Economics, and Proposition 209." *State Politics and Policy Quarterly* 4: 1–17.

Alvarez, R. Michael, and Tara Butterfield. 2000. "The Resurgence of Nativism in California? The Case of Proposition 187 and Illegal Immigration." *Social Science Quarterly* 81: 167–79.

Alvarez, R. Michael, and Thad Hall. 2003. "Whose Absentee Ballots Are Counted?" Working paper. Washington: Century Foundation.

———. 2004. *Point, Click, and Vote: The Future of Internet Voting.* Brookings.

———. 2006. "Controlling Democracy: The Principal-Agent Problems in Election Administration." *Policy Studies Journal* 34: 491–510.

Alvarez, R. Michael, Thad E. Hall, and Morgan Llewellyn. 2006. "Are Americans Confident Their Ballots Are Counted?" Working Paper 49. Caltech/MIT Voting Technology Project. California Institute of Technology.

Alvarez, R. Michael, and Jonathan Nagler. 2001. "The Likely Consequences of Internet Voting for Political Representation." *Loyola of Los Angeles Law Review* 34: 1115–52.

American Association for Public Opinion Research. 2000. "Standard Definitions: Final Disposition for Case Codes and Outcome Rates for Surveys." Ann Arbor, Mich.

Amy, Douglas. 2002. *Real Choices/New Voices: How Proportional Representation Elections Could Revitalize American Politics.* Columbia University Press.

Ansolabehere, Steven, James M. Snyder, and Charles Stewart III. 2001. "Candidate Positioning in U.S. House Races." *American Journal of Political Science* 45: 136–59.

Apollonio, D. E., and Raymond J. LaRaja. 2006. "Term Limits, Campaign Contributions, and the Distribution of Power in State Legislatures." *Legislative Studies Quarterly* 31: 259–81.

Arceneaux, Kevin. 2001. "The 'Gender Gap' in State Legislative Representation: New Data to Tackle an Old Question." *Political Research Quarterly* 54: 143–60.

Argersinger, Peter H. 1980. "'A Place on the Ballot': Fusion Politics and Antifusion Laws." *American Historical Review* 85: 287–306.

Argyris, Chris, and others. 1994. "The Future of Workplace Learning and Performance." *Training & Development,* May: S41.

Arrow, Kenneth. 1951. *Social Choice and Individual Values.* New York: John Wiley.

Atkeson, Lonna Rae. 2003. "Not All Cues Are Created Equal: The Conditional Impact of Female Candidates on Political Engagement." *Journal of Politics* 65: 1040–61.

Atkeson, Lonna, and Kyle Saunders. 2007. "Election Administration and Voter Confidence: A Local Matter." Manuscript. University of New Mexico.

Atkeson, Lonna Rae, and others. 2007. "Using Mixed Mode Surveys (Internet and Mail) to Examine General Election Voters." Paper prepared for the meeting of the American Association for Public Opinion Research. Anaheim, Calif., May 17–20.

Barabas, Jason, and Jennifer Jerit. 2004. "Redistricting Principles and Racial Representation." *State Politics and Policy Quarterly* 4: 415–35.

Barber, Kathleen. 1995. *Proportional Representation and Election Reform in Ohio.* Ohio State University Press.

————. 2000. *A Right to Representation: Proportional Election Systems for the Twenty-First Century.* Ohio State University Press.

Barone, Michael, ed. 1984, 2002. *The Almanac of American Politics.* Washington: National Journal.

Barone, Michael, and Richard Cohen, eds. 2004, 2006. *The Almanac of American Politics.* Washington: National Journal.

Barone, Michael, and Grant Ujifusa, eds. 1986, 1988, 1990, 1992, 1994, 1996, 1998, 2000. *The Almanac of American Politics.* Washington: National Journal.

Barone, Michael, Grant Ujifusa, and Shepard Sherbell, eds. 1982. *The Almanac of American Politics.* Washington: National Journal.

Bartels, Larry. 2002. "Partisanship and Voting Behavior: 1952–1996." *American Journal of Political Science* 44: 35–50.

Beck, Neal, and Jonathan Katz. 1995. "What to Do (and Not to Do) with Time-Series Cross-Section Data in Comparative Politics." *American Political Science Review* 89: 634–47.

Benjamin, Gerald, and Michael Malbin. 1992. *Limiting Legislative Terms.* Washington: CQ Press.

Benz, Matthias, and Alois Stutzer. 2004. "Are Voters Better Informed When They Have a Larger Say in Politics?" *Public Choice* 119: 21–59.

Berinsky, Adam. 2004. "The Perverse Consequences of Electoral Reform in America." Working paper. Department of Political Science, Massachusetts Institute of Technology.

————. 2005. "The Perverse Consequences of Electoral Reform in the United States." *American Politics Research* 33: 471–91.

Berinksy, Adam, Nancy Burns, and Michael Traugott. 2001. "Who Votes by Mail? A Dynamic Model of the Individual-Level Consequences of Voting-by-Mail Systems." *Public Opinion Quarterly* 65: 178–97.

Berman, David R. 2007. "Legislative Climate." In *Institutional Change in American Politics: The Case of Term Limits,* edited by Karl T. Kurtz, Bruce Cain, and Richard G. Niemi. University of Michigan Press.

Berman, Mitchell. 2005. "Managing Gerrymandering." *Texas Law Review* 83: 781–854.

Bernstein, Robert A., and Anita Chadha. 2003. "The Effects of Term Limits on Representation: Why So Few Women?" In *The Test of Time: Coping with Legislative Term Limits,* edited by Rick Farmer, John David Rausch Jr., and John C. Green. Lanham, Md.: Lexington Books.

Bimber, Bruce. 2003. *The Internet and American Democracy.* Cambridge University Press.

Black, Earl, and Merle Black. 2003. *The Rise of Southern Republicans.* Harvard University Press.

Blais, André, and Kenneth Carty. 1990. "Does Proportional Representation Foster Voter Turnout?" *European Journal of Political Research* 18: 167–81.

Boehmke, Frederick J. 2005. *The Indirect Effect of Direct Democracy: How Institutions Shape Interest Group Systems.* Ohio State University Press.

Bowler, Shaun, David Brockington, and Todd Donovan. 2001. "Election Systems and Voter Turnout: Experiments in the U.S." *Journal of Politics* 63: 902–15.

Bowler, Shaun, and Todd Donovan. 1998. *Demanding Choices: Opinion, Voting, and Direct Democracy.* University of Michigan Press.

———. 2002. "Democracy, Institutions, and Attitudes about Citizen Influence on Government." *British Journal of Political Science* 32: 371–90.

———. 2004. "Measuring the Effects of Direct Democracy on State Policy." *State Politics and Policy Quarterly* 4: 345–63.

———. 2006. "Barriers to Participation for Whom? Regulations on Voting and Uncompetitive Elections." Paper prepared for conference, Mobilizing Democracy, Russell Sage Foundation. New York, January.

———. 2007. "Reasoning about Institutional Change: Winners, Losers, and Support for Electoral Reforms." *British Journal of Political Science* 37: 455–76.

Bowler, Shaun, Todd Donovan, and David Brockington. 2003. *Electoral Reform and Minority Representation: Local Experiments with Alternative Elections.* Ohio State University Press.

Bowler, Shaun, Todd Donovan, and Caroline Tolbert, eds. 1998. *Citizens as Legislators: Direct Democracy in the United States.* Ohio State University Press.

Bowler, Shaun, and others. 2004. "Independent's Day: Critical Citizens among the U.S. Voting Public." Paper prepared for the annual meeting of the Southern Political Science Association. New Orleans.

Bowser, Jennie Drage, and Gary Moncrief. 2007. "Term Limits in State Legislatures." In *Institutional Change in American Politics: The Case of Term Limits,* edited by Karl T. Kurtz, Bruce Cain, and Richard G. Niemi. University of Michigan Press.

Bowser, Jennifer Drage, and others. 2003. "The Impact of Term Limits on Legislative Leadership." In *The Test of Time: Coping with Legislative Term Limits,* edited by Rick Farmer, John David Rausch Jr., and John C. Green. Lanham, Md.: Lexington Books.

Boylan, Richard, and Cheryl Long. 2003. "Measuring Public Corruption in the American States: A Survey of State House Reporters." *State Politics and Policy Quarterly* 3: 420–38.

Brace, Kimball, and others. 1988. "Minority Voting Equality: The 65 Percent Rule in Theory and Practice." *Law and Policy* 10: 43–62.

Brambor, Thomas, William R. Clark, and Matt Golder. 2006. "Understanding Interaction Models: Improving Empirical Analysis." *Political Analysis* 14: 63–82.

Bratton, Kathleen A. 2002. "The Effect of Legislative Diversity on Agenda Setting: Evidence from Six State Legislatures." *American Politics Research* 30: 115–42.

Bratton, Kathleen A., and Kerry L. Haynie. 1999. "Agenda Setting and Legislative Success in State Legislatures: The Effects of Gender and Race." *Journal of Politics* 61: 658–79.

Brewer, Paul R., and Lee Sigelman. 2002. "Trust in Government: Personal Ties that Bind?" *Social Science Quarterly* 83: 624–31.

Brians, C., and Bernard Grofman. 2001. "Election Day Registration's Effect on U.S. Voter Turnout." *Social Science Quarterly* 82: 170–83.

Broder, David. 2000. *Democracy Derailed: Initiative Campaigns and the Power of Money.* Orlando: Harcourt Brace.

Brown, Mark R. 1997. "Popularizing Ballot Access: The Front Door to Election Reform." *Ohio State Law Journal* 58: 1281–323.

Brunell, Thomas. 2006. "How Drawing Uncompetitive Districts Eliminates Gerrymanders, Enhances Representation, and Improves Attitudes Toward Congress." *PS: Political Science and Politics* 39: 77–86.

Buchler, Justin. 2007. "The Statistical Properties of Competitive Districts: What the Central Limit Theorem Can Teach Us about Election Reform." *PS: Political Science and Politics* 40: 333–37.

Bullock, Charles S., and Ronald Keith Gaddie. 1993. "Changing from Multimember to Single-Member Districts: Partisan, Racial, and Gender Consequences." *State and Local Government Review* 25: 155–63.

Bullock, Charles, III, M. V. Hood III, and Richard Clark. 2005. "Punch Cards, Jim Crow, and Al Gore: Explaining Voter Trust in the Electoral System in Georgia, 2000." *State Politics and Policy Quarterly* 5: 283–94.

Bullock, Charles III, and Susan MacManus. 1991. "Municipal Electoral Structure and the Election of Councilwomen." *Journal of Politics* 53: 75–89.

Burden, Barry C. 2003. "Minor Parties in the 2000 Presidential Election." In *Models of Voting in Presidential Elections: The 2000 U.S. Election,* edited by Herbert F. Weisberg and Clyde Wilcox. Stanford University Press.

———. 2004. "Candidate Positioning in U.S. Congressional Elections." *British Journal of Political Science* 34: 211–27.

———. 2005a. "Institutions and Policy Representation in the States." *State Politics and Policy Quarterly* 5: 373–93.

———. 2005b. "Minor Parties and Strategic Voting in Recent U.S. Presidential Elections." *Electoral Studies* 24: 603–18.

Burke, Edmund. 1774. *The Works of the Right Honourable Edmund Burke.* London: Henry G. Bohn.

Butler, David, and Bruce Cain E. 1992. *Congressional Redistricting: Comparative and Theoretical Perspectives.* New York: Macmillan.

Cain, Bruce E. 1984. *The Reapportionment Puzzle.* University of California Press.

———. 1985. "Assessing the Partisan Effects of Redistricting." *American Political Science Review* 79: 320–33.

———. 1992. "Voting Rights and Democratic Theory: Toward a Color-Blind Society?" In *Controversies in Minority Voting,* edited by Bernard Grofman and C. Davidson. Brookings.

Cain, Bruce E., John Hanley, and Thad Kousser. 2006. "Term Limits: A Recipe for More Competition?" In *The Marketplace of Democracy: Electoral Competition and American Politics,* edited by Michael P. McDonald and John Sample. Brookings and Cato Institute.

Cain, Bruce E., and Thad Kousser. 2004. *Adapting to Term Limits: Recent Experiences and New Directions.* San Francisco: Public Policy Institute of California.

Cain, Bruce, Karin MacDonald, and Iris Hui. 2006. "Competition and Redistricting in California: Lesson for Reform." Berkeley, Calif.: Institute for Governmental Studies.

Cain, Bruce E., Karin MacDonald, and Michael P. McDonald. 2005. "From Equality to Fairness: The Path of Political Reform since *Baker v Carr.*" In *Party Lines: Competition, Partisanship, and Congressional Redistricting,* edited by Bruce Cain and Thomas Mann. Brookings.

Cain, Bruce E., and Gerald Wright. 2007. "Committees." In *Institutional Change in American Politics: The Case of Term Limits,* edited by Karl T. Kurtz, Bruce Cain, and Richard G. Niemi. University of Michigan Press.

Calabrese, Stephen. 2000. "Multimember Districts Congressional Elections." *Legislative Studies Quarterly* 25: 611–43.

Cameron, Charles, David Epstein, and Sharyn O'Halloran. 1996. "Do Majority-Minority Districts Maximize Substantive Black Representation in Congress?" *American Political Science Review* 90: 794–812.

Campagna, Janet, and Bernard Grofman. 1990. "Party Control and Partisan Bias in 1980s Congressional Redistricting." *Journal of Politics* 52: 1242–57.

Campbell, Angus. 1966. "Surge and Decline: A Study of Electoral Change." In *Elections and the Political Order,* edited by A. Campbell and others. New York: Wiley.

Campbell, Angus, and others. 1960. *The American Voter.* University of Chicago Press.

Caress, Stanley M., and others. 2003. "Effect of Term Limits on the Election of Minority State Legislators." *State and Local Government Review* 35: 183–95.

Carey, John M., Richard G. Niemi, and Lynda W. Powell. 2000. *Term Limits in the State Legislatures.* University of Michigan Press.

Carey, John M., and others. 2006. "The Effects of Term Limits on State Legislatures: A New Survey of the 50 States." *Legislative Studies Quarterly* 31: 105–34.

Carl Vinson Institute of Government. 2003. Peach State Poll, "Georgians Express Confidence in New Electronic Voting System." University of Georgia, February 27.

Carroll, Susan J. 1994. *Women as Candidates in American Politic.* 2d ed. Indiana University Press.

Center for Political Studies. 2004, 2007. *American National Election Study.* Ann Arbor.

Chavez, Lydia. 1998. *The Color Bind: California's Battle to End Affirmative Action.* University of California Press.

Citrin, Jack. 1996. "Who's the Boss? Direct Democracy and Popular Control." In *Broken Contract: Changing Relationships between Americans and Their Government,* edited by Stephen Craig. Boulder, Colo.: Westview.

Clinton, Joshua D., Simon Jackman, and Doug Rivers. 2004. "The Most Liberal Senator? Analyzing and Interpreting Congressional Roll Calls." *PS: Political Science and Politics* 37: 805–11.

Clucas, Richard A. 2003. "California: The New Amateur Politics." In *The Test of Time: Coping with Legislative Term Limits,* edited by Rick Farmer, John David Rausch Jr., and John C. Green. Lanham, Md.: Lexington Books.

Collett, Christian, and Martin P. Wattenberg. 1999. "Strategically Unambitious: Minor Party and Independent Candidates in the 1996 Congressional Elections." In *The State of the Parties,* edited by John C. Green and Daniel M. Shea. 3d ed. Lanham, Md.: Rowman and Littlefield.

Collins, Richard, and Dale Oesterle. 2005. "Structuring the Ballot Initiative: Procedures that Do and Don't Work." *University of Colorado Law Review* 66: 47–128.

Cook, Timothy E., and Paul Gronke. 2005. "The Skeptical American: Revisiting the Meanings of Trust in Government and Confidence in Institutions." *Journal of Politics* 67: 784–803.

Cooper, Christopher A., and Lilliard E. Richardson Jr. 2006. "Institutions and Representational Roles in American State Legislatures." *State Politics and Policy Quarterly* 6: 174–94.

Council of State Governments. 2006. *The Book of the States.* Lexington, Ky.

Cox, Adam B. 2004. "Partisan Fairness and Redistricting Politics." *New York University Law Review* 70: 751–802.

———. 2006. "Designing Redistricting Institutions." *Election Law Journal* 5: 412–24.

Cox, Gary W. 1997. *Making Votes Count.* Cambridge University Press.

———. 1999. "Electoral Rules and the Calculus of Mobilization." *Legislative Studies Quarterly* 24: 387–419.

Cox, Gary W., and Jonathan N. Katz. 2002. *Elbridge Gerry's Salamander: The Electoral Consequences of the Reapportionment Revolution.* Cambridge University Press.

Cox, Gary, and Michael Munger. 1989. "Closeness, Expenditure, Turnout: The 1982 U.S. House Elections." *American Political Science Review* 83: 217–32.

Crisp, Brian, and Scott Desposato. 2004. "Constituency Building in Multimember Districts: Collusion or Conflict?" *Journal of Politics* 66: 136–56.

Dalton, Russell. 1999. "Political Support in Advanced Industrial Democracies." In *Critical Citizens: Global Support for Democratic Government,* edited by Pippa Norris. Oxford University Press.

Darcy, R., Charles D. Hadley, and Jason F. Kirksey. 1993. "Election Systems and the Representation of Black Women in American State Legislatures." *Women and Politics* 13: 73–89.

Darcy, Robert, Susan Welch, and Janet Clark. 1985. "Women Candidates in Single- and Multimember Districts." *Social Science Quarterly* 66: 945–53.

Delli Carpini, Michael X., and Scott Keeter. 1993. "Measuring Political Knowledge: Putting First Things First." *American Journal of Political Science* 37: 1179–206.

———. 1996. *What Americans Know about Politics and Why It Matters.* Yale University Press.

Dillman, Don A. 2000. *Mail and Internet Surveys: The Tailored Design Method.* New York: John Wiley and Sons.

Disch, Lisa J. 2002. *The Tyranny of the Two-Party System.* Columbia University Press.

Donovan, Todd, and Shaun Bowler. 2004. *Reforming the Republic: Democratic Institutions for the New America.* Upper Saddle River, N.J.: Pearson Prentice Hall.

Donovan, Todd, Janine Parry, and Shaun Bowler. 2005. "O Other, Where Art Thou? Support for Multi-Party Politics in the United States." *Social Science Quarterly* 86: 147–59.

Donovan, Todd, and Daniel Smith. 2008. "Identifying and Preventing Signature Fraud on Ballot Measure Petitions." In *The Art and Science of Studying Election Fraud: Detection, Prevention, and Consequences,* edited by Michael Alvarez, Thad E. Hall, and Susan D. Hyde. Brookings.

Donovan, Todd, and Caroline Tolbert. 2007. "State Electoral Context and Voter Participation: Who Is Mobilized by What?" Paper prepared for the Seventh Annual Conference on State Politics and Policy, Austin, February 23–24.

Donovan, Todd, Jim Wenzel, and Shaun Bowler. 2001. "Direct Democracy and Gay Rights Initiatives after Romer." In *The Politics of Gay Rights,* edited by Craig Rimmerman, Kenneth Wald, and Clyde Wilcox. University of Chicago Press.

Dow, Jay K. 1998. "A Spatial Analysis of Candidates in Dual-Member Elections: The 1989 Chilean Senatorial Elections." *Public Choice* 97: 119–42.

Downs, Anthony. 1957. *An Economic Theory of Democracy.* New York: Harper and Row.

Dubin, Jeffrey A., and Gretchen A. Kaslow. 1996. "Comparing Absentee and Precinct Voters: A View over Time." *Political Behavior* 18: 369–92.

Duverger, Maurice. 1963. *Political Parties: Their Organization and Activity in the Modern State.* Translated by B. North and R. North. New York: Wiley.

Dyck, Joshua, and Mark Baldassare. 2006. "The Limits of Support for Direct Democracy: Process-Oriented Preferences and the 2005 California Special Election." Paper prepared for the annual meeting of the American Political Science Association. Philadelphia.

Dyck, Joshua J., and James G. Gimpel. 2005. "Distance, Turnout, and the Convenience of Voting." *Social Science Quarterly* 86: 531–48.

Engstrom, Richard, and Michael McDonald. 1981. "The Election of Blacks to City Councils." *American Political Science Review* 75: 344–55.

———. 1986. "The Effect of At-Large versus District Elections on Racial Representation in U.S. Municipalities." In *Electoral Laws and Their Political Consequences,* edited by Bernard Grofman and Aaron Lijphart. New York: Agathon.

Erickson, Stephen C. 1993. "A Bulwark against Faction: James Madison's Case for Term Limits." *Policy Review* 63: 76–78.

Fiorina, Morris. 1973. "Electoral Margin, Constituency Influence, and Policy Moderation: A Critical Assessment." *American Politics Research* 1: 479–98.

———. 1980. "The Decline of Collective Responsibility in American Politics." *Daedalus* 109: 25–45.

Fiorina, Morris, Samuel J. Adams, and Jeremy C. Pope. 2005. *Culture War? The Myth of a Polarized America.* New York: Pearson Longman.

Fitzgerald, Mary. 2005. "Greater Convenience but Not Greater Turnout: The Impact of Alternative Voting Methods on Electoral Participation in the United States." *American Political Research* 33: 842–67.

Freedman, P., M. Franz, and K. Goldstein. 2004. "Campaign Advertising and Democratic Citizenship." *American Journal of Political Science* 48: 723–41.

Gelman, Andrew, and Gary King. 1994. "Enhancing Democracy through Legislative Redistricting." *American Political Science Review* 88: 541–59.

Gerber, Elizabeth. 1999. *The Populist Paradox: Interest Group Influence and the Promise of Direct Legislation.* Princeton University Press.

Gerber, Elisabeth, Rebecca A. Morton, and Thomas A. Rietz. 1998. "Minority Representation in Multimember Districts." *American Political Science Review* 92: 127–44.

Giammo, Joseph D., and Brian J. Brox. 2007. "Reducing the Costs of Participation: Are States Getting a Return on Early Voting?" Paper prepared for the Seventh Annual Conference on State Politics and Policy. Austin, February 23–24.

Glazer, Amihai, Bernard Grofman, and Marc Robbins. 1987. "Partisan and Incumbency Effects of 1970s Congressional Redistricting." *American Journal of Political Science* 31: 680–707.

Glazer, Amihai, and Martin P. Wattenberg. 1996. "How Will Term Limits Affect Legislative Work?" In *Legislative Term Limits: Public Choice Perspectives,* edited by Bernard Grofman. Boston: Kluwer.

Gomez, Brad, Thomas Hansford, and George Krause. 2007. "The Republicans Should Pray for Rain: Weather, Turnout, and Voting in U.S. Presidential Elections." *Journal of Politics* 69: 649–63.

Gordon, Stacy B., and Cynthia L. Unmack. 2003. "The Effect of Term Limits on Corporate PAC Allocation Patterns: The More Things Change. . . ." *State and Local Government Review* 35: 26–37.

Gronke, Paul. 2004. "Early Voting Reforms and American Elections." Paper prepared for the annual meeting of the American Political Science Association.

Gronke, Paul, and Peter A. Miller. 2007. "Voting by Mail and Turnout: A Replication and Extension." Paper prepared for the annual meeting of the American Political Science Association.

Grose, Christian R. 2005. "Disentangling Constituency and Legislator Effects in Legislative Representation: Black Legislators or Black Districts?" *Social Science Quarterly* 86: 427–43.

Groseclose, Tim, Steven Levitt, and James M. Snyder. 1999. "Comparing Interest Group Scores across Time and Chambers: Adjusted ADA Scores for the U.S. Congress." *American Political Science Review* 93: 33–50.

Guinier, Lani. 1994. *Tyranny of the Majority: Fundamental Fairness in Representative Democracy.* New York: Free Press.

Haider-Markel, Donald. 2001. "Policy Diffusion as a Geographical Expansion of the Scope of Political Conflict: Same-Sex Marriage Bans in the 1990s." *State Politics and Policy Quarterly* 1: 6–26.

Hajnal, Zoltan, Elisabeth Gerber, and Hugh Louch. 2002. "Minorities and Direct Legislation: Evidence from California Ballot Proposition Elections." *Journal of Politics* 64: 154–77.

Hall, Thad E., Quin Monson, and Kelly Patterson. 2006. "The Human Dimension of Elections: How Poll Workers Shape Public Confidence in Elections." Working paper. Institute of Public and International Affairs, University of Utah.

Hanmer, Michael J., and Michael W. Traugott. 2004. "The Impact of Voting by Mail on Voter Behavior." *American Politics Research* 32: 375–405.

Hansen, John Mark. 2001. "To Assure Pride and Confidence in the Electoral Process." Report prepared for the National Commission on Federal Election Reform. Charlottesville, Va.: Miller Center of Public Affairs, University of Virginia.

Hero, Rodney. 1998. *Faces of Inequality: Social Diversity in American Politics.* Oxford University Press.

Hero, Rodney, and Caroline Tolbert. 2004. "Minority Voices and Citizen Attitudes about Government Responsiveness in the American States: Do Social and Institutional Context Matter?" *British Journal of Political Science* 34: 109–21.

Herrnson, Paul S. 2004. *Congressional Elections: Campaigning at Home and in Washington.* Washington: CQ Press.

———. 2006. "Minor-Party Candidates in Congressional Elections." In *The Marketplace of Democracy: Electoral Competition and American Politics,* edited by Michael P. McDonald and John Samples. Brookings.

Hetherington, Marc J., Bruce A. Larson, and Suzanne Globetti. 2003. "The Redistricting Cycle and Strategic Candidate Decisions in U.S. House Races." *Journal of Politics* 65: 1221–35.

Highton, Benjamin. 1997. "Easy Registration and Voter Turnout." *Journal of Politics* 59: 565–75.

———. 2004. "Voter Registration and Turnout in the United States." *Perspectives on Politics* 2: 507–15.

Highton, Benjamin, and Raymond Wolfinger. 1998. "Estimating the Effects of the National Voter Registration Act of 1993." *Political Behavior* 20: 79–104.

Hill, David B. 1981. "Attitude Generalization and the Measurement of Trust in American Leadership." *Political Behavior* 3: 257–70.

Hill, Kim, and Jan Leighley. 1999. "Racial Diversity, Voter Turnout, and Mobilizing Institutions in the United States." *American Politics Quarterly* 27: 275–95.

Hill, Steven, and Hendrick Hertzberg. 2006. *10 Steps to Repair American Democracy: An Owners Manual for Concerned Citizens.* Sausalito, Calif.: PoliPointPress.

Hirano, Shigeo, and James M. Snyder Jr. 2007. "The Decline of Third Party Voting in the United States." *Journal of Politics* 69: 1–16.

Hogan, Robert E. 2004. "Challenger Emergence, Incumbent Success, and Electoral Accountability in State Legislative Elections." *Journal of Politics* 66: 1283–303.

Issacharoff, Samuel, and Pamela Karlan. 2004. "Where to Draw the Line? Judicial Review of Political Gerrymanders." *Pennsylvania Law Review* 153: 541–78.

Issacharoff, Samuel, and Jonathan Nagler. 2007. "Protected from Politics: Diminishing Margins of Electoral Competition in U.S. Congressional Elections." *Ohio State Law Journal* 68: 1121–37.

Issacharoff, Samuel, and Richard H. Pildes. 1998. "Politics as Markets: Partisan Lock-ups of the Democratic Process." *Stanford Law Review* 50: 643.

Jackson, Robert. 1997. "The Mobilization of U.S. State Electorates in the 1998 and 1990 Elections." *Journal of Politics* 59: 520–37.

Jacobson, Gary. 2005. "The Structural Basis of Republican Success." In *The 2004 Election,* edited by M. Nelson. Washington: CQ Press.

———. 2007. *A Divider, Not a Uniter: George W. Bush and the American People.* New York: Pearson-Longman.

Jennings, M. Kent, and Vicki Zeitner. 2003. "Internet Use and Civic Engagement." *Public Opinion Quarterly* 67: 311–34.

Jewell, Malcolm E. 1982a. *Representation in State Legislatures.* University Press of Kentucky.

———. 1982b. "The Consequences of Single and Multimember Districting." In *Representation and Redistricting Issues,* edited by Bernard Grofman and others. Lexington, Mass.: Lexington Books.

Johnson, Douglas, and others. 2005. "Restoring the Competitive Edge." Rose Institute of State and Local Government, Claremont McKenna College.

Karnig, Albert, and Susan Welch. 1982. "Electoral Structure and Black Representation on City Councils." *Social Science Quarterly* 63: 99–114.

Karp, Jeffrey. 1998. "The Influence of Elite Endorsements in Initiative Campaigns." In *Citizens as Legislators: Direct Democracy in the United States,* edited by Shaun Bowler, Todd Donovan, and Caroline Tolbert. Ohio State University Press.

Karp, Jeffrey A., and Susan A. Banducci. 2000. "Going Postal: How All-Mail Elections Influence Turnout." *Political Behavior* 22: 223–39.

———. 2001. "Absentee Voting, Mobilization, and Participation." *American Politics Research* 29: 183–95.

Keith, Bruce, and others. 1992. *The Myth of the Independent Voter.* University of California Press.

Kesler, Charles R. 1990. "Bad Housekeeping: The Case against Congressional Term Limitations." *Policy Review* 53: 20–25.

Key, V. O. 1949. *Southern Politics in State and Nation.* New York: Knopf.

Kimball, David. 2003. "Election Reform Two Years after Florida." Paper prepared for Symposium on Midterm Elections, American Political Science Association.

King, David. 1997. "The Polarization of American Parties and Mistrust of Government." In *Why People Don't Trust Government,* edited by J. Nye Jr., P. Zelikow, and D. King. Harvard University Press.

King, Gary. 1989. "Representation through Legislative Redistricting: A Stochastic Model." *American Journal of Political Science* 33: 787–824.

King, Gary, and Bernard Grofman. 2007. "The Future of Partisan Symmetry as a Judicial Test for Partisan Gerrymandering after *LULAC* v. *Perry.*" *Election Law Journal,* 6: 2–35.

King, James D. 2000. "Changes in Professionalism in U.S. State Legislatures." *Legislative Studies Quarterly* 25: 327–43.

————. 2002. "Single-Member Districts and the Representation of Women in American State Legislatures: The Effects of Electoral System Change." *State Politics and Policy Quarterly* 2: 161–75.

Klain, Maurice. 1955. "A New Look at the Constituencies: The Need for a Recount and a Reappraisal." *American Political Science Review* 49: 1105–19.

Knack, S., and J. White. 2000. "Election-Day Registration and Turnout Inequality." *Political Behavior* 22: 29–44.

Kohut, Andrew. 2006. "Public Concern about the Vote Count and Uncertainty about Electronic Voting Machines." November 6. Washington: Pew Research Center for the People and the Press.

Kousser, Thad. 2005. *Term Limits and the Dismantling of State Legislative Professionalism.* Cambridge University Press.

————. 2006. "The Limited Impact of Term Limits: Contingent Patterns in the Complexity and Breadth of Laws." *State Politics and Policy Quarterly* 6: 410–29.

Kousser, Thad, and John Straayer. 2007. "Budgets and the Policy Process." In *Institutional Change in American Politics: The Case of Term Limits,* edited by Karl T. Kurtz, Bruce Cain, and Richard G. Niemi. University of Michigan Press.

Krueger, Brian. 2002. "Assessing the Potential of Internet Political Participation in the United States." *American Politics Research* 30: 476–98.

Kurtz, Karl T., Richard G. Niemi, and Bruce Cain. 2007. "Conclusion and Implications." In *Institutional Change in American Politics: The Case of Term Limits,* edited by Karl T. Kurtz, Bruce Cain, and Richard G. Niemi. University of Michigan Press.

Lacey, Robert. 2005. "The Electoral Allure of Direct Democracy: The Effect of Initiative Salience on Voting, 1990–1996." *State Politics and Policy Quarterly* 5: 161–81.

Lapalombara, Joseph, and Charles Hagan. 1951. "Direct Legislation: An Appraisal and a Suggestion." *American Political Science Review* 45: 400–21.

Larimer, Christopher W. 2005. "The Impact of Multimember State Legislative Districts on Welfare Policy." *State Politics and Policy Quarterly* 5: 265–82.

Lassen, David. 2005. "The Effect of Information on Voter Turnout: Evidence from a Natural Experiment." *American Journal of Political Science* 49: 103–18.

Lavrakas, Paul J. 1993. *Telephone Survey Methods: Sampling, Selection, and Supervision.* 2d ed. Newbury Park, Calif.: Sage.

Lazarus, Jeffrey. 2006. "Term Limits' Multiple Effects on State Legislators' Career Decisions." *State Politics and Policy Quarterly* 6: 357–83.

Leighley, Jan. 2001. *Strength in Numbers?* Princeton University Press.

Leighley, Jan, and Jonathan Nagler. 1992. "Individual and Systemic Influences on Turnout: Who Votes?" *Journal of Politics* 54: 718–41.

Lem, Steve B., and Conor M. Dowling. 2007. "Picking Their Spots: Minor Party Candidates in Gubernatorial Elections." *Political Research Quarterly* 59: 471–80.

Lentz, Jacob. 2002. *Electing Jesse Ventura: A Third-Party Success Story.* Boulder, Colo.: Lynne Rienner.

Levitt, Justin, and Michael P. McDonald. 2007. "Taking the 'Re' Out of Redistricting: State Constitutional Provisions on Redistricting Timing." *Georgetown Law Review* 95: 1247–86.

Lewis-Beck, Michael S., and Peverill Squire. 1995. "The Politics of Institutional Choice: Presidential Ballot Access for Third Parties in the United States." *British Journal of Political Science* 25: 419–27.

Little, Thomas H., and Rick Farmer. 2007. "Legislative Leadership." In *Institutional Change in American Politics: The Case of Term Limits,* edited by Karl T. Kurtz, Bruce Cain, and Richard G. Niemi. University of Michigan Press.

Lowenstein, Daniel, and Jonathan Steinberg. 1985. "The Quest for Legislative Districting in the Public Interest: Elusive or Illusory?" *UCLA Law Review* 33: 1–75.

Lowi, Theodore J. 1999. "Toward a More Responsible Three-Party System: Plan or Obituary?" In *The State of the Parties,* edited by John C. Green and Daniel M. Shea. 3d ed. Lanham, Md.: Rowman and Littlefield.

Lublin, David. 1999. "Racial Redistricting and African-American Representation: A Critique of 'Do Majority-Minority Districts Maximize Substantive Black Representation in Congress?'" *American Political Science Review* 93: 183–86.

Luechinger, Simon, Myra Rosinger, and Alois Stutzer. 2007. "The Impact of Postal Voting on Participation: Evidence for Switzerland." *Swiss Political Science Review* 13: 167–202.

Lupia, Arthur. 1994. "Shortcuts versus Encyclopedias: Information and Voting Behavior in California Insurance Reform Elections." *American Political Science Review* 88: 63–76.

Luskin, Robert. 1987. "Measuring Political Sophistication." *American Journal of Political Science* 31: 856–99.

———. 1990. "Explaining Political Sophistication." *Political Behavior* 12: 331–61.

MacManus, Susan. 1978. "City Council Election Procedures and Minority Representation." *Social Science Quarterly* 59: 133–41.

Magar, Eric, Marc R. Rosenblum, and David Samuels. 1998. "On the Absence of Centripetal Incentives in Double-Member Districts: The Case of Chile." *Comparative Political Studies* 31: 714–39.

Magleby, David. 1984. *Direct Legislation: Voting on Ballot Propositions in the United States.* Johns Hopkins University Press.

———. 1987. "Participation in Mail Ballot Elections." *Western Political Quarterly* 40: 79–91.

Mann, Thomas. 2004. "Juice Worth the Squeeze." *Pew Trust Magazine* 6.

Mann, E. Thomas, and Bruce E. Cain, eds. 2005. *Party Lines: Competition, Partisanship, and Congressional Redistricting.* Brookings.

Marschall, Melissa, and Anirudh Ruhil. 2007. "Substantive Symbols: The Attitudinal Dimension of Black Political Incorporation in Local Government." *American Journal of Political Science* 51: 17–33.

Martinez, Michael, and D. Hill. 1999. "Did Motor Voter Work?" *American Politics Quarterly* 27: 296–315.

Masket, Seth, and Jeffrey B. Lewis. 2007. "A Return to Normalcy? Revisiting the Effects of Term Limits on Competitiveness and Spending in California Assembly Elections." *State Politics and Policy Quarterly* 7: 20–38.

Matsusaka, John. 2004. *For the Many or the Few: The Initiative, Public Policy, and American Democracy.* University of Chicago Press.

———. 2006. "Direct Democracy and Electoral Reform." In *The Marketplace of Democracy: Electoral Competition and American Politics,* edited by Michael P. McDonald and John Samples. Brookings and Cato Institute.

Mazmanian, Daniel A. 1974. *Third Parties in Presidential Elections.* Brookings.

McCarty, Nolan, Keith T. Poole, and Howard Rosenthal. 2006. *Polarized America: The Dance of Ideology and Unequal Riches.* MIT Press.

McCrary, Peyton. 1990. "Racially Polarized Voting in the South: Quantitative Evidence from the Courtroom." *Social Science History* 41: 507–31.

McCuan, David, and others. 1998. "California's Political Warriors: Campaign Professionals and the Initiative Process." In *Citizens as Legislators: Direct Democracy in the United States,* edited by Shaun Bowler, Todd Donovan, and Caroline Tolbert. Ohio State University Press.

McDonald, Laughlin. 1998. "Redistricting at the Millennium." *Southern Changes* 20: 8–10.

McDonald, Michael. 2004. "A Comparative Analysis of Redistricting Institutions in the United States, 2001–02." *State Politics and Policy Quarterly* 4: 371–95.

———. 2006a. "Drawing the Line on District Competition." *PS: Political Science and Politics* 39: 91–94.

———. 2006b. "Redistricting and Competitive Districts." In *The Marketplace of Democracy: Competition in American Elections,* edited by Michael P. McDonald and John Samples. Brookings.

McDonald, Michael P., and Samuel Popkin. 2001. "The Myth of the Vanishing Voter." *American Political Science Review* 95: 963–74.

McDonald, Michael, and John Samples, eds. 2006. *The Marketplace of Democracy: Electoral Competition and American Politics.* Brookings.

McNeal, Ramona, and Caroline Tolbert. 2004. "Support for Internet Voting in the United States." In *Electronic Voting and Democracy: A Comparative Analysis,* edited by N. Kersting and H. Baldersheim. Houndmills: Palgrave.

Meier, Kenneth, and Thomas Holbrook. 1992. "'I Seen My Opportunities and I Took 'em: Political Corruption in the American States." *Journal of Politics* 54: 135–55.

Mendelsohn, Matthew, and Fred Cutler. 2000. "The Effect of Referenda on Democratic Citizens: Information, Politicization, Efficacy, and Tolerance." *British Journal of Political Science* 30: 669–98.

Moncrief, Gary F., Richard G. Niemi, and Lynda M. Powell. 2004. "Time, Term Limits, and Turnover: Trends in Membership Stability in U.S. State Legislatures." *Legislative Studies Quarterly* 29: 357–81.

Moncrief, Gary, Lynda Powell, and Tim Storey. 2007. "Composition of State Legislatures." In *Institutional Change in American Politics: The Case of Term Limits,* edited by Karl T. Kurtz, Bruce Cain, and Richard G. Niemi. University of Michigan Press.

Moncrief, Gary F., and Joel A. Thompson. 1992. "Electoral Structure and State Legislative Representation: A Research Note." *Journal of Politics* 54: 246–56.

Mooney, Christopher, ed. 2001. *The Public Clash of Private Values: The Politics of Morality Policy.* New York: Chatham House.

Mooney, Christopher Z. 2007. "Lobbying and Interest Groups." In *Institutional Change in American Politics: The Case of Term Limits,* edited by Karl T. Kurtz, Bruce Cain, and Richard G. Niemi. University of Michigan Press.

Morse, Adam, and J. J. Gass. 2006. "More Choices, More Voices: A Primer on Fusion." Brennan Center for Justice, NYU School of Law.

Mossberger, Karen, Caroline Tolbert, and Ramona McNeal. 2007. *Digital Citizenship: The Internet, Society, and Participation.* MIT Press.

Musgrove, Philip. 1977. *The General Theory of Gerrymandering.* Beverly Hills: Sage.

Nalder, Kimberly. 2007. "The Effect of State Legislative Term Limits on Voter Turnout." *State Politics and Policy Quarterly* 7: 187–210.

National Conference of State Legislatures. 2007. "Initiative & Referendum Legislation." Denver.

Neeley, Grant, and Lilliard Richardson. 2001. "Who Is Early Voting? An Individual-Level Examination." *Social Science Journal* 38: 381–92.

Newmark, Adam. 2005. "Measuring State Legislative Lobbying Regulation, 1990–2003." *State Politics and Policy Quarterly* 5: 182–91.

Nicholson, Stephen. 2003. "The Political Environment and Ballot Proposition Awareness." *American Journal of Political Science* 47: 403–10.

———. 2005. *Voting the Agenda: Candidates Elections and Ballot Propositions.* Princeton University Press.

Nie, Norman, and Kristi Andersen. 1974. "Mass Belief System Revisited: Political Change and Attitude Structure." *Journal of Politics* 36: 541–91.

Nie, Norman, Sidney Verba, and John Petrocik. 1979. *The Changing American Voter.* Harvard University Press.

Niemi, Richard G., and Lynda W. Powell. 2003. "Limited Citizenship? Knowing and Contacting State Legislators after Term Limits." In *The Test of Time: Coping with Legislative Term Limits,* edited by Rick Farmer, John David Rausch Jr., and John C. Green. Lanham, Md.: Lexington Books.

Niemi, Richard, and Laura Winsky. 1987. "Membership Turnover in U.S. State Legislatures: Trends and Effects of Districting." *Legislative Studies Quarterly* 12: 115–23.

———. 1992. "The Persistence of Partisan Redistricting Effects in Congressional Elections in the 1970s and 1980s." *Journal of Politics* 54: 565–72.

Norris, Pippa. 1999. "The Growth of Critical Citizens and Its Consequences." In *Critical Citizens: Global Support for Democratic Government,* edited by Pippa Norris. Oxford University Press.

Oliver, J. Eric. 1996. "The Effects of Eligibility Restrictions and Party Activity on Absentee Voting and Overall Turnout." *American Journal of Political Science* 40: 498–514.

Ornstein, Norman J., Thomas E. Mann, and Michael J. Malbin. 2000. *Vital Statistics on Congress.* Washington: AEI Press.

Palazzolo, Daniel J., and Vincent G. Moscardelli. 2006. "Policy Crisis and Political Leadership: Election Law Reform in the States after the 2000 Presidential Election." *State Politics and Policy Quarterly* 6: 300–21.

Pantoja, Adrian D., and Gary M. Segura. 2003. "Does Ethnicity Matter? Descriptive Representation in the Statehouse and Political Alienation among Latinos." *Social Science Quarterly* 84: 441–60.

Patterson, Samuel C., and Gregory Caldeira. 1983. "Getting out the Vote: Participation in Gubernatorial Elections." *American Political Science Review* 77: 675–89.

———. 1985. "Mailing in the Vote: Correlates and Consequences of Absentee Voting." *American Journal of Political Science* 29: 766–88.

Patton, W. David, and others. 2002. *Human Resource Management: The Public Service Perspective.* Boston: Houghton Mifflin.

Peery, George, and Thomas H. Little. 2003. "Views from the Bridge: Legislative Leaders' Perceptions of Institutional Power in the Stormy Wake of Term Limits." In *The Test of Time: Coping with Legislative Term Limits,* edited by Rick Farmer, John David Rausch Jr., and John C. Green. Lanham, Md.: Lexington Books.

Penniman, Howard R. 1980. "Presidential Third Parties and the Modern American Two-Party System." In *The Party Symbol,* edited by William J. Crotty. San Francisco: W. H. Freeman.

Persily, Nathaniel, and Melissa Cully Anderson. 2005. "Regulating Democracy through Democracy: The Use of Direct Legislation in Election Law Reform." *Southern California Law Review* 4: 997–1034.

Petracca, Mark P. 1992. "Rotation in Office: The History of an Idea." In *Limiting Legislative Terms,* edited by Gerald Benjamin and Michael Malbin. Washington: CQ Press.

———. 1998. *California's Experience with Legislative Term Limits.* Washington: United States Term Limits Foundation.

Pew Research Center for the People and the Press. 2004. Mid-October 2004 Political Survey. October 20, 2004. Available at http://people-press.org/dataarchive/.

Pinney, Neil, George Serra, and Dalene Sprick. 2004. "The Costs of Reform: Consequences of Limits Terms of Service." *Party Politics* 10: 69–84.

Pippen, John, Shaun Bowler, and Todd Donovan. 2002. "Election Reform and Direct Democracy: The Case of Campaign Finance Regulations in the American States." *American Politics Research* 30: 559–82.

Pitkin, Hannah. 1967. *The Concept of Representation.* University of California Press.

Polsby, Daniel D., and Robert D. Popper. 1993. "Ugly: An Inquiry into the Problem of Racial Gerrymandering under the Voting Rights Act." *Michigan Law Review* 92: 652–82.

Polsby, Nelson. 1983. *The Consequences of Party Reform.* Oxford University Press.

———. 1997. "Term Limits." In *New Federalist Papers: Essays in Defense of the Constitution,* edited by A. Brinkley, N. W. Polsby, and K. M. Sullivan. New York: Norton.

Poole, Keith T., and Howard Rosenthal. 1997. *Congress: A Political-Economic History of Roll Call Voting.* Oxford University Press.

Powell, Lynda W., Richard G. Niemi, and Michael Smith. 2007. "Constituent Attention and Interest Representation." In *Institutional Change in American Politics: The Case of Term Limits,* edited by Karl T. Kurtz, Bruce Cain, and Richard G. Niemi. University of Michigan Press.

Powell, Richard J. 2003. "The Unintended Effects of Term Limits on the Career Paths of State Legislators." In *The Test of Time: Coping with Legislative Term Limits,* edited by Rick Farmer, John David Rausch Jr., and John C. Green. Lanham, Md.: Lexington Books.

———. 2007. "Executive-Legislative Relations." In *Institutional Change in American Politics: The Case of Term Limits,* edited by Karl T. Kurtz, Bruce Cain, and Richard G. Niemi. University of Michigan Press.

Preuhs, Robert R. 2006. "The Conditional Effects of Minority Descriptive Representation: Black Legislators and Political Influence in the American States." *Journal of Politics* 68: 585–99.

Price, Vincent, and Anca Romantan. 2004. "Confidence in Situations Before, During, and After Indecision 2000." *Journal of Politics* 66: 939–56.

Primo, David M., Matthew L. Jacobsmeier, and Jeffrey Milyo. 2007. "Estimating the Impact of State Politics and Institutions with Mixed-Level Data." *State Politics and Policy Quarterly* 7: 446–59.

Putnam, Robert. 2000. *Bowling Alone: The Collapse and Revival of American Community.* New York: Simon and Schuster.

Rahn, Wendy M., John Brehm, and Neil Carlson. 1999. "National Elections as Institutions for Generating Social Capital." In *Civic Engagement in American Democracies,* edited by Theda Skocpol and Morris P. Fiorina. Brookings.

Reed, Steven R. 1990. "Structure and Behavior: Extending Duverger's Law to the Japanese Case." *British Journal of Political Science* 20: 335–56.

Rhode, David W. 1991. *Parties and Leaders in the Post Reform House.* University of Chicago Press.

Richardson, Lilliard E., and Christopher A. Cooper. 2004. "Legislative Representation in a Single-Member versus Multimember Districts System: The Arizona State Legislature." *Political Research Quarterly* 57: 337–44.

———. 2006. "The Impact of Multimember Districts on Descriptive Representation in U.S. State Legislatures, 1975–2002." Paper prepared for the Sixth Annual Conference on State Politics and Policy. Lubbock, Tex.

Riker, William H. 1982. "The Two-Party System and Duverger's Law: An Essay on the History of Political Science." *American Political Science Review* 76: 753–66.

Robeck, Bruce W., and James A. Dyer. 1982. "Ballot Access Requirements in Congressional Elections." *American Politics Research* 10: 31–45.

Rosenson, Beth A. 2005. *The Shadowlands of Conduct: Ethics and State Politics.* Georgetown University Press.

Rosenstone, Steven J., Roy L. Behr, and Edward H. Lazarus. 1996. *Third Parties in America.* 2d ed. Princeton University Press.

Rosenstone, Stephen J., and John Mark Hansen. 1993. *Mobilization, Participation, and Democracy in America.* New York: Macmillan.

Rosenthal, Alan. 1974. *Legislative Performance in the States: Explorations of Committee Behavior.* New York: Free Press.

———. 2004. *Heavy Lifting: The Job of the American Legislature.* Washington: CQ Press.

Rusk, Jerrold G. 1970. "The Effect of the Australian Ballot Reform on Split Ticket Voting: 1876–1908." *American Political Science Review* 64: 1220–38.

Sarbaugh-Thompson, Marjorie, and others. 2004. *The Political and Institutional Effects of Term Limits.* New York: Palgrave Macmillan.

———. 2006. "Democracy among Strangers: Term Limits' Effects on Relationships between State Legislators in Michigan." *State Politics and Policy Quarterly* 6: 384–409.

Scarrow, Howard A. 1986. "Duverger's Law, Fusion, and the Decline of American 'Third' Parties." *Western Political Quarterly* 39: 634–47.

Schattschneider, E. E. 1975. *The Semi-Sovereign People: A Realist's View of Democracy in America.* New York: Harcourt Brace.

Schickler, Eric, Jack Citrin, and John Sides. 2003. "What If Everyone Voted? Simulating the Impact of Increased Turnout in Senate Elections." *American Journal of Political Science* 47: 75–90.

Schiller, Wendy J. 2000. *Partners and Rivals: Representation in U.S. Senate Delegations.* Princeton University Press.

Schrag, Peter. 1998. *Paradise Lost: California's Experience, America's Future.* New York: New Press.

Senge, Peter. 1990. *The Fifth Discipline: The Art and Practice of the Learning Organization.* New York: Doubleday/Currency.

Sentencing Project. 2006. "Sentencing by State." Washington.

Shah, Dhavann V., Nojin Kwak, and R. Lance Holbert. 2001. "'Connecting' and 'Disconnecting' with Civic Life: Patterns of Internet Use and the Production of Social Capital." *Political Communication* 18: 141–62.

Sinclair, Barbara. 2006. *Party Wars: Polarization and the Politics of National Policymaking.* Oklahoma State University Press.

Smallwood, Frank. 1983. *The Other Candidates.* University Press of New England.

Smith, Daniel. 1998. *Tax Crusaders and the Politics of Direct Democracy.* New York: Routledge.

———. 2001. "Campaign Financing of Ballot Initiatives in the American States." In *Dangerous Democracy? The Battle over Ballot Initiatives in America,* edited by Larry Sabato, Bruce Larson, and Howard Ernst. Lanham, Md.: Rowman and Littlefield.

———. 2003. "Overturning Term Limits: The Legislature's Own Private Idaho?" *PS: Political Science and Politics* 36: 215–20.

Smith, Daniel A., Matthew DeSantis, and Jason Kassel. 2006. "Same-Sex Marriage Ballot Measures and the 2004 Presidential Election." *State and Local Government Review* 38: 78–91.

Smith, Daniel A., and Caroline Tolbert. 2004. *Educated by Initiative: The Effects of Direct Democracy on Citizens and Political Organizations in the American States.* University of Michigan Press.

———. 2007. "The Instrumental and Educative Effects of Ballot Measures: Research on Direct Democracy in the American States." *State Politics and Policy Quarterly* 7: 417–46.

Smith, Mark. 2001. "The Contingent Effects of Ballot Initiatives and Candidate Races on Turnout." *American Journal of Political Science* 45: 700–06.

———. 2002. "Ballot Initiatives and the Democratic Citizen." *Journal of Politics* 64: 892–903.

Sniderman, Paul, Richard Brody, and Philip Tetlock. 1991. *Reasoning and Choice: Explorations in Political Psychology.* Cambridge University Press.

Southwell, Priscilla L. 1998. "Vote by Mail in the State of Oregon." *Willamette Law Review* 34: 345–56.

Southwell, Priscilla, and Justin Burchett. 2000. "The Effect of All-Mail Elections on Voter Turnout." *American Politics Quarterly* 28: 72–79.

Spitzer, Robert J. 2002. "Multiparty Politics in New York." In *Multiparty Politics in America: Prospects and Performance,* edited by Paul S. Herrnson and John C. Green. Lanham, Md.: Rowman and Littlefield.

Squire, Peverill. 1985. "Results of Partisan Redistricting in Seven U. S. States during the 1970s." *Legislative Studies Quarterly* 10: 259–66.

———. 2000. "Uncontested Seats in State Legislative Elections." *Legislative Studies Quarterly* 25: 131–46.

Squire, Peverill, Raymond Wolfinger, and D. P. Glass. 1987. "Residential Mobility and Voter Turnout." *American Political Science Review* 81: 45–65.

Steen, Jennifer A. 2006. "The Impact of State Legislative Term Limits on the Supply of Congressional Candidates." *State Politics and Policy Quarterly* 6: 430–47.

Stein, Robert. 1998. "Early Voting." *Public Opinion Quarterly* 62: 57–69.

Stein, Robert, and Patricia A. Garcia-Monet. 1997. "Voting Early, but Not Often." *Social Science Quarterly* 78: 657–71.

Stein, Robert, Christopher Owens, and Jan Leighley. 2003. "Electoral Reform, Party Mobilization, and Voter Turnout." Paper prepared for the annual conference, Midwest Political Science Association. Chicago, April.

Stein, Robert, and Greg Vonnahme. 2006. "Election Day Vote Centers and Voter Turnout." Paper prepared for the annual conference, Midwest Political Science Association. Chicago, April.

———. 2007. "Turning Out Newly Registered Voters: The Effects of Election Day Vote Centers." Paper prepared for the annual conference, Midwest Political Science Association Conference. Chicago, April.

Straayer, John A. 2004. *Colorado's Legislative Term Limits*. Final Report for the Joint Project on Term Limits (www.ncsl.org/jptl/casestudies/CaseContents.htm).

Strattman, Thomas. 2005. "Ballot Access Restrictions and Candidate Entry in Elections." *European Journal of Political Economy* 21: 59–71.

Sullivan, John L., and Eric M. Uslaner. 1978. "Congressional Behavior and Electoral Marginality." *American Journal of Political Science* 22: 536–53.

Swain, Carol M. 1995. *Black Faces, Black Interests: The Representation of African Americans in Congress*. Harvard University Press.

Swain, John W., Stephen A. Borrelli, and Brian C. Reed. 1998. "Partisan Consequences of the Post-1990 Redistricting for the U.S. House of Representatives." *Political Research Quarterly* 51: 945–67.

Tamas, Bernard Ivan, and Matthew Dean Hindman. 2007. "Do State Election Laws Really Hurt Third Parties? Ballot Access, Fusion, and Elections to the U.S. House of Representatives." Paper prepared for the annual meeting of the Midwest Political Science Association. Chicago, April.

Thernstrom, Abigail. 1987. *Whose Votes Count? Affirmative Action and Minority Voting Rights*. Harvard University Press.

Thomas, Clive S., and Ronald J. Hrebenar. 2003. "Interest Groups in the States." In *Politics in the American States,* edited by Virginia Gray and Herbert Jacob. 8th ed. Washington: CQ Press.

Thomas, Sue. 1994. *How Women Legislate*. Oxford University Press.

Thompson, Joel, and Gary Moncrief. 2003. "Lobbying under Limits: Interest Group Perspectives on the Effects of Term Limits in State Legislatures." In *The Test of Time: Coping with Legislative Term Limits,* edited by Rick Farmer, John David Rausch Jr., and John C. Green. Lanham, Md.: Lexington Books.

Thorley, John. 1996. *Athenian Democracy*. London: Routledge.

Tolbert, Caroline. 1998. "Changing Rules for State Legislatures: Direct Democracy and Governance Policies." In *Citizens as Legislators,* edited by Shaun Bowler, Todd Donovan, and Caroline Tolbert. Ohio State University Press.

———. 2003. "Cycles of Democracy: Direct Democracy and Institutional Realignment in the American States." *Political Science Quarterly* 118: 467–89.

Tolbert, Caroline J., John A. Grummel, and Daniel A. Smith. 2001. "The Effects of Ballot Initiatives on Voter Turnout in the United States." *American Politics Research* 29: 625–48.

Tolbert, Caroline, and Ramona McNeal. 2003. "Unraveling the Effects of the Internet on Political Participation." *Political Research Quarterly* 56: 175–85.

Tolbert, Caroline, and Daniel Smith. 2004. *Educated by Initiative*. University of Michigan Press.

———. 2005. "The Educative Effects of Ballot Initiatives on Voter Turnout." *American Politics Research* 33: 283–309.

Tolbert, Caroline, Daniel Smith, and John Green. 2008. "Strategic Voting and Legislative Redistricting Reform: District and Statewide Representational Winners and Losers." *Political Research Quarterly* (March). See http://prq.sagepub.com/pap.dtl.

Traugott, Michael W. 2003. "Why Electoral Reform Has Failed: If You Build It, Will They Come?" In *Rethinking the Vote*, edited by Ann Crigler, Ed McCafferty, and Marion Just. Oxford University Press.

Uslaner, Eric. 2004. "Trust, Civic Engagement, and the Internet." *Political Communications* 21: 223–42.

Van Vechten, Renee Bukovchik. 2003. "Keeping Lame Duck Legislators in Line: Shirking, Accountability, and Reputation." Paper prepared for the meetings of the Western Political Science Association. Denver.

Verba, Sidney, Kay Schlozman, and Henry Brady. 1995. *Voice and Inequality: Civic Voluntarism in American Politics.* Harvard University Press.

Wand, Jonathan N., and others. 2001. "The Butterfly Did It: The Aberrant Vote for Buchanan in Palm Beach County, Florida." *American Political Science Review* 95: 793–810.

Waters, M. Dane, ed. 2003. *The Initiative and Referendum Almanac.* Carolina Academic Press.

Wattenberg, Martin. 1991. *The Rise of Candidate-Centered Politics: Presidential Elections of the 1980s.* Harvard University Press.

———. 1998. *The Decline of American Political Parties: 1952–1996.* Harvard University Press.

Weberg, Brian, and Karl T. Kurtz. 2007. "Legislative Staff." In *Institutional Change in American Politics: The Case of Term Limits,* edited by Karl T. Kurtz, Bruce Cain, and Richard G. Niemi. University of Michigan Press.

Welch, Susan, and Albert Karnig. 1978. "Minority Representation on City Councils." *Social Science Quarterly* 59: 162–222.

Welch, Susan, and Donley T. Studlar. 1990. "Multimember Districts and the Representation of Women: Evidence from Britain and the United States." *Journal of Politics* 52: 391–412.

Wenzel, James, Todd Donovan, and Shaun Bowler. 1998. "Direct Democracy and Minorities: Changing Attitudes about Minorities Targeted by Initiatives." In *Citizens as Legislators: Direct Democracy in the United States,* edited by Shaun Bowler, Todd Donovan, and Caroline Tolbert. Ohio State University Press.

West, Darrell. 1997. *Air Wars: Television Advertising in Election Campaigns, 1952–1996.* Washington: CQ Press.

White, John P., and Norman C. Thomas. 1964. "Urban and Rural Representation and State Legislative Apportionment." *Western Political Quarterly* 17: 724–41.

Will, George F. 1992. *Restoration: Congress, Term Limits, and the Recovery of Deliberative Democracy.* New York: Free Press.

Winger, Richard. 1997. "Institutional Obstacles to a Multiparty System." In *Multiparty Politics in America: Prospects and Performance,* edited by Paul S. Herrnson and John C. Green. Lanham, Md.: Rowman and Littlefield.

———. 2006. "How Many Parties Ought to Be on the Ballot? An Analysis of *Nader v. Keith.*" *Election Law Journal* 5: 170–200.

Witko, Christopher. 2005. "Measuring the Stringency of State Campaign Finance Regulation." *State Politics and Policy Quarterly* 5: 295–310.

Wolfinger, Raymond, and Steven J. Rosenstone. 1980. *Who Votes?* Yale University Press.

Wolfinger, Robert, Benjamin Highton, and M. Mullin. 2005. "How Postregistration Laws Affect the Turnout of Citizens Registered to Vote." *State Politics and Policy Quarterly* 5: 1–23.

Contributors

LONNA RAE ATKESON
University of New Mexico

DANIEL C. BOWEN
University of Iowa

SHAUN BOWLER
University of California–Riverside

BARRY C. BURDEN
University of Wisconsin–Madison

BRUCE E. CAIN
University of California–Berkeley

CHRISTOPHER A. COOPER
Western Carolina University

TODD DONOVAN
Western Washington University

EVA GALANES-ROSENBAUM
Reed College

PAUL GRONKE
Reed College

THAD HALL
University of Utah

ERIC GONZALEZ JUENKE
University of Colorado–Boulder

BRIDGETT KING
Kent State University

THAD KOUSSER
University of California–San Diego

MICHAEL P. MCDONALD
George Mason University

PETER A. MILLER
Reed College

J. QUIN MONSON
Brigham Young University

KELLY D. PATTERSON
Brigham Young University

KYLE L. SAUNDERS
Colorado State University

JULIEMARIE SHEPHERD
University of Colorado–Boulder

DANIEL A. SMITH
University of Florida

CAROLINE TOLBERT
University of Iowa

Index

science research, 206; scope of, 1–2; socioeconomic differences in outcome, 83, 84, 86; unintentional experiments, 1; venue effects, 205

Registration rules: deadlines, 167–68, 170; deadlines variation among states, 11; effects on minor parties, 167–68, 169–70; electronic voter registration databases, 85; goals of election reform, 12; potential for bias, 12; variation among states, 84–85; voter turnout and, 14. *See also* Election day registration

Reynolds v. *Sims,* 135

Rich, Janice, 56

Rosenstone, Stephen, 57

Russia, 6

Sample ballots and voting guides, 84

Smith, Matt, 59

Socioeconomic status: differences in convenience voting utilization, 83, 84; election reform effects on turnout, 86; turnout effects of referenda and ballot initiatives, 100, 110

Soft money, 3, 201

State and local election administration: Help America Vote Act, 4–5, 21–22; limitations of reform strategies focused on, 196; public perception, 4, 5–6; role in election reform, 197; significance of public trust in, 23; turnout and, 11; variation among states, 11. *See also* Counting of votes, voter confidence in; Polling place operations and characteristics; Poll workers

Stein, Robert, 57, 58

Straight-party voting, 167

Term limits: ballot initiatives, 175; candidate characteristics and, 117, 118–11; career development of legis-

lators and, 119, 120–21; competitiveness of elections and, 14, 117, 119–20; complexity of legislation and, 130; constituency relations and, 122–23; constitutionality, 2, 130–31; demographic diversity of legislatures and, 119, 121; effects on political process, 121–26; as electoral reform, 130–31; fundraising and, 124, 126; future prospects, 130–31; historical practice, 117; influence of ballot initiatives on legislative action, 179–80; legislators' voting choices and, 123–24; lobbyist influence and, 124; outcomes in minority representation, 200; outcomes of past reform efforts, 203; oversight role of legislature and, 129–30; partisan politics and, 122, 125–26; power relations in legislatures and, 124; power relations in state government and, 127–29; public support, 3; purpose, 2, 117; staff influence and, 124; turnover rate of legislatures, 122

Texas: ballot access laws, 163; early voting, 72; redistricting in, 148, 156

Third-party candidates: antifusion law effects, 166–67, 170, 171, 201; competitiveness of two-party race and, 167, 170, 171; nominating petition rules, 162–63, 169–70, 171; obstacles to success, 161; proportional representation in Congress and, 15; prospects for multiparty elections, 201; responsiveness of election system to citizen preferences, 13; state laws, 161; straight-party voting and performance of, 167; voter registration deadlines and performance of, 167–68, 170. *See also* Ballot access laws

Thornburg v. *Gingles,* 135, 200

Trustee function of legislators, 140